PRAISE FOR
LAST WORDS

"*Last Words*, a posthumous autobiography from George Carlin, is a jazzy, inward-looking piece of work . . . as a chronicler of the working of his own mind, Carlin is terrific."

—*The New York Times*

"What *Last Words* ultimately reveals is how Carlin became a political protester, slam poet, cynic, polemicist and performance artist whose messages were delivered under the veneer of humor."

—*The Washington Post*

"The book is at turns biting and touching, and often both, which is what you would expect from a man for whom the sacred was profane and the profane, sacred."

—*Entertainment Weekly*

"Frank and insightful . . ."

—*Time*

"This is not a collection of setups and punch lines, but a candid, fearless accounting of his life and art . . . *Last Words* shows a comic master at the height of his storytelling powers and with no limit to what he had left to say."

—*Los Angeles Times*

"For comedy fans, this book is vital. It's easily worth its weight in gold for the biting observations on showbiz and its personalities."

—*San Francisco Chronicle*

"[*Last Words*] sounds as if he is still with us, rested and ready to ridicule the latest cultural hypocrisies."

—*The Washington Times*

"Seven particular words are associated with the late comedian George Carlin, and sentimental is not one of them. But that's the surprising portrait that emerges from *Last Words*."

—*Houston Chronicle*

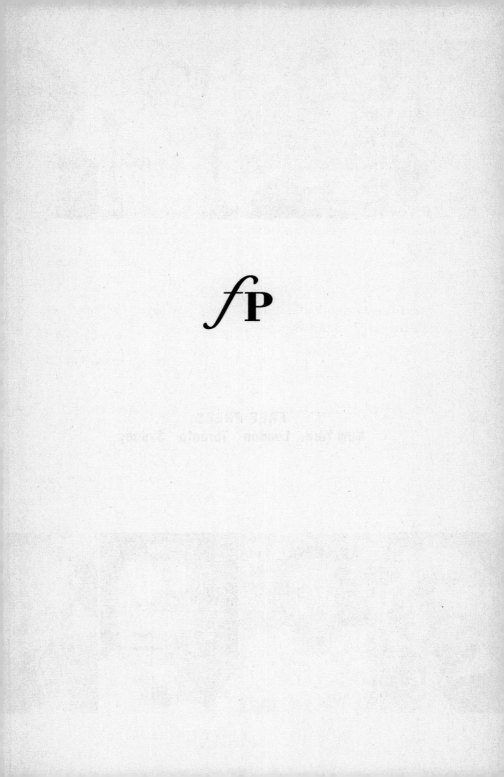

FREE PRESS
New York London Toronto Sydney

FREE PRESS
New York   London   Toronto   Sydney

LAST WORDS

GEORGE CARLIN
with Tony Hendra

FREE PRESS
A Division of Simon & Schuster, Inc.
1230 Avenue of the Americas
New York, NY 10020

First Free Press trade paperback edition November 2010

FREE PRESS and colophon are trademarks of Simon & Schuster, Inc.

For information about special discounts for bulk purchases,
please contact Simon & Schuster Special Sales at
1-866-506-1949 or business@simonandschuster.com

Manufactured in the United States of America

1   3   5   7   9   10   8   6   4   2

The Library of Congress has cataloged the hardcover edition as follows:
Carlin, George.
Last words / by George Carlin.
p.   cm.
1. Carlin, George.   2. Comedians—United States—Biography.   I. Title.
PN2287.C2685A3   2009
792.7'6028092—dc22
[B]
2009037036

ISBN 978-1-4391-7295-7
ISBN 978-1-4391-9110-1 (pbk)
ISBN 978-1-4391-8293-2 (ebook)

CONTENTS

Introduction by Tony Hendra   xi

1 The Old Man and the Sunbeam   1

2 Holy Mary, Mother of George   15

3 Curious George   23

4 The Ace of Aces and the Dude of Dudes   41

5 Air Marshal Carlin Tells You to Go Fuck Yourself   51

6 Two Guys in Their Underwear   67

7 Introducing the Very Lovely, Very Talented—Brenda!   85

8 Those Fabulous Sixties   97

9 Inside Every Silver Lining There's a Dark Cloud   117

10 The Long Epiphany   135

11 Wurds, Werds, Words   155

12 High on the Hill   175

13 Say Goodbye to George Carlin   191

14 Death and Taxes   209

15 I Get Pissed, Goddamit!   223

16 Working Rageaholic   241

17 Doors Close, Doors Open   259

18 Being, Doing, Getting   277

19 New York Boy   289

"Gee, he was here a moment ago . . ."

—(What George wanted on his tombstone—
if he'd had one.)

INTRODUCTION

Tony Hendra

I have this real moron thing I do? It's called thinking.
—GC

For the last half century, somewhere in America, night in night out, George Carlin stood on a stage, raging, explaining, berating, sniping, purring questions, snarling answers, kicking holes in the polyester pants of hypocrisy, puking down the nice clean tux of conventional wisdom, doing what none of the interchangeable comics who shuffle across Comedy Central's various interchangeable performance areas ever do: "this real moron thing—thinking."

A mild-mannered and approachable man offstage, the riled-up, baffled Everyman he played onstage was the final step in the evolution of an intelligence that, like no other, got under the skin of the American Dream.

"It's called the American Dream because to believe it, you have to be ASLEEP!"

All his life he yanked the Band-Aids off that bruised and battered carcass, and poked savagely away at what he found underneath. In the seventies he did it by probing his own history in classic works like *Class Clown*, becoming a prime mover in a kind of comedy saddled with the term "nostalgia" but which was actually something far more interesting and ambivalent, fond memories of absurd repression. During the Reagan imperium his attention began turning outward to politics, violence, language, especially official and pseudo-official language, not to mention that central social issue, pets. In the nineties and the Bush years—the zeros—he took on more general symptoms of the folly of his species: war, religion, the planet, consumerism, cataclysm, death, divinity, golf.

Unlike many of his peers, he died uncorrupted, uncompromised and unbowed. He was urban not suburban, live not prerecorded, raw not precooked. His voice always vibrated with the energy of the Harlem streets from which he sprang, cutting through middle-class crap like a fine old ivory-handled straight razor. Because he did this alone, without fanfare, live, often in lowbrow locales like blue-collar clubs and Las Vegas, the proposition that George Carlin was a major artist may raise the brows, even the hackles, of the artist-ocracy. But that is what he became in his maturity: a unique creative force, equal parts actor, philosopher, satirist, poet—a real man of the people, not a multimillionaire media travesty of one. An artist whose designation "comedian" describes his work as inadequately as "painter" describes Francis Bacon or "guitarist" describes B.B. King.

It isn't the purpose of this book to make that case, though I have tried to shape the narrative—as far as another's first-person narrative can be shaped—to show how an acutely perceptive young performer with an ear as sharp as surgical steel became first an accomplished writer, then a master craftsman and finally a mature artist who could not only make you laugh till you were gasping but then take your breath away once you'd caught it, with the hard-edged poetry and coruscating variety of his language. No one I ever met in the business of being funny, and I've met a few, was more the antithesis of Happy the Carefree Clown than George; no one understood better that comedy at its finest is a dark and beautiful art.

For me this book is first and foremost a labor of love. More than fifteen years ago George asked me to help him tell the story of his life, and for a variety of mostly logistical reasons, I never got to finish the job. And while George told many bits and pieces of his story to various people at various times, he always wanted to get the whole thing down in one place at one time, packaged, polished and perfect. He made no secret of being anal in his habits, and he liked his works put away neat and tidy up on the shelf of his lifetime achievements. This book is one of the very few that never made it up there. Until now.

I first met George in mid-1964 when he was starting out as a comedian and I was too (actually half of one: my partner Nick Ullett and I were a comedy team). It was in the legendary, if unfortunately named, Café Au Go Go on Bleecker Street in Greenwich Village. The Go Go *was* Greenwich Village in the sixties. Grotty and gloomy, with black walls and a bare-board stage, it was dark enough that at a corner table, you could actually suck on a furtive joint. Music greats as diverse as Stan Getz and the Blues Project recorded classic albums there, folkies like Stephen Stills transitioned into rockers there, up-and-coming comedians like Richard Pryor and Lily Tomlin cut their comedic milk-teeth there.

George was one of them: the Go Go was his New York base—"my laboratory." Off and on for a year, he'd been developing material for what would soon be an Apollo mission of a television career. Nick and I had also appeared at the Go Go a couple of times, notably opening for Lenny Bruce earlier in the year. It had been our first booking in America—and a delightful introduction to America it was. The third night of the gig, undercover NYPD cops arrested Lenny as he came off stage—allegedly for obscenity but as likely for being too funny about Catholics. He made bail and went back to work the next night with the same act. So the next week they busted him all over again.

The Go Go was one bond with George; Lenny was another. We'd gotten to know him quite well during his disastrous run; and Lenny had given George his start in showbiz four years earlier when he too had been half of a comedy team (with TV producer Jack Burns). We all idolized Lenny's brilliant, risk-taking material, the Zorro-like satiric slashes he left on the asses of his targets. Lenny was who we all wanted to be when we grew up.

Throughout the rest of the sixties George and we were friendly competitors. We played the same nightclubs as he did across America—Mister Kelly's in Chicago, the hungry i in San Francisco. We got our first TV break like him, on the old *Merv Griffin*

Show. We endured the same vapid wasteland of sixties variety TV—especially the purgatorial torments of *The Ed Sullivan Show.* Shows that censored out all mention of the social turmoil and revolutionary tumult going on outside their studio doors.

George was a hit in the wasteland (more than us), but the repressive environment triggered in him—and me—a major self-reinvention as the sixties became the seventies. George transformed into the groundbreaking satiric stand-up we knew and loved; I signed on as an original editor of the brand-new humor magazine *National Lampoon.* Again we were competitors—this time for the vast campus audience the Baby Boom had created. The only time I saw George now was in Atlantic Records' ads for his comedy albums in our pages; they were often next to house ads for the *Lampoon's* own hit comedy albums, the first two of which I produced. Then, for a decade, our paths diverged.

In the mideighties, I took a sabbatical from satire to write about satire: a book called *Going Too Far,* dealing with the antiestablishment humor that had emerged in the midfifties and given rise in the sixties and seventies to an extraordinary generation of comedic voices. In an unguarded moment I described this to my editor as "Boomer humor"; he insisted I use the wretched term throughout the book. Among the many comedy stars I wanted to interview, George was by now in the top rank.

George best typified a crucial element of my premise: that Boomer humor—because of its fundamental message of dissent—had always had an adversarial relationship with Official America's most powerful weapon, television. In its origins it had tended to be a humor of the page or the stage—whether concert, nightclub or theater. A live, largely uncensored affair, often improvised and by definition unrepeatable, the very opposite of recorded entertainment. To get it, you hadda be there.

Like a few other major comedians—Richard Pryor, Lily Tomlin, Steve Martin—George had remained faithful to this principle, working almost exclusively in live performance since the early seventies, appearing on television only as "an advertisement for myself." His most notorious comic essay, "Seven Words You Can Never Say on

Television," deftly defined the antagonism—and Boomer humor's core appeal. And he'd stuck to his guns—except for a brief lapse in the late seventies when he was at risk of becoming Johnny Carson's doppelganger. By the mideighties he was almost alone among major comedians who still worked live all the time.

For George the stage hadn't been stasis or stagnation. Quite the contrary: the uncensored freedom of live performance was what fed his ever-broadening and deepening work, gave it such flair, range and demotic force. He sharpened his art for and with real people, not the anonymous zero of a camera lens. He disseminated his comic vision by spoken word, gesture, inflection, the raised shoulder or eyebrow, the pause, the beat, the word not spoken, all those elements of performance the camera cheapens, falsifies or simply misses. He was building a devoted following of millions, a few thousand at a time. He had learned that laughter, like politics, is always local. To get George, you hadda be there.

And George gave good interview. He was the most articulate of all my subjects about his craft, his artistic development and his comedic view of the world. Furthermore, his life onstage and off were one and the same. This was a man who lived through his craft and his material.

Even with giants of Boomer humor like Dick Gregory or Jules Feiffer, my interviews usually ran around an hour. With George we became so engrossed in our conversation that we recorded cassette after cassette over a period of a week or more, covering his development from his childhood in wartime Manhattan to the movie he'd just completed (*Outrageous Fortune*, starring Bette Midler): a more than forty-year period for which his recall was phenomenal.

Great for my book. Far more exciting though was discovering, after a decade in very different areas of comedy, how much we had in common. We'd both had Catholic backgrounds, we were both loners obsessed with the nature and practice of comedy. We shared comic loves, hates, preferences, insights and experiences, for instance those ghastly sixties variety shows. (There was no one in my rather literary comedic circle with whom I could share the terror recollected in tranquillity, of *The Ed Sullivan Show*.) This time around we weren't just professional colleagues. We really hit it off. And laughed a lot.

George turned fifty in 1987 and soon after caught the autobiography bug. In 1992 he asked me to read what he'd written so far. He wasn't happy with it. "It" was a hundred double-spaced pages covering the first six years of his life in copious, often funny detail, interlarded with many rather self-consciously "writerly" passages. The hundred pages were continuous: they were the opening chapter. I pointed out that by this math, his first sixty years would run a thousand pages. Even in an era of morbidly obese memoirs it would stand out. That was why I was reading the fucking thing, said George. He needed someone to help.

So began the long, wild, meandering, erratic and almost always hilarious process of documenting the life, times and oeuvre of George Denis Patrick Carlin. I already had ten to twelve hours of great stuff from *Going Too Far*. Over the next ten years we added forty to fifty hours more of taped conversations and as many unrecorded ones. It was an unpredictable process. Right after we'd done our initial sessions, I became editor in chief of *Spy* and George went into preproduction on his Fox sitcom, *The George Carlin Show*. Work was limited to spur-of-the-moment meetings when we happened to be in the same city. After a year, *Spy* expired, followed not long after by *The George Carlin Show*. Work resumed—the body of material grew both on tape and other notes and I began to rough out some early chapters.

The genre of what we were creating, since it intersected somewhat with our modus, came up. George didn't want to call it an autobiography: only pinheaded criminal business pricks and politicians wrote autobiographies. We also tossed the narcissistic Gallicism "memoir," which we decided was a linguistic mongrel of "me" and "moi." Because George wanted to place himself in the context of important movements in comedy over what was nearly a forty-year career, I started adding interstitial pieces of that cultural history. So a few years in, with a book emerging that was part biography, part autobiography, we hit on our genre: it was George's *sortabiography*. And that's what we called it ever after.

INTRODUCTION

In early April 1997, George's wife Brenda was diagnosed with terminal liver cancer. She declined rapidly and died just five weeks later, the day before George's sixtieth birthday. Partly because she had figured fairly prominently in the sortabiography, partly because of the yearlong depression he went through in the aftermath, we put it aside for a while. That year he also published his first hardback humor book, *Brain Droppings*. It was a big best-seller and George relished the role of author. He began planning a second book, *Napalm & Silly Putty*. We'd get to the sortabiography, all in good time. We continued to see each other in our normal ad hoc way, discussing new developments in his life and work for possible inclusion and refining what we already had.

Napalm & Silly Putty was to come out in late April 2001. Part of the planned launch was an event at the Writers Guild Theater in L.A., one of a prestigious lecture series called Writers Bloc. George asked me to do the evening with him as an onstage conversation about the book, but also about his life and work. We set the intellectual bar quite high—the audience included a number of distinguished members of the WGA—and after some initial discomfort, relaxed into a fascinating dialogue. As it developed, both of us realized the same thing: we were good at this because we'd been doing it for years. It was a public version of the free-ranging conversations we'd had about the sortabiography, which would often take us to completely unexpected places. The audience seemed to enjoy the ride and the evening was a success. (Though the distinguished Writers' questions didn't quite make it over our intellectual bar: "What do you watch on TV?" was one; "What do you think of the current crop of comedians?" was another.)

The experience put the sortabiography back front and center and we began discussing doing it as George's next book. This back-and-forth generated a classic George Moment.

He usually initiated contact with me by sending me an e-mail of mind-bending prurience. Whenever I saw on AOL the screen name "sleetmanal" (for Al Sleet, the Hippy-Dippy Weatherman) I knew I was in for some truly revolting images. I would try to top him and disgusting e-mails went back and forth until we'd

decided on a place and time to meet or to have a phone conference.

This time George decided to cold-call my New York apartment.
I wasn't there, but my eleven-year-old son, Nick—who as a kid always had an unusually deep voice—was. The conversation went as
follows:

NH: Hello.

GC: Is Tony there?

NH: No. Who's this?

GC: This is George Carlin. Who's this?

NH: This is his son, Nick.

GC: Hey, Nick, how the fuck are ya?

NH: Pretty fucking good. How the fuck are you?

An hour later when we finally spoke, George—not as a rule exactly pro-kid—said he was impressed by Nick's lightning powers of
repartee. I said it was hardly surprising: Nick had grown up roaming
the same Upper West Side streets and basketball courts George had
fifty years earlier.

We discussed what was needed to bring the book up to date.
George seemed to feel his work on it was largely done. He'd covered
the first sixty years of his life in great detail and depth; he'd told
me many things about himself and his life he'd never told anybody
else and we'd uncovered a lot of other stuff in our conversations.
Nothing that remarkable had happened in the last few years except
Brenda's death. We could either deal with that or cut the book off
before it. There was no rule you had to include everything in your
life in a book like this. By that logic, anyone who wrote an autobiography couldn't finish it until they were dead.

INTRODUCTION

We decided to see how *Napalm & Silly Putty* did and regroup in the fall. On top of his book tour and normal concert load, George had an upcoming HBO special in November to plan. As things turned out, we never did regroup. 9/11 intervened, causing George major headaches for his HBO show (and adding a darkly comic episode to the sortabiography). *Napalm* became another huge best-seller, staying on the *New York Times* best-seller list for twenty straight weeks; the audiobook won George his fourth Grammy. Meanwhile I was on the best-seller list too, having become involved with a fast-track 9/11 book, a photographic tribute to the FDNY and the 343 firefighters who died at the World Trade Center, called *Brotherhood*, which I edited and cowrote with Frank McCourt. (Rudy Giuliani and Thomas van Essen provided forewords. The proceeds went to FDNY charities.)

By the time I next saw George, at his HBO special in November, our literary landscape had changed. His publisher wanted another humor book like *Napalm*, and by now I was in the process of selling my own semiautobiographical book, the account of a lifelong friendship I'd had with a saintly and funny Benedictine monk named Father Joe. Not to worry, said George, our book was great and it wasn't going anywhere. It would get done.

It was mid-'03 before I surfaced from writing *Father Joe* and made contact with George again. In the meantime he'd experienced more heart problems—arrhythmia, requiring a procedure called an ablation. He was also doing a new humor book, *When Will Jesus Bring the Pork Chops?*, a title designed to be offensive to all three Abrahamic faiths. (When it came out in 2004, the only religious institution it offended was Walmart. Because the cover lampooned the Last Supper with George seated at the table, waiting for Jesus, they refused to rack the book.)

George was always a long-term planner, and a new idea now entered the picture, involving an ambition of his we'd discussed occasionally, of capping his career with a Broadway show. The model for it would be Lily Tomlin's brilliant, virtuosic performance in Jane Wagner's *The Search for Signs of Intelligent Life in the Universe*, which she'd premiered in 1985 and had since performed all over the world. His new idea was to use childhood stuff from the book as a basis for the Broadway show; then when it opened, finally publish the sortabiography itself. The success of one would feed the success of the other. This seemed an excellent approach, especially since he wanted me to work on the Broadway end of it too.

2004 came and went, and by the time we spoke again, George had been through rehab and was working again as hard as ever. But he had begun to talk more and more about slowing down, about someday soon getting off the road. Then he could devote the time he needed to the "Broadway thing." His health began to decline—after the 2005 HBO special he suffered heart failure—but whenever we spoke the plan for the next stage in his long and extraordinary career remained the same.

George didn't live to fulfill his dream of homecoming, of taking his hometown by storm on Broadway, the magical place where he scampered as a boy from stage door to stage door, filling a fat autograph book. But at least the story of his life has made it to the light. In his own words.

Words—the thing he loved most.

1

THE OLD MAN
AND THE SUNBEAM

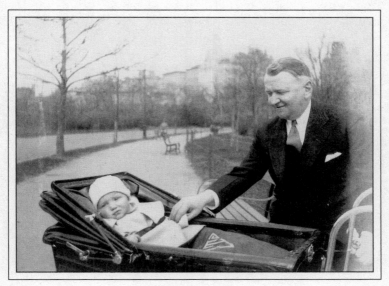

Patrick Carlin Sr.
(Courtesy of Kelly Carlin-McCall)

Sliding headfirst down a vagina with no clothes on and landing in the freshly shaven crotch of a screaming woman did not seem to be part of God's plan for me. At least not at first. I'm not one of those people who can boast of having been a sparkle in his mother's eye. A cinder comes closer.

I was conceived in a damp, sand-flecked room of Curley's Hotel in Rockaway Beach, New York. August 1936. A headline in that Saturday's *New York Post* said "Hot, sticky, rainy weekend begins. High humidity and temperatures in the 90s send millions to the beaches." At the Paramount Theater in Times Square, Bing Crosby and Frances Farmer starred in *Rhythm on the Range*. Meanwhile at Curley's Hotel on Beach 116th Street, Mary and Patrick Carlin starred in yet another doomed Catholic remake of *Rhythm in the Sack*.

For several generations Rockaway Beach had been a favorite weekend retreat for New York's alcohol-crazed Irish youth in search of sex and sun. Popular ethnic slurs to the contrary, the Irish do enjoy sex—at least the last ten seconds or so. But we must admit that Irish foreplay consists of little more than "You awake?" Or the more caring, sensitive "Brace yourself, Agnes!"

Not that my conception was the tale of two young lovers, carried away by passion and strong wine. By the time my father's eager, whiskey-fueled sperm forced its way into my mother's egg-of-the-month club, she was forty and he was forty-eight—certainly old enough to be carrying rubbers. The odds against my future existence were even longer: this particular weekend was a single isolated sex-fest during a marital separation that had lasted more than a year. In fact the preceding six years of my parents' marriage had consisted entirely of long separations, punctuated by sudden brief reconciliations and occasional sex-fests.

The separations were long because my father had trouble metabolizing alcohol. He drank, he got drunk, he hit people.

My mother told me that my father hit her only once. (My older brother, Patrick, can't say the same.) His first marriage ended disastrously when his first wife died of a heart attack not long after one of his beatings. My mother's theory was that while my father had been very free with his hands where his first family and Patrick were concerned, he didn't abuse her, because she had four brothers and her dad was a policeman.

Their reconciliations were sudden because my father had a terrific line of bullshit. And because my mother really loved him. The two of them were crazy about one another. According to those who knew them they were one of the great pairings of all time. So while I sprang from something good and positive, by the time I showed up I was a distinct inconvenience. This marriage had gone south long before. As in Tierra del Fuego.

Getting conceived had been hard enough. Staying conceived literally required a miracle. My next brush with nonexistence came two months after the sweaty sex-weekend in Rockaway Beach.

During the five years between the birth of my brother and my tiny embryo glomming on to a few square millimeters of her uterine wall, my mother had made several visits to a certain Dr. Sunshine in Gramercy Square. Never for an abortion, mind you. Holy Mary Mother of God, no! The procedure in question was called a D&C: dilation and curettage—literally "open wide and scrape." A wonderfully delicate euphemism for quasi-Catholics with a little money. Really high-tone too. Gramercy Square was *the* place to get opened wide and scraped. No back-alley abortions on my father's salary.

Legend has it that my mother was seated in Dr. Sunshine's waiting room with my father who, being a family man, was reading the sports pages, apparently just fine with my being less than a hundred feet from Storm Drain #3. The good doctor's instruments were ster-

4

ile and standing by. The old dilator-and-curettager had selected a nice new pair of rubber gloves and was whistling cheerfully as he pulled them on preparatory to my eviction.

Then it happened. My mother had a vision. Sometimes when you're trying to be born, that religious shit can come in handy. Not a full-blown vision, like Jesus' face being formed by pubic hairs in the bottom of the shower. But real enough to save my embryonic ass. My mother claimed she saw the face of her dear, dead mother—who'd died six months earlier—in a painting on the waiting-room wall. She took this as a certain sign of maternal disapproval from beyond the grave. (Catholics go for that sort of thing.) She jumped up and left the abortionist's office, with me still safely in the oven. On the street below she delivered these momentous words to my father: "Pat—I'm going to have this baby."

And so I was saved from an act frowned on by the Church through an experience smiled on by the Church. It's a wonder I'm not more devout. In fact you might be surprised that I support a woman's right to an abortion. But I do. Absolutely. So long as it's not *my* abortion.

My father's response to this dramatic development is unrecorded. No doubt it included something about finding a place nearby that had qualified for a liquor license. After all, this was a man who, riding home from the hospital where my brother had just had a tonsillectomy, said: "Know how many beers I could've bought with what it cost to take your damn tonsils out?"

In October 1936, shortly after my aborted abortion, Mary and Pat decided to try and make a go of marriage again. So here they were, this time at 155th and Riverside, with another nice home, a maid and of course the same old problems. And I have to say that while my father's drinking must have made a sizable contribution to the chaos, my mother was an extremely difficult person to live with. She was spoiled, self-centered, strong-willed and demanding; no matter who you were, she'd find out how to press your buttons, God bless her sainted memory.

Somehow though, while I waxed and multiplied within her, things sailed along smoothly enough for them to stay together. One day in May 1937 she decided to take a recreational stroll on the then new George Washington Bridge. The exertion brought on labor pains sooner than expected and a couple days later I came barreling down the birth canal, a nine-pound behemoth, requiring the use of forceps. My mother insisted care was taken not to grip my temples lest in her delightful words, it caused "the creation of an idiot." This was almost as important to her as the fact that the obstetrician was Dr. James A. Harrar, the "Park Avenue doctor" who'd delivered the Lindbergh baby.

The day I was born was auspicious. It was the day King George VI of England was crowned and a commemorative stamp was issued with the king's head on it—along with my birthdate, May 12th, 1937. How about that? A New York Irish kid named George rates a fucking stamp for his birthday! No wonder I've always been a devout monarchist. I was also born about a week after the Hindenburg disaster. I've often wondered whether I'm the reincarnation of some charbroiled Nazi CEO.

Lying there in New York Hospital, my first definitive act on this planet was to vomit. And vomit and vomit and vomit. For the first four weeks of my life I lived to projectile vomit. My mother later told me with great pride: "They would feed you and you would shoot formula clear across the room. You couldn't keep anything down." And I still can't. This remarkable inability to hold anything back and to spew it clear across a public space has served me well my whole life. At New York Hospital, I also survived circumcision, a barbaric practice designed to remind you as early as possible that your genitals are not your own.

My first home—the Vauxhall, 780 Riverside Drive at 155th Street—was, according to my brother, "opulent." Expensive new furniture, a sunken living room, a dramatic view of the Hudson River and—Amanda, a very large, strong black woman who was actually capable of backing my father down. She became Patrick's and my protector when Dad got out of line—which was plenty. The bar at Maguire's Chop House on Upper Broadway got regular and strenuous workouts. Meanwhile my mother had settled into her Marie Antoinette period, sitting at the dinner table, tinkling her little bell to cue Amanda that the next course should be served. In fairness to my old man, that sort of behavior in a New York City cop's daughter would be enough to drive anyone out to the boozer for a few pops.

One night Pat the Elder sailed in, ethanol-powered and very late, and Mary had a few choice things to say about "what good is it having all this nice stuff if we can't have meals together, blah blah blah." During the subsequent debate, to emphasize an abstruse point he was making, Pat carefully dropped a tray of silver-and-crystal tea service from their sixth-story window to the street below. He said something on the order of "This is what I think of your nice stuff" and headed Maguire-wards.

Mary, who was capable of making life-changing decisions on a dime, made one now. She was leaving for good. Despite my father's promises, the pattern hadn't changed. There was a new baby on the scene. Who knew when I might be scheduled for a taste of the character-forming "discipline" my brother had endured since infancy? Three months? Six? As soon as I had hair I could be hauled around our living space just like him.

That night, Mother Mary headed for the one place she knew we'd be welcome and safe—her father's house. Dennis Bearey, the gentle ex-policeman, lived not far away at the corner of 111th Street and Amsterdam. Two days after our arrival there, my father was spotted across the street watching the building, hoping to collar my mother on her way out and stage one of his specialties—getting back in her good graces with that terrific line of bullshit. But this time Mary was having none of it. Three days later she, Patrick and I went out Grandpa's fire escape, down four stories and through the backyards of 111th Street to Broadway, where my uncle Tom was waiting in his car. He drove us up to South Fallsburg in the Catskills and a farm owned by a couple of my mother's friends.

There we stayed for two months. I was barely sixty days old but my life on the road had begun. And my first stop was the Catskills.

A week later, my father forced his way into Grandpa's apartment by breaking down the door. The tough old cop, now seventy-four, was helpless to stop him. The next day he was dead of a stroke. Chalk up Number Two to my Dad. Technically he may not have been a killer but he sure was good at causing death.

Dennis Bearey had come from Ireland to be a New York City policeman and, over the years, prided himself on the fact that he never used his gun. A strong man, he used to play with his four sons by extending his fist and telling them "Run up against that and kill yourself." After seventeen years on the force, he was retired on a disability from injuries he sustained struggling with a street criminal. A few weeks before, he'd passed the test for first lieutenant and was told by his immediate superior that a payoff of a thousand bucks was expected if he wanted the promotion. He refused to pay the bribe and told his family, "Principle—if it comes out of a dog's ass!" My mother said that when I was just a few weeks old he would look at my tiny hand and say, "Future district attorney." Sorry, Pops—it took a different turn. But I sure wish I could've known you.

Mary was the first of his six children, all born in either Greenwich Village or Chelsea. She was frail as a kid and among other things was given a glass of Guinness stout each night to build her up. It worked. The physical strength she ultimately developed was matched by mental toughness. When she was ten she sent a box of horseshit to a girl on her block who had neglected to invite her to a birthday party. She was small, vivacious, made friends easily, played piano, was a great dancer, laughed loudly . . . and you didn't want her for an enemy. She always knew who she was and what she could do. She was never "the least bit backward about coming forward." She brooked no shit from the world—clerk, waiter, bus passenger. Anyone who crossed her would get a verbal broadside and a bellyful of The Look, a thing of such withering dismissal it could strip the varnish from a paratrooper's footlocker.

This all served her well in the business world—in forty-plus years of work she had only five bosses. Her second job was great—at a then hot ad agency called Compton. These were the Roaring Twenties and she was a flapper—she played the field shamelessly, a self-admitted cockteaser. "I'd lead them on but never come across." Yet in spite of this intense partying, she never drank, unusual at a time when so many people's livers were swelling to the size of beach balls.

While her friends soaked up the gin, she soaked up culture. She read widely in the classics with a special fondness for—of course—

tragic heroines like Hedda Gabler, Anna Karenina, Madame Bovary. I don't mean that this cop's daughter was a cultural snob. She almost single-handedly kept the Broadway theater afloat in the twenties and had as well developed a taste for the thin rot of American pop culture as the lowbrows she tried to distance herself from.

While she genuinely appreciated serious playwrights, her pursuit of high culture was also part of a pattern of social ambition—and certainly of her plans for me. She often called on her command of literature when later our lives had become a running battle. I think my early aversion to reading can be traced to the importance she placed on it and to her use of literary references in the middle of an argument. Maternal monologues would include stuff like: "How sharper than a serpent's tooth is the ungrateful child!" or "What a tangled web we weave when first we practice to deceive!" all delivered with the melodramatic flair of a Sarah Bernhardt. From an early age I was unimpressed, which was part of a larger pattern in our relationship. She insisted, I resisted. But one message did fall on fertile ground—she passed on to me the love of language, an immense respect for words and their power.

The long struggle between Mary and Patrick entered its final stages in December 1937 when the court awarded her a legal separation. My father fought the action, contending that he was a loving father and husband. He was brought down in court by his own flair for melodrama. At a key point in the proceedings my mother's lawyer had my aunt Lil bring my six-year-old brother Patrick into the courtroom. My father sprang to his feet, flung out his arms extravagantly and cried: "Son!" Patrick cringed like a whipped puppy and clung to Ma's skirt. Bingo! Thirty-five bucks a week!

He didn't want to pay, natch, and over the next two years they fought through lawyers until my father simply quit his job to deny her the money. My guess is his alcoholism was probably catching up with him as well. With time on his hands and liquor on his brain his harassment worsened. My mother—a policeman's daughter—had the remedy. Patrick remembers many evenings when the three of us would arrive from downtown at the 145th Street subway stop, she'd call the precinct and a patrol car would shadow us all the way home. More often than not my father could be seen standing across the street.

These sad and sorry performances were the final act of the drama—one that in many ways was a tragedy. My father's children by his first wife swear to his loving attention; his letters to them are shot through with gentle, jovial affection. Even my mother had to admit he could be an absolute joy to be with—thoughtful, romantic, tender, funny.

And he'd done very well for himself. In the mid-1930s at the zenith of his career he was national advertising manager for the *New York Post*, at that time part of the Curtis chain and highly respected—a broadsheet, not a tabloid. Several years running he was among the top five newspaper ad salesmen in the country. Remember, this was the 1930s, before television and with radio still in its ascendancy, when newspapers were still paramount in the area of advertising. Pat Carlin was at the hub of it all—a nationally known figure. All through her working life my mother would come across ad execs who'd started in newspapers and would tell her, "Pat Carlin taught me everything I know."

In 1935 he won first prize in the National Public Speaking Contest held by the Dale Carnegie Institute, beating out 632 other contestants. Throughout the thirties he was in great demand as a luncheon and after-dinner speaker. In those days public speaking was a big deal. At one time, according to my mother, between salary, commissions and public speaking fees my dad was bringing home a thousand dollars a week—a film-star-sized sum at the time.

His set speech was "The Power of Mental Demand"—which also served as the defining theme of his life. The title was that of a book written in 1913 by Herbert Edward Law. I still have his copy of it; on the inside cover is an inscription: "This is my bible. Please return to Pat Carlin, 780 Riverside Drive NYC." The speech itself depended on its dramatic ending. After a forceful inspirational talk, he'd slowly bring the tone and tempo down until by his penultimate line he was almost whispering. "The power . . . of mental . . . demand." He'd point around the room at various members of the audience.

"Each of you . . . in this room . . . has it." Then the big finish. He'd practically shout, "PUT IT TO WORK!"

Electrifying, my mother said.

He was a dynamo, well matched to his live-wire wife. At its best their marriage was a great romantic adventure filled with energy, excitement, sparkling repartee. My mother claimed that when she and my father were married, "Madison Avenue said, 'That's not a marriage—that's a merger.'" He called her Pepper after her spunky personality; she called him Ever Ready after his sexual drive and availability. Several times she told Pat and me how great the sex in their marriage was, and when she did a wistful look would come into her eye. Dad's approach was uninhibited for such prim and proper times. According to Ma she'd sometimes hear him call from another room, "Mary, is this yours?" go in and find him standing in the nude, holding his penis with the ice tongs.

She told me once about the last day he ever saw me. I was only a few months old. He came to whomever's home we were staying with at the time, and began playing with me on the living-room floor. Then he picked me up, held me above his head and sang this song to my mother:

> The pale moon was rising above the green mountain
> The sun was declining beneath the blue sea
> 'Twas then that I strolled to the pure crystal fountain
> And there I met Mary, the Rose of Tralee
>
> She was lovely and fair as the rose in the summer
> But 'twas not her beauty alone that won me
> Oh, no, 'twas the truth in her eyes ever dawning
> That made me love Mary, the Rose of Tralee

Early in their courtship they'd made "The Rose of Tralee" their own song. I'm sure it poured absolutely sincerely from his great sentimental Irish heart. But it didn't work. The Rose of Tralee was determined and he was history. He never saw me again.

Something—I don't know what—happened in 1940 or early 1941 that changed his course. It must have been related to his alcoholism because the next trace I have of him he was working as a kitchen assistant at the monastery of the Graymoor Friars in Garrison, New York. In a letter to his daughter Mary—by his first marriage—he chirps:

> *My new job is assistant to Brother Capistran who is in charge of the cafeteria. On Sunday I attend the steam table, dishing out food. During the week I have charge of the men who mop, clean up and get the place ready for the following Sunday. I have a private bedroom and I eat with five privileged characters in a small dining room, the same food as the priests and brothers . . . I have lost thirty pounds, mostly around the waist. I feel swell— not a drink in over six weeks and there is plenty available. Oh yes!*

I first saw this letter in 1990 when I was fifty-three, the exact age he was when he wrote it. Besides the eeriness of that, there were other things that struck me. His spirit seemed completely unaffected by the change in his financial circumstances—this was a man who only five or six years earlier had been at the top of his game, promoting and employing the Power of Mental Demand and commanding a small fortune doing it. But he seemed to be a person who defined himself and his self-worth in terms of his own relationship to the universe at large—not the material world and its narrow standards. It made me proud of him and gave me reason to believe that my own very similar sense of what's important had come directly from him. It's a connection, a profound one. I don't have many.

By the fall of 1943 he was writing to his other daughter Rita from Watertown, New York, where he'd landed a job at radio station WATN, selling commercial time and playing records on the air— the same thing I'd be doing just thirteen years later. "Well here I am a veteran 'cowhand' with twelve days' experience lousing up the air. I think I've set radio back twenty years . . . This old horse is learning something new. I'm going to stick it out until I develop enough technique to up myself." Best of all there was a station sign-off he said he'd like to deliver; and this was at the height of World War II and its patriotic fervor:

"I pledge allegiance to the people of the United States of America and all the political crap for which they stand. Big dough shall be divisible with union dues for all."

As conclusive evidence it's scanty, but suggests to me that my father saw through the bullshit that is the glue of America. That makes me proud. If he transmitted it to me genetically, it was the greatest gift he could have given.

His enthusiasm for radio didn't lead anywhere except home a year later, with daughter Mary in the Bronx. He might have had an inkling his health wasn't good and kept it from his family. Anyway he died at her house, aged fifty-seven, in December 1945, of a heart attack.

I remember walking up the hill to our house—by now we'd had a home on West 121st Street for several years. It was a few days before Christmas. I was singing "Jingle Bells" and thinking of the presents my uncle Bill had let me pick out the week before, wrapped and waiting under the tree—an electric baseball game, an electric football game, a real leather football.

The kitchen was quiet and my mother more serious than usual. She sat me down on a little stepladder that doubled as a chair—I still have it—and handed me a death notice from that day's *New York Journal-American*. I didn't need to read beyond his name; I knew what death notices looked like. I don't recall any emotion. I just knew my brother would be happy and my mother relieved.

Years later I came across the only record I have of his feelings for me. It's a telegram he sent to my mother on my first birthday in May 1938. We'd been separated from him for about ten months by then but my mother hadn't found work yet, so he was probably still fanning the hope things might work out. He wrote to her: "Just to let you know that one year ago today, I shared every moment of your anguish and prayed that I might share each pain—while your present advisors said nothing and cared less. Thank God and you for the sunbeam you brought forth, whom I pray will outlive all the ill-founded gossip."

He did have a terrific line of bullshit: praying to share the pains of childbirth sounds like vintage Pat Carlin. But he called me . . . a sunbeam.

And he got his wish, though there are very few people alive to whom it matters. Not only did I outlive the gossip—by which I'm sure he meant my mother's quite public and vocal negative opinion of him—but I lived to write this book which will serve as testimony to my old man's great heart and soul.

A sunbeam. Imagine that!

2

HOLY MARY,
MOTHER OF GEORGE

Mary Carlin with a young George
(Courtesy of Kelly Carlin-McCall)

My mother's visit to the funeral home was a frigid affair for both sides—her family and the Carlins. She had always kept her distance from Patrick's folks, considering them shanty Irish, and I'm sure they saw her as a climber, an uppity gold digger. They weren't far wrong.

My mother's capacity for good living had long been blunted by the realities of salaried employment, but she retained her class pretensions and tried to realize some of them by using us kids as advertisements for her taste. Pat, when he was young, had always been dressed like a little sissy in Eton collars and short pants, explaining in part why his fighting skills developed so rapidly. I escaped the worst of that because she couldn't afford it, but she still took me to have my hair cut at Best & Co. on Fifth Avenue, because she knew that was where "the better people" had their kids' hair cut. The better people went to Best.

Much of the struggle between Mary and her sons revolved around her "plans" for us and our strongly developed instinct for independence. She was a woman with decidedly aristocratic pretensions, indoctrinated with the idea that she was "lace-curtain Irish," as opposed to the shanty kind with its stereotypes of drinking, lawlessness, laziness, rowdiness, all the things which—to the degree that ethnic generalities have any meaning—come from that side of their national character that makes the Irish fun.

There was a fierceness to my mother's striving typical of her generation (she was born in 1896). William Shannon in *The American*

17

Irish writes: "Social rules and conventions in America are set by women, and the standards women enforced in late Victorian America as to what was 'nice' behavior . . . could be cruel and rigorous. And to these standards the Irish mothers and maiden aunts often added exacting requirements of their own because resentment and competitiveness impelled them not only to want to be accepted and well thought of but also superior and invulnerable." Voilà! Mary Bearey in a nutshell.

She felt she had detected a diamond beneath my father's rough shanty-Irish exterior, and could clean him up, polish the gem. It's a common courtship fantasy. That mission thwarted, she turned her sights to the more malleable Silly Putty of her sons. Pat the Younger quickly screwed up that strategy. One time in the elevator of our building on Riverside Drive they encountered a lady of particularly regal bearing. "What a lovely little boy," she purred. "And what is your name?" "Son of a bitch!" answered the lovely little boy. Pat was dismissed early on by Ma as "being a Carlin" and having the "dirty, rotten Carlin temper" and I became in her eyes "a Bearey," a scion of her superior, cultured, lace-curtain ancestry. My quiet nature as a little boy became "the Bearey sensitivity." She had even named me for her favorite brother, George, a sweet, gentle soul who played classical piano.

(George, by the way, spent most of his life in the nuthouse. He had taken all his clothes off on the crosstown bus and they said don't do that, but he did it again two years later. So they put him in Rockland State Hospital, Building 17, diagnosed with dementia praecox. He would come home at Thanksgiving and Christmas and play the piano. One Thanksgiving he turned to me and said, "I'm an admiral. I sail out of Port Said." He pronounced "Said" as the past tense of "say," not with the vowels separated. I thought it was wonderful that he'd spent his life in Rockland and claimed to be an admiral. But he never told me any more about his seafaring days.)

Part of my mother's strategy for advancing her life-agenda and realizing her material dreams demanded careful control of the development of her children. I don't mean moral guidance or practical life-advice but a code that would make her look good and feel comfortable. "Everything you do is a reflection on me." She was obsessed with appearances, utterly dependent on the approval of the outside world, in particular that segment of society for whom she worked and that met her approval, the ruling class. Her vocabulary was full of tripe like "A man is judged by his wife," "When you speak you judge yourself," "You are judged by the company you keep." Judgment, judgment, judgment. Judgment of others, judgment by others.

The other control factor was guilt—how our behavior made her feel. She turned everything into a test of how considerate or inconsiderate we were being. She carried it to melodramatic lengths—infused it with a sense of martyrdom. It wasn't just "I give you everything." It was "I trudge home night after night, my arms loaded with bundles for you boys, my poor arms loaded with bundles and the doctor says I may drop on the spot because my blood pressure is 185 over 9,000 and the garbage isn't even out." I know lots of people heard that shit but there was some extra dimension for me—it was frightening. I had the normal need to differentiate from the parent, especially one of the opposite sex, but she was repelling me with these aspects of her behavior and of her dreams for me.

When her marriage broke up, her living with a maid on Riverside Drive and having nice crystal and all that shit went away. It was unfinished business. I think she wanted me to finish the job. On one occasion I overheard her saying to Patrick that he would amount to nothing because he was a Carlin and so on, but . . . "I'm going to make something out of that little boy in there." It gave me steel. It made me determined that she wouldn't make something out of me. I would be the one that would make something out of me.

And yet she was my mother, so she's deep in my art, both for what she gave me—especially that love of words—and for what I rebelled against in her. And she made me laugh, she had a way with a punch line. Once she told Pat and me about coming home on the bus that day. A big fat German man plonked down beside her. "A big Hun sat next to me," she said, "a big mess! He was taking up far too much room. So I took out my hatpin and showed it to him and said: 'Condense yourself!' "

I'll never forget the moment when I made my mother laugh for the first time. That I actually took an idea and twisted it and she laughed. And it was real—not just cute-kid stuff. I provoked a laugh in her by means of something I thought of. How magic that was, the power it gave me.

Even after I'd made the break—made it pretty clear that I wasn't going to let her make something of me—she hung on. She'd find excuses to come visit me on the road when I was playing these little nightclubs in the early sixties. She'd show up in Boston or Fort Worth or Shreveport. "I just want to see if you have nice linens." By then I'd begun to claim my independence and my manhood and was able to accommodate that—we hadn't wound up killing each other after all.

But then she showed up on my honeymoon! My partner, Jack Burns, and I were working at the Miami Playboy Club, and my brand-new wife, Brenda, and I were living at the motel next door—and I get a call: "I'm coming down with Agnes" (Agnes was her sister). My mother and my maiden aunt on my fucking honeymoon!

Mary got on well with Brenda. Almost too well. A little later when we lived with her in New York—I was getting started on my own by now and things were pretty tight—she would often try to drive a wedge between Brenda and myself. I would go out drinking with the guys from the old neighborhood, and while I slept it off in the morning, she'd give Brenda twenty bucks and say, "Go on downtown, and go shopping—don't let him know where you are." Anti-man, anti-husband stuff. It was the diametric opposite of the old mother-in-law joke.

As Shannon says, Victorian standards of niceness could be cruel. It wasn't just that the linens had to be nice. And while Mary must have been dismayed that her son chose the career I did, she made the most of it. When I was a regular on *Merv Griffin* in the mid-sixties, she came on the show and upstaged everybody—including me. In a way I hadn't yet made a break with Mary's niceness. The sixties were my nice years, my nice suit, my nice collar, my nice tie, my nice haircut—and my nice material.

When I really made the break in 1970, really put that niceness behind me, she had a remarkable—but typical—reaction. She came to the Bitter End on Bleecker Street right around the time of the *FM & AM* album. I was doing "Seven Words" by then, and so for the first time she saw me saying "cocksucker" and "motherfucker" on stage and having people laugh and applaud.

Mary was never a prude. She liked to tell a dirty joke—but she'd make believe she felt ashamed and embarrassed. She'd give you a look like "Aren't I awful? Am I the bad girl?" and then tell it. But I was taking things very far—plus I was attacking two of the things she held most dear: religion and commerce. She was mortified that I would be rewarded for these attitudes. But she was incredibly happy I was successful. It was the payoff. The fulfillment of "Everything you do is a reflection on me." She was a star's mother. "Hi—I'm Georgie's mother."

But here's the most telling thing. On the block of 121st Street where I grew up was our church, Corpus Christi, and Corpus Christi School. It was run by Dominican nuns and they all knew Mary. Throughout my nice years the sisters got to know me from television; they knew I was an alumnus of Corpus Christi, and my mother would visit with them and it would be "Yes, he's doing so well," "Yes, I'm so proud of him," "Yes, you should be."

Now comes shit-piss-cocksucker-tits and God-has-no-power. So one day she's walking past the church and runs into a couple of the nuns and they comment on the new surge in my popularity and say, "Corpus Christi was all over the *Class Clown* album." So Mary says, "Yes, but isn't it awful, sisters, the language he's using." And they say, "No, don't you see? What he's saying is these words are part of the language anyway and they're kept off in their own little section and their own little closet. He's trying to liberate us from the way we feel about these things." My mother says, "Oh yes, yes, of course." She's okay now. She's fine. Shit, piss, fuck, cunt, cocksucker, motherfucker and tits have just received the imprimatur of Holy Mother Church. Now they're nice words.

When I threw my mother out of my life figuratively as a teenager, I threw out the good with the bad. To make a clean break you eliminate everything, but I still find her ambitions hidden in mine—and they're not necessarily bad. An important goal of mine is to do a one-man Broadway show. And it was Mary who used to take me to Broadway shows and in the lobby would point to people and say: "See that man's hand? Look at that. He's cultured. He's refined. Look how he holds his cigarette. Look at the angle of his leg. That's what I want for you." In some way my desire to go to Broadway and the legitimate stage is to impress the people my mother admired. I still have this longing to be Mary's model boy. She is hidden in every cranny of my workroom, requiring me to do things. What I have to do constantly is to take Mary out of things and leave only myself in them. Then decide if I want to do them.

My mother wanted me to learn the piano. Like her, like Uncle George the admiral. And I did take lessons and play at recitals and shit, but I hated practicing. I had this dream one night not long ago. I'm trying to learn these piano pieces and I'm very frustrated because I haven't got time, and I'm trying to learn them. Then right there in the dream I say to myself, "Hey, I don't even take piano lessons!"

When I woke up I wrote that down. I stuck it up on the wall of the room where I work. Whenever I get goofy and my OCD kicks in, I look at it and say: "Mary, Mary! Get out of the room!"

3

CURIOUS GEORGE

George Carlin, 1959
(Courtesy of Kelly Carlin-McCall)

One blazing Sunday in July 1941, my mother and I and an older woman named Bessie, who was our housekeeper, went to Mass at Corpus Christi Church on 121st Street, between Broadway and Amsterdam. Usually we went to Our Lady of Lourdes, a gloomy neo-Gothic barn on 143rd Street, but the good Catholic ladies had been attracted to Corpus Christi by its pastor, Father George Ford. It wasn't physical attraction, although Father Ford was, by contemporary Catholic standards, doing something quite indecent. He was delivering intelligent sermons that credited his congregation with having minds of their own.

As well as the church he ran an eponymous parochial school of eight grades—an oasis of enlightenment in the wasteland of Ascensions, Nativities, Blessed Sacraments and Our Ladies of Unbearable Maternal Grief, where retrograde clergy routinely hammered on the bodies and minds of the children entrusted to their care.

After Mass we strolled up the hill toward Amsterdam. There outside 519 West 121st was a sign: "Vacancy—5 Rooms." Just what we needed! An address my father didn't know about. And only a few doors from a school I could walk to without crossing the street. Of course I was only four, so I still had two years to shop for a really cool pencil box. Mary always was a visionary.

Most people would've considered this a random piece of good luck, but not Mary Carlin. She pointed out to me many, many times afterward that God's mother had been directly responsible for finding our apartment, because we moved in on August 15th, the Feast of the Assumption.

For Catholics the Feast of the Assumption was a Holy Day of Obligation, which meant you had to attend Mass on that day or be guilty of a mortal sin. I certainly hope we found time to attend Mass, because mortal sins are far worse than venial or "regular" sins. If you die with a mortal sin on your soul you will burn in inconceivable torment in hell for all eternity. Dying with a venial sin on your sheet merely costs you a few aeons of flaming agony in purgatory. There the fires are as hot as hell but you're consoled by knowing it's only for a few hundred thousand million years. God hands out these hideous, agonizing punishments because He loves you.

The Assumption of Our Lady by the way doesn't mean she assumed she was going to heaven. That would be a sin of pride and August 15th would be the Feast of Our Lady's Presumption. Our Lady could not commit a sin. She was conceived immaculate, meaning "free of the stain of original sin" (which has nothing to do with whether your sins display any originality). She was the only human ever to give birth without being fertilized by a male sperm—otherwise known as the Virgin Birth—the reason being that the standard male sperm-delivery system comes very close, in the eyes of the Church, to mortal sin. We have to assume—there's that word again—that Mary's husband, Joseph, never came close to getting into the Immaculate Pants.

Why Mary the Immaculate had so keen an interest in the living arrangements of Mary the Carlin was never explained, but right around the time the United States was laying plans to sucker Japan into attacking Pearl Harbor, we three Gypsies (my mother's name for herself, Pat and me) plus Bessie tucked ourselves safely away in our Morningside Heights apartment.

We soon discovered we'd moved into one of the greatest neighborhood concentrations of educational, cultural and religious institutions in America. The centerpiece was Columbia University with its many colleges, including, just a few yards from my front door, Teachers College, from which it was once said every superintendent of schools in America had been graduated. Across Broadway was Barnard, one of the Ivy League's Seven Sisters. Down the street from our house was Union Theological Seminary, America's foremost training ground for Protestant clergy.

Two blocks farther west, towering over the neighborhood, was Riverside Church, a twenty-eight-story Gothic cathedral endowed by the Rockefellers, and known locally as Rockefeller Church (a sure sign of what Americans really worship). It soared over our heads at the foot of our street—a three-hundred-foot phallus with seventy-four bells in its head, the largest carillon in the world.

Just around the corner were the Jewish Theological Seminary and Juilliard School of Music, where I walked in at the age of ten to ask if I could get piano lessons. Close by was International House, not of pancakes but of foreign Columbia students; Interchurch Center, HQ of the National Council of Churches, and a few blocks away Grant's Tomb, where many a night we smoked pot while that old juicer Ulysses and his wife dozed away inside.

Our neighborhood quickly became a metaphor for my mother's cultural dilemma: the clash between her self-image as a lace-curtain businesswoman and the reduced circumstances in which her shanty-Irish husband had abandoned her. Downtown, up on the hill, was the intellectual center which embodied her cultural aspirations. Uptown, down the hill, on the Broadway which Jesus tells us "leads to destruction," lay a mostly Irish neighborhood beginning around 123rd Street, known back then as White Harlem.

White Harlem was tougher and more crowded than the streets around Columbia. Its buildings were older and many didn't have elevators. The whole area had a decidedly working-class flavor and, of course, was a lot more fun. You can guess in which direction Mary wanted her sons to head. And which direction *they* wanted to head.

At the beginning she didn't have to worry about me—I was only four when we moved into 519. The highlights of my life were my trips to midtown with Bessie, listening to the radio and thumb-sucking. I was a world-class thumb-sucker. My specialty at bedtime was to loosen part of the bottom sheet, wrap it around my thumb and cram the whole thing into my mouth for extended, overnight sucking. By morning this would create yet another circular, pleated saliva stain in one corner of the sheet, which must have caused some speculation at the local Chinese laundry: "Aha! Irish form of birth control! No wonder so many of them!"

The big old Philco radio in the living room fascinated me from the beginning. I couldn't get enough of it. I didn't care what was on: quiz shows, soap operas, newscasts, interviews, plays, comedies. That all these voices could magically enter my house fired my imagination and nurtured my obsession with words, inflections, accents. On a more basic level it provided company. I harbored a distinct loneliness as a little kid, growing up with no grandparents, no father, a part-time mother and a hired friend—Bessie, who, kind, sweet and mothering though she was, wasn't blood. My adored older brother— the problem child—was away at boarding school. For an embryonic loner the radio was deeply associated with warm feelings—comfort, security, companionship. More than half a century later it still is.

Safe, cared for, nurtured—and mere minutes away from the wild, noisy, vast and exciting world of New York City. Bessie and I traveled at least three days a week to midtown where we haunted the racks and counters of cathedrals of consumerism like Macy's, Gimbels and Klein's. Noontime we'd go to Mass at the Franciscan church on 32nd Street. Then we'd attend the most sacred ritual of all: lunch at the Automat. Squirming around for long hours on hard wooden benches in a church basement couldn't hold a candle to the celestial joys of mashed potatoes, peas and creamed spinach. And these hundreds of pilgrimages to the world's busiest urban center gave me something more—a sense of vast possibility. You could get on a train and in a matter of minutes entirely change who and what you were. A subconscious lesson at the time but one I'd put to good use before long. I mastered the Broadway–Seventh Avenue IRT at a very early age.

When I was six Bessie left us to work for a Japanese family, an interesting move in 1944. ("How could she do this to me?" Mary wailed. "Leave me for a Jap family?") I didn't care. I was in Corpus Christi by now and my Bessie period was behind me. After-school without Bessie or Mary or even Patrick was an unparalleled education in street life. I started exploring early. I had a mile-square playground of colleges and churches and their grounds at my disposal: a thousand hallways, classrooms, labs, theaters, lounges, libraries, dorms, gyms, chapels and lobbies just asking to be terrorized by me and my playmates. Security—a more recent American obsession— was minimal and a handful of small kids can scoot, scatter, disappear and reappear with amazing ease. In addition of course we were in our pre-vandal stage and attracted little attention.

When we got tired of being little pests, there were games: Chinese and American handball, boxball, ring-a-levio (called ring-a-leary-o in my neighborhood), blacksmith, Johnny-ride-a-pony, kick the can, roller hockey and a strange game called three steps to Germany. Plus all the city-street variations of baseball: stickball, punchball, stoopball, curb ball and baseball-off-the-wall.

We had three parks nearby: Morningside Park, Central Park and Riverside Park, which stretched five miles along the sewage-laden Hudson, where we bathed in summer with no apparent ill effects. All the parks were dotted with playgrounds, many recently installed by Mayor La Guardia and called Tot Lots. Basketball courts, baseball diamonds, wading pools, thousands of trees to climb, countless hills for sliding, sledding, rolling down and running up and miles and miles of paths for riding bikes. Not *designated* bike paths, not *shared* paths. Paths where pedestrians had to get the fuck out of the way.

Actually I rarely rode my bike in the park—it was more stimulating when ridden in the streets, weaving adroitly through fast-moving vehicles. "Go play in traffic" wouldn't have been a put-down for us—just another glaringly obvious suggestion from an adult. Heavy traffic as an obstacle to play offers a level of stimulation simply not found on the farm or in nice suburbs where kids enjoy the innocent idyll of American childhood. Heavy traffic focuses the mind. Going out for a long pass on a busy crosstown street develops impressive coordination skills unknown in Iowa.

Heavy traffic as a form of transportation is even better. Grabbing a hitch on a fast-moving truck when you're on roller skates or a bike is idiotic, spectacularly dangerous and every bit as thrilling as it sounds. Techniques vary. With a bike you only have one hand to control the bike and must stay beside, not behind, the truck or risk massive head trauma. On roller skates the fun is all in tiny metal skate-wheels going thirty miles an hour over Upper Manhattan's cratered streets. I'm ashamed to admit that we did not wear safety helmets, kneepads, elbow pads, shoulder pads, gloves or protective eyewear. We could at any time have put our eyes out or broken our necks; curiously none of us ever did. And those lightning-fast, hip-swiveling maneuvers we learned dodging two-ton automobiles trying to cut inside and make the light blossomed later on the dance floor.

By the time I was seven I was slipping into the subway to head downtown to Central Park, Times Square, Rockefeller Center, Wall Street, Chinatown, the waterfront—great tracts of unexplored territory, an urban El Dorado, just sitting there waiting for an adventurous child. Afternoons of collecting autographs, sneaking into movies, browsing in department stores, walking up the stairs to the observation decks of the RCA and Empire State Buildings, stealing stuff from novelty stores, climbing trees in Central Park, riding elevators on Wall Street or simply walking around taking in the big show—the greatest entertainment on earth. It gave me the feeling I belonged, I was entirely at home in the vast city I was growing up in.

Sometimes after a few hours of goofing I'd show up at my mother's office around five-thirty and talk her into taking me to the Automat for a cocktail of creamed spinach. Often, during the meal, she'd give me a quarter and ask me to bring it over to some person she'd spotted sitting alone, nursing a cup of coffee with no place to go. Being down on your luck, she called it. She really did have a generous heart. She just made it so goddam difficult to love her.

New York City was a great education, but first grade with Sister Richardine in Room 202 also meant other awesome new experiences: sex, music and the roar of the crowd.

First grade generated first kisses. Two of them. The first first kiss was one afternoon when Sister Richardine announced the imminence of the annual church bazaar. This so aroused a little girl named Julie—clearly a future shopaholic—that she threw her arms around me and planted a big wet kiss on my cheek. An uproar ensued in the class. Small as I already was, I shrank even further—a tiny, beet-red creature in short pants.

But deep down under those ill-fitting shorts, something was stirring. My second first kiss came not long after, alone in the clay room with Ilda Muller-Thym. I bided my time, then made my move—and gave her a big wet kiss. My only memory was that it was good, she didn't hit me and we didn't get caught. To this day I can't see a child's poorly made clay bunny without a vague churning in my loins.

Room 202 possessed an odd homemade musical instrument consisting of rows of glass bottles filled with varying amounts of water, suspended in a wooden rack. The player struck the bottles with soft wooden mallets, producing a musical note. After much effort I learned "Frère Jacques" and one day played it for the class. My first ever public appearance! A real charge! Having thirty people (okay, six-year-olds, but they had pulses) sit without fidgeting and watch something you were doing—which they *couldn't do*—was intensely satisfying. Having them applaud at the end, even though many had difficulty bringing their hands together with any accuracy, produced an odd sense of power. It was an intoxicant. As would be the case with many intoxicants, I immediately wanted more.

Actually my attraction to the spotlight had begun earlier when my mother taught me to do two things: an impression of Mae West—whom I'd never seen—and a dopey little dance popular in the thirties called the Big Apple. Whenever we had company or I visited my mother's office, she asked me to do my little act. I never needed to be coaxed. I even added another impression I'd worked up on my own—Johnny, the Philip Morris midget. Philip Morris cigarettes featured a midget dressed as a bellboy who walked around upscale hotel lobbies yelling, "Call for Philip May-ray-us." Since I was in effect a midget my impression was flawless.

Second grade brought my next big career move. Our teacher Sister Nathaniel had organized the class into a band. A big band, though not quite in the Duke Ellington sense: the thirty-odd children had a single form of instrumentation—sticks and clappers. The band was in effect a large percussion section with one actual instrument, a really crappy xylophone. Still, it was the only thing that could play a melody, and I leaped at it. After incredible effort I mastered "March of the Little Lead Soldiers" and became the featured soloist.

The highlight of our band's schedule was an invitation to perform at the Horace Mann School in Teachers College, across 121st Street. The occasion was a tribute to Joe Louis and the First Lady of the United States, Eleanor Roosevelt. At seven years of age I was about to do my first liberal benefit.

Two ensemble stick-and-clapper numbers brought the audience to the REM portion of the sleep cycle—and my big solo. I stepped out in front of the band for "March of the Little Lead Soldiers," and without false modesty I have to say I nailed it to the wall. A great rendition—tasteful, restrained and yet spirited. I may have made xylophone history with my daring, cross-hand four-mallet ending. I glanced across the stage to where the guests of honor were seated. Thank God they were awake—and applauding! I did notice that one of the First Lady's stockings was drooping rather badly. At that stage of her life it was probably just part of a larger pattern.

Corpus Christi School, revolutionary for its time, had no report cards or grades. There was none of that cutthroat competitive spirit which so improves our American way of life. We were encouraged to study and excel simply for the joy of discovery. If we were inculcated with anything it was the simple idea that the future would take care of itself if you did right by yourself today.

I grasped the work easily and had a lot of time for daydreaming. If there'd been a course in "What's Outside the School Window" I would have been head of the class. But idle classroom time can lead to more than just looking for brassieres on the rooftop laundry line next door. It is the breeding ground of the class clown.

Class clowns are dedicated to attracting attention to themselves. Traditional Freudians might attribute my chronic need for attention to the fact that I had no father and half a mother. Naaah. The truth was much simpler. Then as now, I was a consummate show-off.

Disgusting tricks are the key components in the class clown's repertoire. These are useful not only in subverting the whole process of elementary education, but in making girls sick. That's really all you wanted to do when you were nine or ten—if you could get Margaret Mary to throw up on her desk in the morning, you knew it was going to be a good day. And though I doubt I deprived my schoolmates of much of their education, I certainly curtailed my own. My entire public-school education ended at ninth grade and I barely made it through that. On the other hand, the credentials I earned disrupting class and making girls throw up stood me in good stead a quarter century later on my 1972 album *Class Clown*.

I had several disgusting tricks I could do: I could bend either thumb backward till it lay flat on my lower forearm. I could crack every one of the twenty-eight finger knuckles officially recognized by the Knuckle Institute. I could also control each eye independently. First both eyes left, then keeping right eye left, move left eye right, then right eye right. Done at high speed, with the right girl, this will definitely make her vomit. But I was outclassed in this category. Ernest Cruz could turn his upper eyelids inside out. Wow. Even I would heave. "Don't do that, Ernest, you look like a devil, man!"

My class clown arsenal included all the standard weapons: weird faces, fart sounds, belching, mimicry, random wisenheimery and sickening physical contortions. I had an unusual additional talent: blowing small bubbles of saliva about a quarter inch in diameter off the tip of my tongue. (Pat taught me this.) Here's how you too can be a bubble blower: With jaw slack, tongue relaxed and mouth open you form the bubble by drawing the tongue away from the floor of your mouth and quickly wedging your tongue under the bubble. Once the tongue holds the flattened, nascent bubble, you exhale gently, releasing the bubble in an eccentric little arc. It will usually travel anywhere up to three feet, making it hard for anyone in front of you to ignore. The flying spit bubble's virtue is stealth. Unless the student sitting in front of you takes exception to the mounting layer of saliva on the back of his or her collar, it goes undetected—until it's too late.

Making faces had the same silent power. I was gifted with a rubbery face and took pride in contorting it in the most revolting ways.

The trick here is to identify students with minimal self-control and loud or goofy laughs. This goes to the heart of being a class clown, because class is one of those places you're not supposed to laugh— like kneeling in front of a casket—so it's the one place the urge to laugh is uncontrollable.

First you get your target's attention with a rubber-band-powered paper clip to the neck. When you have their attention, you whip some interestingly twisted face on them. They explode in giggles, you relax your face into a mask of innocence and they get reamed out. You're off the hook. You're ready to strike again. This time instead of depriving only one child of his or her education, you can stunt the development of the entire class. Welcome to the world of revolting sounds—a symphony of bodily functions, pre-eminent of which is the fart.

Class clown was always the first to discover the artificial fart under the arm. You place your palm vertically in your armpit (under the T-shirt and against the skin) and snap your elbow sharply downward against your side. The air escaping from the armpit pocket erupts in an impressive blatt. (I've never understood why this action, which involves no actual bodily fluid, results in such a deliciously liquid-sounding fart.)

The fart sound is an important sound when you're a kid, so you find as many ways as possible to make it. You can do it in the crook of your arm or by blowing against your forearm. I didn't need any of the fancy ones because I was into the bilabial fricative. In plain English, I could blow a fart with my mouth. I was so glad when I found out it had an official name. "Raspberry" and "Bronx cheer" never made it for me. It was always the bilabial fricative.

I had competition. There was John Pigman, Grandmaster of Gross-out, who could belch at will and for what seemed like five or six seconds at a time. He had a large oral cavity and so the belch would resonate and gather force inside his mouth before making its majestic exit. There was something about the texture of his throat that gave the impression of little food particles rattling around down there. As a bonus he would recite as much of the alphabet as he could while the belch lasted.

Sometimes John would be in the movie theater and you didn't know he was there. If anyone on-screen opened their mouth without saying anything—John provided the dialogue. John was an artist. He taught me something about guerrilla theater long before there was such a thing. I once saw him sneak up behind two old ladies who were walking arm in arm on our block. He got behind and be-tween them and pulled back each one's inner shoulder so they were both facing him, then loosed a horrific, interminable belch right in their faces. They were so stunned I'm surprised they didn't drop dead on the street.

They should've. Because he pulled another, even better stunt. (John Pigman, as natural a performer as ever lived, knew how to top himself.) Same scene, same two old ladies, same buildup. This time instead of belching, he unzipped his fly, pulled out one of those gray-white wieners and cut it in half with a pocketknife. Is it any wonder I idolized this man?

Probably the most disgusting thing I could do I learned from Pat. Here those of you who are parents might want to exercise that age-old method of sheltering children from the real world: as they read this passage, put your hands over their eyes. Or if you're reading this to them at bedtime, skip the next paragraph.

This simple, intensely satisfying stunt involves gathering a gob of spit in your mouth with a "clam" or "lunger" mixed in with it to give it elasticity. Tilt the head slightly forward. Let the spit dribble slowly from your mouth until it hangs down in a long string, like a bungee cord of saliva—then suddenly suck it back into your mouth the sec-ond before it breaks off. This was so disgusting it even grossed me out. And I was the one doing it.

Besides a budding talent for what you might loosely call physi-cal comedy, I was also a pretty good mimic. I could do anonymous character voices like drawls and brogues but I could also do many of the adults us kids had to deal with, especially the nuns and priests of Corpus Christi. Later I branched out to include storekeepers, local characters, the parents of my friends—a minefield that one—and the friends of my parent. I also did the standard celebrity repertoire of the time—Peter Lorre, Jimmy Cagney, Sydney Greenstreet—

even though my voice was an octave too high for accuracy. They were a generous audience on the stoop.

But the exciting thing was the discovery that I could create funny dialogue for these characters and voices. Plenty of people can do imitations, lots of kids can mimic grown-ups. The real power is in making up stuff for your impressions to say. And the most exciting thing of all was to try this stuff on my mother and have it work. I knew her laugh and I knew when it was sincere. It felt great to be able to say, in answer to her question "Where did you hear that?" "I made it up."

Around fifth grade I began to feel I might have a future as some kind of performer. "Some kind" because my thinking on the matter was scattered. A fifth-grade autobiography assignment I still have required a closing paragraph on "What I want to be when I grow up." I wrote, "When I grow up I'd like to be an actor, impersonator, comedian, disc jockey announcer or trumpet player."

Disrupting class made school more bearable once lessons had been mastered, but after-school—that longed-for part of the day that belongs to the kid alone—was what counted for me and the kids of my generation. Small screens hadn't yet co-opted the play of children and it was out on the streets with us, exploring neighborhoods, hopping the subway downtown, hanging out, stealing . . .

I remember so much from those days. Like the Turds. A guy named Bob Cross ran the playground at Riverside Church. He was one of these nice midwestern guys studying PE at Teachers College and this was a local project that gave him a credit. He had a softball league and asked us street kids if we'd like to be in the league. We said yes, so he asked the name of our team. We said, "The Turds." He might have let it pass because we spelled it t-e-r-d-s. (We didn't know any better.) So there up on the board in chalk, for the nice Protestant congregation to see and enjoy, was: "First Game This Evening: The Panthers v. The Terds."

I remember my fedora. It was black and this is how I got it. You would go into the IRT subway at 116th Street and in the nice weather when the trains came in, some of the windows would be open. This was way before air-conditioning, and the vertically oriented windows would open from the top down. So if a guy was sitting inside with a hat on, you would wait until the doors closed and then just as the train had begun to lurch forward you'd reach through the window and grab his hat. Then you'd trot alongside and wave and give him the finger. If you got lucky you got one that fit. I got a fedora of the low-rent variety where it's almost as flat as a porkpie. But it was a fedora, it was black and it fit.

So long as we're into stealing, there were also my magnificent pegged pants, or more accurately, pistol-pocket pegged pants. Another kid and I discovered that the Chinese students who lived in International House at Columbia played tennis and volleyball down on Riverside Drive on these makeshift courts at the bottom of a hill we called Greenie, which used to be our sled-riding hill. They took their civilian clothes off and laid them down alongside the court, and we found out by sitting there—making believe we were really interested in their games—we could steal their wallets.

One day we made a big killing—around eighty dollars—and we split it. With my forty bucks—a small fortune in the 1940s—I went to Fulton Street in Brooklyn to buy my dream item of male haute couture: "Guinea" pegged pants. I'd seen guys at Coney Island with colored pants—bright red or green or electric blue pants but with different-colored cuffs and belt loops, high rises and pistol pockets (back pockets with a flap and shaped like a pistol). All these details had to be in a color that contrasted with the pants proper but coordinated with all your other accessories. Very complex, very important, very impressive.

So in seventh grade in a Catholic school I sported electric blue pegged pants with gray pistol pockets, a two-inch rise, gray belt loops and saddle stitching with a fourteen-inch peg and exaggerated knees. Topped off with—I almost forgot—an orange leopard-skin shirt. When I showed up in class with them the nun who was our home-room teacher said, "I'm so pleased you're working now."

She thought I'd gotten a job as an usher in a movie theater.

There was my first group sex. It was that time of year when it's getting cold enough that you hang around in the hallway rather than out on the stoop. I'm with the guys—maybe six or seven of us. One of the neighborhood girls who was well developed for her age came by. And someone said, "Let's feel her up." What did I know? I run in the hallway with them. While she's not struggling, our schoolmate is trying to make it known that this is not her first choice of activity. The guys are taking turns putting their hands inside her blouse and feeling her tits for a couple seconds and then it's the next guy. Both sides working. "Georgie, go ahead, go ahead." So I felt her tit and thought, "Hey, wow, that's it? That's what it's like? That's nice." My first experience of group sex.

Now we'd be called "delinquent," "troubled," "alienated" or worse; certainly some of the guys from the neighborhood later did time. But there was something innocent about running wild on the streets back then. For one thing the streets were pretty safe. There were no weapons and no one ever got hurt.

A good deal of this activity I did in the company of Brian McDermott, Roger Hogan and Johnny Sigerson. Ah, those magical names. Let's have some more of them:

Arthur Dempsey, David and Susan Foley . . .
Bobby, Demmy, Dido and Gerry Brennan . . .
Cecilia Pineda, Floyd Conant, Danny Kim . . .
Una Clausey, Joanie Sheridan, Bill and John Peck . . .
Condit Allstrom, John, Mary, and Jill Birnam . . .
Gertie and Peggy Murphy, Pierce and Marian Mulrooney . . .
Levitra Schwartz, Charlotte and Sarah Firebaugh . . .
Agnes Stack, John Wendell, Bill Pigman . . .
Johnny, Judith, Theodora, Clailia and Jedidiah Steele . . .

What poetry in a mere list of New York names. Just typing them is a profoundly nostalgic connection to those sweet days. My childhood, the block I grew up on are instantly embodied in the young faces that go with them. They mean nothing in the world of hype and showbiz. But they mean everything to me. They're the All-Stars in my Hall of Fame.

I stayed a night recently in New York and I didn't know it had snowed, so when I opened the drapes I was immediately back in that wonderful childhood world of waking up with snow. All those little things you noticed as a kid: the way the mortar that sticks out between the bricks picks up a little snow on each level. Those weird porcelain insulators screwed into the window frame that the people before you left behind: they have little piles of snow on them. The clotheslines strung between the buildings on every floor have a fine line of snow all the way across. And suddenly, for no reason, a little bit falls off.

There's one other thing with snow. Even when you're fifteen or sixteen and you just want to get laid and snowballs no longer hold the slightest interest for you—or even for that matter if you're never going to see sixty again—when it snows you've always got to make one snowball. Only one, but you gotta.

Just to see if it's good packing.

4

THE ACE OF ACES
AND THE DUDE OF DUDES

Patrick Carlin Jr. and George
(Courtesy of Kelly Carlin-McCall)

My brother, Patrick, is what shrinks call a self-installed role model. I went to his high school, I followed him into the air force, I learned to dance from him. He's the one who taught me: "George, if you're gonna steal, never get caught." His idea of honesty. We took care of each other and fought my mother and were partners in that struggle.

When I started first grade at Corpus Christi, Patrick was in seventh grade. One day he showed up in my classroom. Not because my mother had gotten sick or our house burned down. No, he'd been acting up in class, so Sister Marion had sent him down to first grade where he could be with children "closer to his own emotional level."

He perched on one of those tiny first-grade chairs and settled in. I came over and offered him a hunk of clay. We made little balls out of them and pegged them at the other first-graders. Yeah. He's always been my best pal.

My mother's primary motive in leaving my father was to protect me from the beatings he gave little Pat. It was the central fact determining the shape of our lives—and it certainly shaped Pat. My father, beaten by his father, was one of the many Americans who thought—and still do—that inflicting physical pain will persuade a child to act a certain way—beginning when they're, say, two.

My father's chosen weapon of discipline was a slipper, leather, bedroom, hard heel equipped with. He was a stocky, powerful guy and he felt no need to hold back. Especially with a couple of drinks under his belt and an opponent who weighed almost thirty pounds.

From the start Pat took his torture in the most honorable way—he didn't break, he didn't fold, he didn't give Dad what he wanted. Little two-year-old Pat's view was that when his father got home from work, he'd be simply itching for an excuse to take Pat and the slipper into the bathroom and get on with the fun. Patrick Senior's first question as he came through the door was always: "And how was my little man today?" To the credit of his unbowed spirit, Pat invariably told the truth about how the little man had been that day. And walked right into the teeth of the beatings. My mother, appalled by the violence, would always try to get him to lie to spare himself the slipper. But that wasn't Pat's way. He once described to me a typical day:

My mother and Leone, the family's black maid, try to get little Pat to wear his little sunsuit for a trip to the park. Little Pat doesn't want to wear his little sunsuit. Little Pat wants to wear his little sweatshirt. Little Pat throws a monumental tantrum lasting several hours, which finally ends when he's confined to his crib, where he resolutely refuses to sleep. Toward nightfall, my mother pulls him out of his crib, makes him look presentable and implores him to tell his father he'd been a good boy.

Patrick Senior comes sailing in from work and/or Maguire's Chop House. Sure enough, his first words are: "And how was my little man today?" Patrick Junior looks him in the eye and repeats the words he's learned at his father's knee: "I called Leone a nigger son of a bitch."

And off they go into the bathroom, father and son, to continue the grand American tradition of beating the shit out of someone weaker than you.

My mother subscribed to the same parental tradition, but she knew how to delegate. When he was only seven, she sent Pat away to Mount Saint Michael boarding school so that the Marist Brothers could provide "male discipline": a euphemism which translated as a hope that the brothers would "beat the rotten temper out of him." Wonderful logic. Five years of beating by his father had produced a little monster, so more violence, this time at the hands of strangers, ought to straighten him out. Ah, the Irish.

Not surprisingly my brother saw my mother as a big zero who'd failed to protect him from his father and had now given up on him. Mary made no bones about it: "You've got your father's dirty, rotten temper and you always seek out the scruff. You'll never amount to anything." And so my big brother set out to do exactly that: in her eyes at least, not to amount to anything.

Pat had his own way of dealing with all this antagonism, of embracing it, of enjoying it almost, so that the bastards never had the satisfaction of grinding him down. He would say he had no hard-on for those dedicated men of the cloth, the priests and brothers of Mount Saint Michael. Every time one of them whacked him it was for good cause: he'd looked the guy full in the face and made some subversive comment.

Patrick spent four years with the men of the cloth so I'd only see him on Easter and Christmas vacation. But we were good pals. The age discrepancy actually worked to my benefit, especially in the all-important area of words. One time right after he came back from boarding school—I would've been about four at the time—we were doing something together and I said, "That dirty cow-sucker!" I had heard it somewhere and it made sense to my little mind that you'd suck a cow. Being a grizzled veteran of nine, my bro knew better: "Not cow-sucker, George. Cocksucker!"

In a good Irish neighborhood we were into bad shit. If there was a rule, Patrick's religion required him to break it. Anything I did wrong he would encourage. We both resisted our mother because she had these delusions of grandeur: she was determined to make a couple of geniuses out of us. Or fruits. The way Patrick puts it is concise: Mary wanted two Little Lord Fauntleroys. What she got was a pair of hardened dog turds.

Nothing made him prouder than the fact that I was always getting kicked out of schools (though Corpus Christi had to take me back in eighth grade because they wanted me to write the school play). I was going down the road he'd already blazed. My mother wanted Pat to go to a school called Regis on the East Side which was for bright kids, but of course he balked. He wanted to go to Cardinal Hayes High in the Bronx: THE cool school. He was more interested in football and dances than "a goddam book report."

Even at Cardinal Hayes he was the same old Patrick. He most admired Brother Philip, the littlest guy in the school and the best hitter. He used to hit Pat right in the nose with a full fist. "Just fucking beautiful," my brother used to say.

He'd be sitting at his desk with his algebra book open and Brother Philip would ask: "Carlin, you know how many homeworks I've assigned this year?" "No, I don't, brother." "Thirty, and you know how many you've handed in?" "No, I don't, brother." "None—and why is that?" Patrick would say, "Because I ain't got no book." Bop! He hits Patrick full in the nose. His nose bleeds easily so to fuck with the good Brother, Pat holds his nose over the algebra book so it can catch the drips. Bam! Bam! Bam! The bantamweight hits him three more in the back of the neck and says, "Go wash up! Don't make a martyr outta yourself!"

We didn't get to do as much together as I would have liked because of the age difference. Still, I knew his buddies and he knew mine. It was a tight neighborhood. Sometimes he'd be going to some party uptown and his friends would say, "Bring Georgie and tell him to bring his tape recorder." My mother had given me a tape recorder for my eighth-grade graduation and on it I'd record all these imitations of people in the neighborhood. I did one Pat loved of Dottie Murphy kicking her grandson: "Take that, you little bastard! Just because your father's a bastard don't mean you can be a bastard too!"

Once when he was home from the air force—he'd just gone in, so he would've been nineteen—I begged to go to the bar with him, though I was much too young. (You had to be eighteen in those days.) He said, "You can't get fucking served. You shouldn't be in there." I offered him a deal: "If I imitate Dottie Murphy talking to Charlie Mallon with Rudy Madden chiming in, will you take me then?"

Rudy Madden was one of those guys with about fifty tattoos and a dark tan. Big on fishing and a voice like a backhoe. Charlie Mallon was a younger brother of a guy named John Mallon, who was the toughest motherfucker in the neighborhood.

I whipped these imitations on him—of Charlie talking to Rudy talking to Dottie Murphy; and I cracked Patrick up. He took me down to the bar.

It was a very hip neighborhood if you wanted it to be—or you could just be a little stay-at-home square and clean house. I wasn't into that any more than Pat had been. I was too busy trying to score reefer off the Puerto Ricans. It drove my mother up the wall because she saw me following in Pat's footsteps. She did try to head me off. She got me a job in a swank New York men's clothing store called Rogers Peet that had been around practically since the Declaration of Independence. A place where rich business pricks felt secure enough while trying on fancy suits to leave their wallets in their pants pockets. Just begging to be stolen. I answered their call and raked in the stuff, but eventually got caught—the cardinal sin according to Patrick, perhaps the only thing he and Mary agreed on.

It was probably good she didn't know what Pat was up to. By then he was down on the waterfront with his dudes stealing flare guns and first-aid kits from Liberty ships and selling them on Riverside Drive. That was a federal rap—ten years and a ten-thousand-dollar fine. Unlike me, Patrick never got caught. He used to say: "I could be looking at you and steal the boots right off your fucking feet."

I had my own crowd and he had his but it was sometimes useful for people to know my older brother was Pat. When we'd go down to Columbia to steal the freshmen's beanies and the students dared to bother us, Pat and the boys would kick the shit out of them.

We hated the Columbia students. It was our neighborhood—Irish Catholic with a lot of hostility on every corner. Out of every twenty Irish kids there were probably thirteen or fourteen getting their asses kicked regularly back home. They felt the need to pass that along.

The students came in from Nebraska and Iowa and they'd run around like they owned the place. Patrick and his pals just devoured them. The students had this dumb song: "Who owns New York? Who owns New York? Some people say we do! Who owns

New York? Who owns New York, who? COLUMBIA!" So one night the guys kicked some students' asses for singing it. Pat said it was beautiful to see the Columbia assholes lying in the street while he sang the song back at them, but with his own words: "Who cleans the streets? Who cleans the streets? Some people say we do! Who cleans the streets? Who cleans the streets, who? WE DO!"

From an early age, he and the guys would "hit up cars." They'd go up to the 120s where the Columbia dorks parked their cars without bothering to lock them. All you had to do was pop the doors till a handle opened, get in the glove boxes and strip them. Amazing what people leave in glove boxes. In the fullness of time I followed suit.

Patrick has always shown the way and I've followed in his footsteps. I went into the air force, just like him, and between the two of us we amassed five court-martials. He had three. I had two. My mother really loved that.

Over the years our relationship has shifted. Back in the sixties Patrick was still slogging away with Catholicism, getting his kids baptized and so on. He was a conservative Southern California car dealer in those days. Then he saw how much my Catholic rap on *Class Clown* and my attitudes toward big business upset our mother. And concluded I must be right.

I encouraged him to write. Long ago when I heard him shooting the shit with the guys at the car dealership I knew he'd be great at it. And he was. I hooked him up with a terrific shrink, Dr. Charles Ansell, and he found out he wasn't fucked up. He was well. The world around him was fucked up.

Patrick likes to say that the relationship has almost inverted: that I'm the main dude now. But it's subtler than that. Earlier on, Pat and I lived in different parts of the world—which is to say he lived in places like Vermont and Trinidad, while I lived in L.A. But over the last twenty-five years, we've spent a lot of time together. He's influenced me perhaps without even quite knowing it, enticed out of me very final and violent and harsh judgments. I articulate them better than he does and I'm obsessive-compulsive about getting them out where they can be heard. But for a long time now he's struck a deep chord in me. He writes wonderful dialogue, great earthy stuff. Talk about the sledgehammer—this is a steam-driven pile driver.

I share his feelings, his ideas and passions, but he kicks them up into a higher gear. Once upon a time, I would never have done stuff like "I Love It When a Lot of People Die" or "People Who Oughtta Be Killed." I didn't have a place in my garden for that stuff. His presence is a sort of reinforcement. It's less an inversion than that the wheel has come full circle. Almost like the old days: if my big brother feels like that, it must be okay. Not that different from when I graduated eighth grade and Mary wanted me to go to Regis just like she'd wanted Pat to. And I said forget it. Just like Pat.

At the end of eighth grade you get this little eighth-grade book that everybody signs with things like "Happy Graduation George from The Girl Who Sat Next to You," the stuff of fond memories decades later. Patrick happened to be home on leave from the air force and I asked him to sign my graduation book. This is what he wrote: "Go to Cardinal Hayes and be a cool guy." Signed: "The Ace of Aces and the Dude of Dudes, Your brother, Patrick."

5

AIR MARSHAL CARLIN TELLS YOU TO GO FUCK YOURSELF

George in uniform, circa 1954

(Courtesy of Kelly Carlin-McCall)

Weird how the military touches so many aspects of your life. It's like the Church in that way. You hate it but it forms you. It's a parent. Mother Church and Father Military.

"Father" might seem a bit affectionate for someone who's on record more than once as having no respect for the business of war. But I don't. I don't feel about war the way we're supposed to, the way we're told to by the United States government. A large part of which is the United States military, whose business is war. So the military is telling us how to feel about war—so *they* can stay in business. Something is fucked up here.

But I confess, Father, to being conflicted about the military. I was four when we got into World War II. Its memory is precious to me, a central fact of my young life. The slogans, the uniforms, the newscasts, the songs: "The White Cliffs of Dover," "Don't Sit Under the Apple Tree," "I'll Never Smile Again." I can never hear them without being overwhelmed by nostalgia. Weirdly enough, the songs of war make me feel . . . safe.

Then there were the blackouts. I loved the blackouts. They gave me a sense of danger: little five-year-old me fighting the war on the home front. The whole idea of blackouts was that if everyone turned their lights out, the Germans wouldn't be able to find New York City to drop bombs on it. Fair enough. The Germans were probably itching to fly three thousand miles across the Atlantic on one tank of gas and reduce us to rubble. They're crazy, those Krauts.

Every week, we'd hear the keening rise and fall of the air-raid siren at 116th and Broadway, signaling air-raid drill and blackout. We'd turn off the lights and gather in the hall—no windows there—where Mary had put a single low-watt amber bulb. I'd wait hopefully for explosions and my mother would tell me how my father was far away in the Pacific, "helping General MacArthur win the war."

The super, Andy McIsaac, would prowl around the building's courtyards, flashlight in hand, wearing an official air-raid warden's hard hat, courageously checking to make sure everyone had turned their lights out so the Germans would be fooled into thinking New York City was just another harmless stretch of marshland.

One time I slid up the window to steal a peek and catch the action of The World At War. Andy wheeled at the sound and blinded me with his flashlight. "George, get yer head back inside unless you want to get it blown off!" I hustled back to the dark hallway as quick as my jammie-clad little legs would carry me. The last thing I needed was to get hit by shrapnel and have a plate in my head for life.

What did you do in the war, Daddy? I did my part. Like bringing the butcher the cans of hardened bacon fat my mother filled from the breakfast skillet. They gave us eleven cents a pound. I've often wondered, what did they do with it? Ship it to those lonely boys overseas? What did THEY do with it? Come to think of it, I don't want to know.

And if everyone else in our front-line advance post had been wiped out by a direct hit, I was ready to serve. As a plane spotter. Thanks to the board game Spot-a-plane I could identify by silhouette any aircraft of any combatant nation, even Italy. Focke-Wulfs, Messerschmitts, Mitsubishis, Vickerses, de Havillands, Martins, Douglases, Boeings, I knew them all. No one could fool me. I could distinguish them from front, side, above and below. Some Kraut cocksucker in a Messerschmitt pretended to be a Spitfire by flying upside down: I'd have the artillery blast him to kingdom come.

Columbia had a Naval Officer's Training School where college graduates attended a ninety-day course before being shipped overseas as ensigns. On Sunday evenings, after supper hour, the midshipmen, assembled in separate ranks of Catholics, Protestants and

Jews, marched through the streets to the local churches and synagogues for evening services. Us kids used to march along beside them for several blocks and they sang as they marched. I can still hear their voices bouncing off the buildings:

> Farewell and goodbye
> There's no need to cry
> Sally and Sue don't be blue
> We're comin' right back
> We're comin' right back to you

The Protestants had a longer march than the Catholics and Jews—down to Riverside Church—so they got my attention more often. Many years later I found out that one of the midshipmen I'd marched alongside was a young guy fresh out of the University of Nebraska—Midshipman Johnny Carson.

Then there were bombs. I've always had a thing about bombs and they were a big part of my childhood. By the last year of the war, I was eight and already riding downtown on the subway by myself; often to the Chrysler Building on 42nd Street where the army had a permanent display of military hardware: jeeps, artillery pieces, a tank, uniforms, insignia, all sorts of good stuff. But the centerpiece was a huge five-hundred-pound bomb called the Blockbuster. It sat vertically in a rack, in its falling orientation, packed with explosive possibilities.

I imagined the rising high-pitched whistle as it screamed to earth—perhaps from a B-17 my uncle Tom had worked on—falling down, down, down, onto the heads of those German people I'd seen in the newsreels. But what I remember most vividly is that previous visitors had scratched their names on the bomb's casing: "Vito—Brooklyn," "Gloria & Eddie," "Sonny USN." Anonymous, powerless people trying to associate themselves with the bomb's vast impersonal power.

Why not? Everyone should try to scratch their name on the bomb of life.

A few hundred yards from my house in Columbia's Pupin Physics

Labs, another bomb—the Big One—began its charmed life. That same year our own homegrown bomb was tested on a few hundred thousand Japanese and came through with flying colors. We all went down to Times Square to celebrate V-J Day: the end of one war and the beginning of the next—the Cold War, which would last ten times as long and cost a hundred times as much. But which we'd win also. Damn, we're good at war.

In due course the time came for me to do my part in winning the Cold War: the draft. One problem with the draft in a large population like New York City was that they had so many volunteers, you often didn't get a draft notice until you were twenty-one or twenty-two. That was more disruptive than getting one at eighteen, so guys often joined up earlier. A lot of them didn't want to be in the army so the chic way to get out of military service was to go into the air force.

The air force seemed a pretty good deal. You could be part of a group whose job it was to go out and drop bombs on brown and yellow people, then come home, take a shower and catch a movie. Plus my brother was in it and they had cool blue uniforms—not that pukey khaki shit—and a lot of off-base privileges. The way it came down to me the air force sounded a lot like a country club.

But mainly I joined the air force with a clear goal: using the GI Bill to train myself as a disc jockey at disc jockey school. Funny how a teenager thinks: I had it all mapped out. I'll become a disc jockey someplace and I'll be so good in that town I'll get famous enough to appear in a nightclub. I'll become a comedian there and get funny enough to be a comedian on Broadway and after that I'll be in movies! Piece of cake.

In August 1954, in I went. My mother had to sign me in, because I was only seventeen. My fiancée, Mary Cathryn, and I went down to 39 Whitehall Street at five in the morning for reporting and swearing in. They put us on a bus for a three-hundred-mile ride to Sampson Air Force Base near Rochester, New York. Weird again: what's running through my head is "Off we go into the wild blue yonder!" I'm on a fucking bus going into a dark hole called the Holland Tunnel.

Right from the get-go in the air force, I gravitated to the black guys. On that bus, I struck up a conversation about black music with a guy from Staten Island named Bishop. He clued me in about the cha-cha-chá versus the mambo, which I thought was the in dance. He told me: "Nah, the mambo's out. Watch for the cha-cha-chá. That's coming next." The first lesson I learned in the military.

Basic training was grueling but I was prepared. You've always got to weed out the amateur slackers and leave the field to professional, dedicated slackers like me. I volunteered for an experimental flight of seventy men used as medical subjects to track the spread of germs. We didn't live on the open base but in our own section, in real rooms. Every so often the medics came around and swabbed our throats with long Q-tips. The first time, they said, "We're trying to see if there's any colds in the outfit."

Later we found out from Flight Sergeant Vanelli what they were really doing. They took cultures from the throats of all the men, marking what room they were in and where they slept in that room so they could track the spread of colds and viruses. So along with the swabs that went in to take stuff out, there were swabs with germs from other guys they put in. Not on the same Q-tip, but still. Disgusting!

We got out of a lot of duty. We didn't even have to get up in the morning for reveille. Reveille is when every flight in the squadron has to fall in, dressed, with their teeth brushed, in parade formation, and they have roll call. We guinea pigs had standing permission to fall out if we wanted or even just fuck off. Early morning, still dark out, September/October, upstate New York? We did a lot of fucking off.

We would go on bivouac, where you go out for three days in tents and camp. It rained one night and they immediately sent us back to the barracks, because they didn't want to compromise their important virus-research unit.

I didn't consider flying for a moment. I had no high school diploma, so I wasn't going to be an officer or a pilot. I quickly discovered that officers were assholes anyway: the bosses and managers of the operation. I definitely didn't identify with them. I might have wanted the things they could buy with their salary but I certainly didn't want to get them that way. I was strictly GI.

I gravitated to the black airmen, some of whom were from around my neighborhood in Harlem. Others came from the South Side of Chicago or the Hough neighborhood in Cleveland. I had more in common with them—jazz, R&B, stuff I could talk about. The white kids were mostly farm kids from upstate New York, Ohio and points west. No "bonding" with them.

At this level your flight commander was the same rank as you. He too was going through basic training to get his one stripe. But if they'd had some military experience, like the National Guard, they were made flight commander. First among equals. Same deal as the pope.

The flight commander had his own room to live in at the end of the hall. Ours was a big black guy, called Don, with powerful shoulders who'd been a swimmer in high school in Chicago. He was half full of shit but he did get to choose the squad leaders—the front-rank marchers, who led each column and had a little bit of clout. Don chose two black guys and me, because I was a cool guy.

A lot of basic training is sitting through classes, listening to life-or-death lectures like how to behave in uniform. If you're in uniform you never push a baby carriage. If you're in uniform you never carry an umbrella. If you're in uniform you always take off your hat indoors. You have to salute this guy and that guy. And lectures on military history: endless fucking battles, all of which we'd won.

Don would give me off a lot of classes. I'd been selected for a more important mission. In the morning he'd hand me a list—my orders for the day: "Go down to the BX [the Base Exchange] and steal these records." Don was a shrewd tactician: being a big-city kid, I was good at stealing. Being white, I was less likely to be scrutinized while browsing the racks. My skill put me in his good graces. He'd let me hang in his room after the other guys had lights-out, and listen to the records I'd stolen.

One day in the BX on a search-and-acquire mission, I spotted this one-striper I could swear I'd met somewhere. Then it hit me: he was from my neighborhood and I'd scored pot from him once. He was a rank above me, almost a god: anyone with a stripe could order you to do things and you had to obey. Here was a real dilemma: does the Uniform Code of Military Justice allow me to approach him or not? Does it allow me to score pot from him or not? I needn't have agonized. Apparently it allowed me to do both.

He was in a different barracks, exclusively for one-stripers. I went to his room at a prearranged time just before lights-out. And I was blown away. Not only does this dude have a 45 rpm record player, playing a Stan Kenton record, he has a lit joint in the ashtray, casually left there between hits. Lit! Just sitting there!

I'd never seen that before in my life. A joint had to go around fast so not a single milligram burned away. Forget ashtrays. You stood on the stoop and zipped it around quick, a process called "one and go" or "two and go." He was just letting it sit there and burn! What a motherfucking classy guy! I bought a ten-dollar bag and some papers and that night I was the hit of Don's room.

Thus we skated through basic, serving our country by smoking pot, stealing records and giving each other colds.

And they gave me a stripe for it.

Next it was off to Denver and "set school." Here you learned a set: in my case the K-2 bombing and navigation system used in the hot new B-47 Stratojet medium-range bomber. The B-47 was a brainchild of General Curtis LeMay, whose earlier World War II brainchild had been incinerating German and Japanese citizens by the hundreds of thousands from the air. (He was also the model for George C. Scott's psychotic General "Buck" Turgidson in *Dr. Strangelove*.) By now he commanded the Strategic Air Command and the B-47 was key to his new mission of incinerating Russian citizens from the air. By the millions this time. My kinda guy.

The B-47 was the first bomber in history that flew as fast as a fighter. It was also a high-altitude aircraft. So the K-2 system—which was analog—had a lot of navigational problems to solve in getting a bomb to its target and releasing it in a timely manner. It had to take into account factors like drift at subsonic speeds, ballistics, the nature of the casing, how the bomb fell and a host of other variables.

You set in certain values at the beginning and fed in other values along the way: where is your BRL (Bomb Release Locus), your AP (Aimed Point) and your GR (Ground Range)? Then K-2 computed them and solved them so that the nuke would actually hit its target. I loved this shit, partly because I got to use my brain for a change but also because I found I loved data flow, the technology, the problem solving. And the jargon. There was one great acronym associated with the K-2: IRAN. Someone with a glimmer of humor must've come up with that. It stands for: Inspect and Repair As Necessary.

Plus all of it was about one of my favorite things—bombs.

I turned eighteen in May 1955, and having been in the service eight or nine months, I got to pick where I would now be based. Actually you got to pick three bases and they picked from those. I tried to get as close to home as possible. I chose Plattsburgh, New York, Columbus, Ohio, and some other SAC base in New England, at any of which I would've been able to defend sacred American freedoms like freedom of choice. Predictably they ignored all my choices and sent me to Barksdale Air Force Base, across the Red River from Shreveport, Louisiana, which, according to my friend José, was "the fucking armpit of the fucking nation."

I didn't do much off-base socializing at first. The barracks life was pretty cool. It was three people in the room, your own single beds, and you could drink and smoke. If you had a Class A pass, you could leave the base anytime you wanted. So there was a certain freedom. I disappeared into my music, jazz and R&B. And before long I got to put my master plan into action.

Every base has an NCO club and an officers' club, but this was the fifties Deep South and segregated. So there was an annex in the club for black NCOs. Lesser mortals could also go there: one-, two- and three-stripers. That's where I began to hang out. They had "radar" hotdogs: the franks had cheese injected in the center and were heated in some kind of radiation-powered oven—an early version of a microwave. Who knows how much radiation we ingested with our dogs? There was malt liquor and Carling's Black Label and a jukebox and dances and other good stuff. There was me and a lot of black guys from various squadrons. I saw another white guy in there maybe twice. I was ostracized by the mainstream white culture in the barracks as being one of them "crazy white nigger-lover guys from New York City."

Socializing with black airmen came very naturally to me. On the Harlem streets I grew up on as a kid, we were cheek by jowl with blacks and Latinos of all kinds: Dominicans, Puerto Ricans, Cubans, and we all got along pretty well. We had to. I heard plenty of prejudicial and discriminatory remarks from guys on the corner and on the stoops in my teenhood. But they never sat well with me, they never took hold. When I heard "spades," I started using that more, because it was softer than the prevailing slurs. The offhand racist remarks and attitudes didn't go with the way I felt. My mother wasn't prejudiced either, so it wasn't in my background as it was for a lot of guys. (Although she leaned toward anti-Semitism. She referred to Jews as "Norwegians." The code between her and her sister, Agnes, was: "Ag, couple of Norwegians on the bus.")

I once spent a night in jail just for being in a car with a black guy driving. I had a black roommate named Connie who owned a little car. Which was nice; a total reversal of what they'd expect down there. Walters, a white guy from San Jose who lived across the hall, and I needed a lift into town. We were going to a white bar and Connie was going to a black one.

So a black guy is driving in Louisiana in a little coupe with one white guy sitting next to him and another white guy—me—in the back. We're heading down Barksdale Boulevard toward Shreveport and suddenly there are two local police cars with lights flashing. They put us through the usual kind of verbal harassment. They had to treat us a little bit differently, because we were airmen. They knew they could harass us for one night and then our base would get us out the next morning. But for a few hours they got to put us through some Southern shit, full of the usual hatred and insults.

We wound up spending the night in jail, for no reason, except DWB and DWBWWG (Driving While Black With White Guy). They put Connie in one cell with the black guys, Walters and I in an adjacent cell. Through the bars we could talk to and touch the black guys. The window had no glass in it, because it's a real sultry climate.

I had three joints in my sock and they hadn't searched us. So we smoked pot all night, in 1955, blacks and whites together, in the

Bossier City jail. Blew the fucking smoke out the fucking window. That felt good!

There was a freedom to hanging with blacks that ran counter to the structured life of the military. In one way it was part of my training for a comedic career, picking up a looseness and directness I wouldn't have had if I'd stuck with "my own kind." Plus the music led to radio and a stint as a deejay, which in turn led to my becoming a performer. In another way that rebelliousness ensured an impressive record of court-martials and near-court-martials.

Barksdale was an SAC base with a lot of real live B-47s, each one of which was worth a fortune. In 1955 there was no nuclear triad yet, no land-air-sea capability. They were just beginning to build the submarines and they hadn't yet dug the silos. B-36s had been phased out and the B-52s weren't yet being delivered. So B-47 medium bombers were it: our only deterrent against the demonic designs of the Evil Empire. I was one tiny but crucial part of the thin line between America and Armageddon. Peace, as our psychopathic commander used to say, was my profession.

You needed a SAC pass to walk the flight line, with your picture on it, and coded for whatever you were allowed access to. I'm walking the flight line one day and an air policeman my age, if not younger, is on duty. My SAC pass was under my field jacket so he couldn't see it. He says, "Where's your SAC pass?" I said, "Fuck you. I'm going to work," and kept walking. He draws his gun and says, "Spread-eagle on the pavement," and I said, "Fuck you, you cocksucker."

Then logic takes over: "Wait, I have it, here it is, leave me alone." But it was too late. I'd said "Fuck you." I had defied authority. And I got an Article 15, a punishment just short of a court-martial. They can dock your pay and reduce you in rank. So I lost my stripe and went back down to airman basic.

I earned the stripe back after a while, but now along came a military exercise which simulated "enemies" trying to breach the perimeter of the base. The game is you defend the bombers. They try to get in and tag the bombers. The idea of Soviet troops getting as far as Bossier City, Louisiana, and sabotaging our B-47s made about as much sense as Germans flying across the Atlantic on one tank of gas. But this stupid schoolyard shit was taken very seriously.

It's night and just before Christmas. Even in Louisiana it's freezing on the flight line. There's a power unit going by one of the bombers, keeping it nice and warm inside. I'm stationed near it and I'm full of alcohol so I figure I'll take a little nap. I put my gun—I refuse to call it a rifle, it's a gun—next to the power unit, go into the plane and crash. Some sector guy drives by checking on us, and sees my fucking weapon. Abandoned! They haul me out and this time I'm court-martialed for "deserting my post in a Unit Simulated Combat Mission."

Military justice—an oxymoron if ever I heard one—saves time, money and gets convictions. Forget about that stupid due process stuff. The colonel who presided over my court-martial was the only other man present: he's judge, jury, prosecutor, defense attorney. He says: "We find you guilty." What "we," motherfucker?

But he decides to be lenient: "You have Christmas leave coming up so I'm going to take it easy on you. I'm letting you off the brig. But we're taking two-thirds of your pay for ninety days and you lose your stripe."

My air force record on stripes was this: I got one stripe, lost one stripe, got one stripe, got two stripes, lost one stripe, got two stripes, lost one stripe, lost another stripe. I earned six stripes and lost four stripes. By the time I got out I felt like a fucking zebra.

So now my rep was starting to be: "It's not just he's hanging out with these boogies. He's a fuckup too." Then something happened that changed my life. I'm sitting in my room one night and a guy named Mike Stanley from Mississippi comes by and says, "Hey, George, know what I'm doing? I'm in a play. I play the boxer in *Golden Boy*. There's this little theater group downtown called Venture Theater and they got other parts to fill. You'd be good at that, you're a clowny guy." So I went down and got a part in one act as the trainer and as the photographer in the next. With a different hat.

But the guy who was playing Tom Moody, the fighter's manager, was Joe Monroe, morning disc jockey on KJOE, the most popular station in town. Everybody listened to KJOE and everybody talked about it, because it played Top 40, when quick-format Top 40 was brand new, the hot thing. What I didn't know was that Joe Monroe was also a 50 percent owner of the station. So I said, "Joe, I wanna be a disc jockey when I get out of the air force. I'd love to come down and just watch your show someday." He said, "Anytime."

I go down to KJOE, and when he signs off he says, "Take these texts, go into that studio with the glass wall and read them for me." So with my New York accent, in the Deep South, I'm reading: "Hey, Hackenpack Store is open seven days a week! Twenty-four hours a day!" Then I read news about the Suez Canal crisis. He hires me on the spot, sixty cents an hour to do the weekend sustaining newscast.

Soon I expanded. There was a one-hour show from twelve to one, where they didn't do the formula—they just played Nice Music at Noontime or whatever. I got that hour, twelve to one. The next step was he decided to cut out the twelve-to-one slot: "That stuff's bullshit, we're not doing that anymore." He went to a 6–9, 12–3, 3–6 daily format. I got the twelve-to-three slot, every day.

The air force was incredibly pleased that I'd finally found something constructive to do. I was downtown in a very visible position. I was not spreading venereal disease or raping people. Excellent PR for the USAF.

They gave me an off-base permit. Because I needed to be away from the base so much, they took me out of my career field as a 32130E K-systems mechanic and made me a dispatcher. Every other night at midnight I wrote up work orders for the next day. It took an hour some nights, some nights longer. But once I was done, I could leave. Tops I did three hours of work out of every forty-eight, lived in my room, kept my bunk area clean. That was all they demanded of me.

I had one more court-martial—in England. We were there for ninety days, the whole wing, forty-five planes, every piece of equipment. What SAC often did to prove that they were worth their money was to mobilize an entire wing and fly it to a "forward position" like Morocco or England, which were only 1,500 or so miles from the godless Soviets instead of 3,500 miles away in Louisiana. So they'd save a few bucks on gas.

While we were in England, the Dodgers, whom I'd loved all my life and had never won a World Series, beat the Yankees in the World Series. A friend and I listened to it on Armed Forces Radio. We were five hours later in England of course, but when the Dodgers won, we got royally hammered. I stagger back to the base and it's the middle of the fucking night and I'm still celebrating. The barracks chief, the tag sergeant, starts raining on my parade, yelling, "Shut up, Carlin!" To which I replied with my standard "Go fuck yourself, cocksucker!"

Gross insubordination. Grounds for my second court-martial.

So that's two court-martials, and four more Article 15s after the first one, in my air force career to date. A grand total of seven major disciplinary offenses. Pretty fucking impressive.

And I still had a year to go. I'd signed on for four years of active duty. Then you automatically had to do four years more in the reserves. They had your ass for eight years. But they didn't want mine.

There were four ways to get out: dishonorable discharge, bad conduct discharge, honorable discharge and general discharge. I didn't fit any of them. They decided I was something called a 3916, which was like a no-fault divorce. A tacit acknowledgment that it wasn't working out between you and the air force. You had to meet three criteria: One, you'd been out of your career field for two years or more. Two, you'd been reduced in rank more than two times. Three, you did not plan to reenlist. I fit the profile perfectly.

The air force let me out after three years and one month, with all my pay allowances and all my GI rights. And they didn't want me in the reserves. Basically they said: "You don't mention you were here and we won't either." An early form of don't ask, don't tell.

I absolutely beat the game. I was twenty, I had a year and a half of radio under my belt, I was clear of all obligations to the military. It was just a great feeling.

So I do have this ambivalence. Obviously I'm against militaries, because of what militaries do. In many ways though, the air force was unmilitary-like. They dropped bombs on people, but . . . they had a golf course.

I'd conquered the fucking system this whole squadron revolved around. I knew everything there was to know about the K-2 system: 1,600 pounds of equipment, 41 major components, 370 vacuum tubes and close to 20,000 separate parts. I'd learned how not to get in fights. I'd learned how to get just drunk enough to get home okay. I'd learned how to stay just within the confines of regulation.

In a way, the air force was the father I never had. It was an all-male entity that took care of me, gave me a room of my own, fed me and helped get the childhood part of me finished. It brought me to a place where I could step off into my life and career and rejected me at just the right moment.

So I want to thank the Pentagon, the Soviet Union and the military-industrial complex from the bottom of my heart. Without them, I could never have become the man I am today.

6

TWO GUYS
IN THEIR UNDERWEAR

Jack Burns (left) and George
(Courtesy of Kelly Carlin-McCall)

The most important milestone in my early career was meeting Jack Burns at WEZE in Boston in 1959.

After the air force and I parted ways, I continued as a deejay at KJOE back in Shreveport for a few months. But I wanted to be nearer New York and in a larger market, and when one of the guys from KJOE moved up to Boston, I asked him to get me a spot there, no matter what kind of station it was.

WEZE was a far cry from KJOE. An NBC network station, they still carried soap operas, quiz shows and other antiquated programs. I got on the air as a board announcer, doing live copy and running the board when network came in. I did have a two-hour music stint late at night but I had to play shit like Sinatra, Vic Damone, Keely Smith and Louis Prima.

Jack was a newsman at the station. He and I hit it off immediately. We both did much the same Irish street character—who later became my Indian Sergeant and all the other Sergeants he spawned. Jack's version was a Boston-Irish bigot who later became famous in his classic taxicab routine with Avery Schreiber.

Jack's guy had more of an edge. My guy had a more human side to him. These two guys would talk together for hours. They were great characters for saying things you weren't quite willing to say yourself. Jack and I found ourselves being very inventive in each other's company. We thought fast on our feet and struck up a great friendship. Even dreamed a little about doing a comedy act . . .

Then, as usual, I got canned.

I caused two major crises at WEZE. The first was the Cardinal Cushing Rosary Incident. In 1959 Cardinal Cushing was a big deal in the Catholic Church and, being very close to the Kennedys, an even bigger deal in Boston. Every evening from 6:45–7:00 he said the rosary on the air and was a longtime favorite of the Catholic-Irish faithful.

So I'm riding the board and Cardinal Cushing is in his palace or wherever the fuck they live. He's on remote—a phone line. This evening he's doing the Five Sorrowful Mysteries. Before he began the rosary he would always say a little something about life in the Boston archdiocese. This evening he starts in about the Little Sisters of the Poor. "The Little Sisters of the Poor have been working selflessly for years in the Boston wards where children with chronic diseases . . ." He gets carried away by the wonderful saintly Little Sisters and starts the Five Sorrowful Mysteries late.

Now seven o'clock is creeping up and His Eminence is only at the Third Sorrowful Mystery. ("The Crowning of Our Lord with Thorns," for those who care.) I'm faced with a major executive decision. At precisely seven o'clock an Alka Seltzer–sponsored newscast is due from the network. Alka-Seltzer and NBC versus Cardinal Cushing and the last two Sorrowful Mysteries? A no-brainer. I lower the cardinal's pot. He's off the air.

The news comes on with that little NBC jingle. Not a minute goes by before the phone rings and I hear a voice of thunder: "I'd like to speak to the young man WHO TURNED THE HOLY WORD OF GOD OFF THE AIR!"

Apparently he had a fucking air-check monitor in his ear and he'd heard NBC News coming in. I said: "Cardinal Cushing, this is George Carlin. I'm on duty. I have a log to follow and the FCC . . ."—you know how you go for everything in a crisis situation—"This is a Federal Communications Commission regulation I have to follow . . ."

The station backed me up, but it was a huge black mark. Crisis Number Two—the News-Unit Incident—was even huger and blacker. Several times, on weekends when I needed to score pot, I'd taken the station's mobile news-unit, a vast boat of a station wagon stuffed with equipment and gaudy lettering along the side reading "WEZE 1260, News of the Moment!' and driven it to New York.

This particular weekend, there were about six or seven of us, crowded in with the equipment, driving through Harlem looking to score. Everyone knew someone: "Let's go see if Paco is around 111th and Madison." No dice with Paco, so now it's "Georgie, Georgie, I know, Santos! Let's try Santos!" and off we cruise to 145th and Amsterdam. All over the city in a huge fucking car with huge fucking letters on it, trying to score illegal drugs. Great PR for NBC News.

When I get home there's a call from the station manager in Boston. He says: "Guess what? We got a prison break at Walpole State Prison. Started last night. We couldn't find the news-unit. I assume you have it?" "Yeah, I got it. It's fine!" "Well, it's not doing us any good down there in New York." I said, "They have a shitload of prison breaks at Walpole. There'll be another within a month. Don't sweat it."

He didn't appreciate that. Sayonara, George.

KXOL, the number one station in Fort Worth, took me in and gave me a great spot: the seven-to-midnight segment doing Top 40. The "homework shift," they called it: kids doing their homework and listening to the number one station playing all the cool records.

Before long I got to be a bit of a local celeb so I had a lot of contact with those kids. And for the first time I got a whiff of that unnamed, unspoken, unformed conspiracy of the young against authority and old rules that seemed to be fermenting in the heartland. In Fort Worth, of all places! ("*Cowtown! 'N proud of it!*") At sock hops you could see the degree of influence black music and dance had had, even on these white—basically segregated—Protestant kids. They were trying to learn cool moves even if they weren't doing them as freely as their role models.

Then after about six months at KXOL, who comes floating in the door one day but Jack Burns.

He'd quit WEZE, while doing the early morning news with a massive hangover. The station was in the old Statler hotel, which had long windows like the *Today Show* does now, through which the public could peer in and be part of the exciting world of radio—

like newsman Jack Burns doing the early morning news. In the middle of reading the headlines Jack looks up to see an old wino pissing on the window right in front of him. If there were no glass he'd be pissing on Jack.

And Jack thought to himself: "I do not want to be pissed on while delivering important news of the day." And quit.

Now he's on his way to Hollywood, "to give them one more chance." But he's broke and his tires are bald and he's taken a detour to Cowtown to see if I could find him work.

In more ways than one it was something that was meant to be. A guy had just quit our newsroom without notice and they were looking for a newsman. Authoritative, knowledgeable newsman Jack got the job on the spot.

We picked up right where we'd left off (as did our Irish alter egos), and started rooming together. And Jack resumed his steady radicalization of me that he'd begun in Boston.

In my home, Republicanism was a given. Both my mother and my aunt had worked for William Randolph Hearst and were terminally infected with the Westbrook Pegler–J. Edgar Hoover–Joe McCarthy virus. My mother was always happy to proclaim that while her dad had been a lifelong Democrat, she'd become an Eisenhower Republican.

Part of the reason was that she rubbed shoulders with big business, working as executive assistant to Paul B. West, the president of the Association of National Advertisers, a lobbying outfit for the advertising industry. (She was his executive assistant, *not* his secretary. No taking dictation for Mary.) She was on first-name terms with the marketing chiefs of big corporations like Philco, Ford, General Motors, General Foods, General Electric, U.S. Steel. She loved to throw their names around. And had taken on board their Republican beliefs lock, stock and barrel.

Then there was McCarthy. In 1954, between high school and the air force, when I briefly worked at Western Union, his Senate hearings were really boiling. Because of what I'd absorbed at home I was very pro-Joe. I was surprised at how many of the WU managers— who'd come up through the union ranks—were not. Nonetheless, after I left home, I continued to assume his ravings were correct. Of course there were Communists everywhere! And if you were commies wouldn't you try to get into the State Department?

These feelings (rather than opinions) weren't really part of my overall personhood. My mother had simply grafted them on to the personality of an outsider and rebel.

At WEZE I still had that conservative graft. It would come out on air sometimes. On one particular occasion Jack called me on it. I can't remember why I did this on an easy listening station in an ultraliberal town—some news event must have provoked it—but right in the middle of the Mantovani-style music mush I issued a call for the preemptive bombing of Red China.

When I came off the air Jack was waiting for me. He said: "How the hell did you work nuking China into an intro for Andre Kostelanetz?" I had no idea what he was talking about: it seemed normal enough to me. Jack said: "Let's go get a beer. There's some things I gotta talk to you about."

From Jack I heard a very different slant than the one I'd grown up with. That the Right was interested in things but the Left was interested in people. That the Right defends property and property rights, while the Left fights for civil and human rights.

Jack turned me on to Castro, who'd recently ousted the Cuban dictator Batista. Jack had been in Cuba back when he was in the Marines and "just another right-wing Irish reactionary" (like me), but after the revolution he'd gone back and been really impressed with Castro. He even interviewed Castro when he came to Boston, one of the first English-language interviews Castro gave in the United States.

I began to realize the error of what had been handed to me through the Catholics, the Irish, my mother, through the Hearst legacy in our family. It didn't take much reasoning. It immediately struck a chord. Of course that's how I feel! Of course I'm for the underdog! Of course it's right-wing business assholes who've been keeping me down! The first time those doors opened for me was thanks to Jack.

We started going to a coffeehouse called the Cellar on Houston

Street where you could get drinks even though Fort Worth was dry. In white Protestant Texas Cowtown, a bunch of beatniks at an all-night coffeehouse with illegal alcohol was really living on the edge. (There was one guy there who wore a blanket and an eagle on his shoulder. A fucking eagle!) These were Cowtown's outcasts. That was attractive somehow. All food for these new feelings.

One night we got up and started riffing on the bits we'd played around with at home, letting our Irish guys talk, improvising on the floor. We heard laughs, amazing, real laughs. And that was the beginning. The genesis of everything that came afterward. The first time I ever stood up in front of an audience of complete strangers and intentionally made them laugh. There is nothing like that feeling. Nothing. Nearly half a century later it's still as powerful as ever.

We continued to get up at the Cellar and continued to get laughs. And a great deal more confidence. Some of it was because we were local favorites from the radio. But we were also doing these things with great abandon. The Cellar was our gymnasium, our laboratory. It belonged to us. And it allowed us to develop an expansive onstage collective personality, which in turn led to taking chances.

JB: Hi, kids, it's time for Captain Jack . . .

GC: And Jolly George!

JB: What a show we've got for you today, kids. Remember yesterday on cartoon time we left Clarabelle the clown and Hermie the hermaphrodite all hung up in the back room? What were they trying to do, kids? That's right—hide the booze before Clarabelle's Mommy came back!

GC: How about you, kids? Manage to get the booze hidden before Mommy staggered home? Watch out: Mommy don't wanna see you getting smashed too. Tell you what you do. You watch where Daddy hides his booze, then you put yours in the same place! If Mommy finds it, he gets busted, not you!

JB: Hey, kids, listen up! Today is absolutely the last day to send off for your Captain Jack and Jolly George junior junkie kit!

GC: Boy, you've gotta have this kit, kids!

JB: Why is this the last day? Well, we were down in Tijuana and our dealer's been busted by the fuzz. So we're running a little short of the stuff. Now—this is pure heroin you get. No cuts. No milk, sugar, flour. Dy-no-mite stuff, kids!

GC: Captain Jack and I shot up a bag right before the show. Lemme tell you, kids, I'm TWISTED! Look at my EYES! One taste and I'm STONED!

JB: In the kit you get a U.S. Army surplus 12 cc hypodermic needle . . .

GC: And a genuine Roger's silverware bent spoon. That's to mix the fix . . . The bent spoon is available in Modern, Traditional, Provincial or Rosemead. Make sure you specify which pattern you want when you send in the cash.

JB: AND—you get 3,669 feet of rubber tubing to wrap around your arm to get that vein popping out there.

GC: AND you get a thirty-day supply of cotton to keep the spike clean. Don't want to get no abscessed vein. You know, Captain Jack—we've gotten a lot of letters from kids shooting up with a dirty spike—and getting abscessed veins. You keep that spike clean, kids. And when you see that big bluish, purple splotch creeping up your arm it's time to switch to the main vein.

JB: Now, this is just for the girls! You boys, out of the room! Okay, girls, today is your last day to send for your Lolita kit. You get an autographed picture of Vladimir Nabokov and the original

*Lolita. You also get an instruction booklet. If you girls read those
instructions and do the exercises prescribed . . .*

GC: *That's kind of fun in itself, girls . . .*

JB: *. . . in just two weeks you'll be walking and talking and acting like girls twice your age. Then you can pick up a little cash
after school. Call those boys back in!*

GC: *Okay, kids, time to go. We want to leave you with our
thought for the day:*

JB/GC: *Whatever you do—don't forget to PRAYYYY!*

Something else happened during that period that had a nice wistful, romantic flavor. We would watch *The Jack Parr Show* ("where
dreams are made"), and be full of fantasies about appearing on it.

We'd sit around in our underwear—it was very hot in Texas so
we'd always be sitting around in our underwear—and improv getting on *Parr*. One would play Parr, the other Burns or Carlin. "So
tell us, guys"—that soft, serpentine hiss Parr had—"how did you two
get together?" "Well, I was dating Jack's mother. She's black, by the
way. So I'm going down on her one night and Jack walks in . . ."

We decided we had to leave Fort Worth. I went to the station
manager, Earl. (Earl was one of these periodic alkies who wake up
in Seattle and call the office: "I'll be in, in about a week.") I tell him
we're going to Hollywood to become nightclub comedians. He says,
"Well, George, a lot of people have left here to go to Hollywood and
a lot of them had to come back. We put a lot of money into promoting you and taking your picture just right. And now you're just going
to leave." I said, "I gotta do what I gotta do." He said, "George, if you
do come back we're going to have to use the same picture." I said,
"Okay."

We bought a Dodge Dart, real good-looking two-door, light blue
car. Tinted windows and everything. We just got in the car and
drove west on old Highway 80 toward El Paso. Mike Ambrose, the

midnight guy (who went on after my shift was over), kept saying goodbye to us as we drove out of the signal's reach. Talking to us on the air, "They're on their way. On their way to Hollywood. They're going to be big stars." Then he played "El Paso" by Marty Robbins. Just a wonderful feeling.

We went to El Paso, Las Cruces and points west. It was *On the Road* with Jack Kerouac. One night we found ourselves driving through some desert landscape working on a six-pack and there was a full moon. So we turned off the lights and drove for miles and miles. Hurtling through the Great American Night in the late fifties. Wonderful. Crazy. Taking chances.

We decided to go into Mexico and drive the rest of the way to California through Mexico. There was a Highway 2, but we weren't sure if we were going the right way. There weren't enough signs, and if there were they were in a fucking foreign language. Night fell and I looked up and there was the Big Dipper. And I said, "The Big Dipper was over there last night when we were going west. It's over there tonight. So we're still going west." And I felt I really knew how to take care of shit.

Eventually we turned north and came to the outskirts of L.A. on the Hollywood Freeway. There's one section of the Hollywood Freeway, coming from the Harbor Freeway, where you suddenly see all these tall, tall palm trees, the ones that have nothing on top but the little fronds.

Right afterward there's the sign that reads: "Next Six Exits: Hollywood." The ultimate moment! The ultimate destination of all those movie dreams I'd had in the dark of the Nemo Theatre on 110th Street.

What I remember most about the ambience of Hollywood was this amazing *morning* feeling. This promise of wide-open possibility. Something about the way the air smelled. And tasted good—and no, this is not a smog joke. There was a goldenness to the atmosphere. Even with all the traffic, a kind of quiet, a peace free of hustle and agitation. You felt safe but at the same time able to have different dreams every day. Or picture a hundred futures.

The reality was that we checked in to the YMCA and immediately hit places like Villa Capri hoping Frank Sinatra would come in. Or that someone would say, "Look at those two interesting young men at the bar. Shouldn't they be in show business?"

We had some money saved so we bought suits at Sears, cool Rat-Packy three-button deals. The kind of suits that in one light look green and in a different light look brown. So it's like having two suits.

We hit the Brown Derby on Vine Street. Going in we met Rock Hudson coming out. My first realization that everything is not what you're led to believe in the fan magazines: Rock was so light in his loafers he barely touched the sidewalk.

Another night in the Brown Derby we spotted this guy in a banquette with two or three women, an older guy, sharply dressed. And he had a telephone at his elbow! Actually in the banquette! We figured he must be a really fucking cool agent guy. A few weeks later our new manager arranged to have somebody come into the nightclub we were working and take photos of us while we were on stage. It was the really fucking cool agent guy.

We continue this way for about a month and come back one day to the YMCA to find the remainder of our money missing from the sock drawer. We'd been robbed—presumably by some Young Christian Man. Disaster. We had to get some dough, get work. But unfortunately we'd made a mutual pact not to ever really work. We would not park cars or wait tables. It was show business or starve.

We had to get back into radio. Like I said, we weren't going to *work*. The first place we went—a daytime station called KDAY—was looking for a morning comedy team. Only in Hollywood! We did an audition tape and got the gig. They called us the Wright Brothers, put aviator helmets on us and we did our first show from an airplane.

We had trouble getting up at five in the morning. If we were late we had a trick in case the station owner had been monitoring us and had heard dead air. We'd upcut ourselves—chop the first letters off a word to make it sound as if there was something wrong with the transmission. ". . . 'ack Burns, here! 'd morning Los Angeles!"

The studios—in a little building on Vine—didn't occupy the entire floor. There were also small offices where song publishers, song pluggers or other small offshoots of showbiz could have an address and get phone messages.

The station went off the air at sunset. Jack and I used to stay at the station and work on nightclub bits there. One night we're rehearsing and a guy came out of one of these little offices. His name was Murray Becker.

Murray watched us for a while, then said, "I used to manage Rowan and Martin and Ford and Hines, I know a lot of the teams, I know agents, I got connections, I worked with a lot of comics. You guys are nice, you're hip, you're young, you're clean, you got that hip tip, it's in, it's hip, why don't you let me manage ya?"

Well, why not?

A week or so before, we'd found work at a coffeehouse called Cosmo Alley. We were there without a contract. Murray said, "You gotta have a contract." First things first, he drew up a management contract between Burns and Carlin and Murray Becker. Then he went to the coffeehouse and got everything down in writing. He got us into AGVA, where he knew people. Murray was a little Jewish guy, a lovable man who knew his way around. Incredibly loyal. If you were his act, man, you got talked about in glowing terms all day to everyone.

Two things now happen. First: Murray knows a guy at Era Records, Herb Newman, and he gets Herb Newman to record us. Three hundred bucks advance, but . . . we're only in L.A. for a month and we've recorded an album!

Second: an important part of our act was an imitation of Mort Sahl and one of Lenny Bruce. I did them both because I was a better mimic than Jack. And to imitate them in 1960 was something of an act of defiance. So we felt far out—that was the term of the time— these guys are really FAR OUT! They do Lenny and Mort Sahl!

Murray says, "I know Milt Ebbins [Mort Sahl's manager], I know Lenny Bruce. We were in the navy together. I think I can get them to come in and see you guys and we can get a blurb or something. We get a little talk going, you guys are young, you're sharp, you're hot, you're hip . . ."

So Mort came in to see us. Mort was encouraging. He called us "a cerebral duo" and later he recommended us to Hugh Hefner for the Playboy Clubs. They called us a "duo of hip wits . . ."

A few nights later in comes Lenny with his wife, Honey, and while we didn't quite realize at the time the legendary nature of this encounter, I do remember that for eveningwear Lenny had chosen a powder-blue sport jacket.

Lenny was incredibly important to me. I'd come across his album *Interviews of Our Times* when I was in Shreveport and I was changed forever. The defiance inherent in that material, the brilliance of the mimicry, the intellect at work, the freedom he had. I had no sense I could approach it ever, but I wanted to emulate it in any way I could.

One simple way: mimic him. I got aspects of him that were very good although I didn't really have the voice. But he liked us! He was partly flattered I think and partly liked the brash edge we had. So he was friendly and wished us luck (*"Emmis!"*). The next thing we know, we get a telegram from Jack Sobel, the head of GAC, which was one of the biggest agencies of the day. (General Artists, we handle everybody!) The telegram read: "Based on Lenny Bruce's rave reaction, New York office hereby authorizes West Coast office GAC to sign Burns and Carlin under exclusive representation contract, all fields, Jack Sobel." Phew.

It was June 1960. We'd been in the business five months. We had an album, a manager and a big agency. And Lenny Bruce liked us! L.A. seemed to have delivered big-time on that morning feeling.

By now I had politically crossed the street. There'd already been several months of a campaign in which a new young liberal candidate was on the horizon and getting clearer all the time. Jack was a Kennedy man from way back. When Kennedy won the Wisconsin primary, Jack said: "He's on the glory road." That made my skin prickle.

We got booked, properly booked for once, into a legitimate nightclub: The Cloister Inn in Chicago. A first-line place that was regularly reviewed by *Variety*. Right on Rush Street in the heart of Chicago's nighttime scene with the Happy Medium across the street, the Living Room, the Playboy Club, Mister Kelly's farther down. We were opening for Bobby Short. "How come we're open-ing for a pianist?" Jack asks. "He ought to be opening for us."

We do great. We get held over. Hefner sees us. Hefner likes us. We're in the Playboy Club. And *Playboy* at that time was on its way up, the polite side of the revolution, if you like, fighting for sexual freedom and freedom of speech. The guys who bought keys were actually kind of lame—they only thought they were hip because Hef told them they were. But still, it felt good to be in that mix.

And we got the *Paar Show*. Just ten months after we'd been sitting in our underwear in Fort Worth fantasizing about it. We did Hunt-ley and Brinkley interviewing Kennedy and Nixon. I did Nixon in 1960 (before anyone, I think, and I did Kennedy better than Vaughn Meader. Ha!). We didn't get Paar as host: we got Arlene Francis. So we didn't get to tell our story about our having met when Jack caught me going down on his African-American mother. But we did get to be part of the Kennedy power structure that night: Arthur Schlesinger Jr. was also a guest.

Burns and Carlin were on their way.

Our goal, if we had one, was to be a crossover act, somewhere between the disrespectful, irreverent comedy of the coffeehouses and the smart, sophisticated Blue Angel school. Shelley Berman, Mort Sahl, Nichols and May had already accomplished this, Bob Newhart and Dick Gregory were beginning to. That was what we aspired to.

But there was some other element to what we did—a certain amount of risk taking. We weren't quite what was becoming a stan-dard type. We weren't clean cut, campus bred.

We were urban, rough-edge Irish kids. In nice suits, with what seemed like a decent vocabulary and a bit of social conscience, but cut from a coarser cloth. And when we later auditioned live at the Blue Angel, which was a very big deal (besides being in my home-town), those sophisticated East Siders, who fell off their chairs at Shelley and Mort and Nichols and May, just stared at us.

Another miscalculation was at the Playboy Club in Chicago. Hef told us that Joe Kennedy—JFK's father—was in the club and would we do a special show in the library for him? We said we weren't sure Joe Kennedy would go for our humor. But Hef dismissed that: "They've all got a great sense of humor. All the Kennedys."

So we did the bit, with Jack interviewing me as Jack Kennedy. Now, the trouble with doing humor in front of somebody who's the subject of it is the whole audience waits for that person's reaction before they laugh. Or don't. So they didn't. Because Joe was steamed. No Kennedy sense of humor in evidence. Not about his boy.

"No Time For Comedy," said the *Variety* headline next day: "Joseph Kennedy sat stonily through George Carlin's impresh of the Chief Executive . . . Kennedy père was heard to remark as he was leaving, 'I don't see anything funny in making fun of my son.' Translation: the whole room went down in flames."

In reality our political material was pretty harmless. We had a veneer of hipness, even of daring, but we were more interested in playing characters—especially these lower-class Irish guys—than we were in making a statement. We let our comedy serve our politics rather than have our politics drive what we did and said. And the Irish characters were in charge. They did the writing. There was always the chance at any moment that one of these characters might say something unplanned and might say it in an uncomfortable, disturbing manner. Shock, not titillate. That's exciting, the high-wire stuff.

These guys came from deep in our street experience: they were cops, dads, bartenders with baseball bats. The first-line authority figures we'd grown up with as opposed to Congress, big corporations and more impersonal authorities. Putting bigoted or violent language in their mouths was fun and funny and even to a degree satirical, exposing them for what they were. In a way they were the forerunners of later mainstream Irish bigots like Peter Boyle's Joe and Carroll O'Connor's Archie Bunker. Later still, throughout the eighties, my Irish street guy was a powerful element in the evolution of what finally became in the early nineties my authentic voice. He and his White Harlem relatives are the core of the family of characters that still live inside me.

For the next two years, Jack and I played first-line nightclubs like the Embers in Indianapolis, Freddie's in Minneapolis, the Tidelands in Houston. Bill Brennan, the owner of the Racquet Club in Dayton, flew into Chicago to see us and booked us for the next month. The Racquet Club was a hugely important booking. Not professionally—after all, this was fucking Dayton, Ohio. But it was where I met my wife, Brenda.

The nightclub circuit was unpredictable. Some places got what we were doing. In the Playboy Clubs, for the most part, we did okay. There were other places where we died. At one club outside Detroit, the owner said, "I haven't booked a live act since Bobby Clark in 1941. You guys better be good. My softball team's coming in tonight."

It was a cinder-block bar with a jukebox and tables and a little dance floor. The softball team comes in still in uniform and off we go. We do the Kennedy bit. Stuff about the European Common Market. They don't get it or like it. No laughs, nothing. Sweat is pouring off us. About ten minutes in, somebody puts a quarter in the jukebox and they start dancing to the music—while we're still halfway through the act.

The owner came over as we were wrapping up: "I'm taking a bath with you guys. Don't you work dirty?" We said, "Like Lenny Bruce?" He said, "Who the fuck's Lenny Bruce? You better get some tits and ass in this act. You got two more shows and the room don't turn over." Holy shit. We ran out and bought a fright wig for me and for the second show did a bit with Jack as Ed Murrow and me as a waitress in the club. We did stuff we'd never done before—or ever again. We were there for a week. We didn't get fired. A nightmare.

Sometimes it worked the other way around. There was a club in Allentown, Pennsylvania, whose owner was a great Lenny Bruce fan. And because Lenny liked us, he booked us. In the ad in the paper it said: "Lenny Bruce's favorite comics." Nobody in Allentown, Pennsylvania, knew who the fuck Lenny Bruce was either and if they had they would have hated him. Every night there were maybe five, six people in this cavernous room. Still the guy booked us back. And it was the same story every time we played there.

Deep down I didn't want to work. I was lazy because I knew I was going to be a single at some point. Jack and I being together was just a stepping stone. I had no idea what the timing would be but I knew it was inevitable. We developed a show of solid stuff and a second show (for when those fucking people in the front tables wouldn't leave). But once we had that under our belts, we essentially coasted.

Jack used to say that the reason Burns and Carlin didn't work was because we were very much the same person. We did the same characters. We were strong willed, Irish, Catholic, veterans. We had many things in common that made us great buddies, but didn't explode onstage.

The truth was more harsh: I didn't want to expend my best ideas on the team. I was selfish about my creativity. I refused to put out my best effort for, and with, Jack.

We broke up in March 1962—or I broke us up. It was at the Maryland Hotel in Chicago, where we'd had our first big booking. Jack seemed a bit stunned at first, but I think subconsciously he'd known for a while it was coming. We got pretty stoned and were clowning around and for some reason that seemed funny at the time Jack threw this paperback out the window into the freezing night. As he did he suddenly realized all his pay was in the book. He'd put it there for safekeeping. We ran to the window and watched the twenties and fifties floating down through the snow and we both knew that by the time we got to the street it'd all be long gone. So we split my half.

Jack joined the Compass Players in St. Louis (he auditioned with another hopeful named Alan Alda: both of them made it in) and then moved to Second City, where he later formed a comedy team with Avery Schreiber that did far better than Burns and Carlin. He ended up as a hugely successful TV writer and producer. We've stayed the best of friends.

A few years ago Jack said that without Burns and Carlin he would've been working at the A&P as a stock boy for the rest of his life. Maybe. And quite possibly without Jack I would've ended up as some dopey old radio cocksucker spewing bigotry into the night.

7

INTRODUCING
THE VERY LOVELY, VERY
TALENTED—BRENDA!

George and Brenda, 1961

(Courtesy of Marion Rife)

Brenda was born in Dayton, Ohio, in 1939 at St. Elizabeth's, an open-door hospital run by the Franciscan Sisters. Forty-odd years later I wound up there one night, after totaling my car. And experienced a nose-related miracle.

She was the elder of two sisters and Daddy's little girl. Art, his name was. He took her everywhere, including his favorite saloons, where he'd sit her on the bar while he drank. Art had been a singer in Chicago speakeasies during Prohibition and went by the name "The Whispering Tenor." His wife, Alice, made him quit. He hung out with these gangsters who, according to her, forced drinks on him so that he developed a drinking problem. From what I could tell when I got to know him Art didn't need much forcing. But Alice didn't like gangsters or alcohol so Art had to give up being the Whispering Tenor.

Alice was the dominant figure in the family and Brenda was scared of her. She did stuff like marking Brenda's periods on the calendar with an X. She was nice enough but very controlled and severe. I think she was Lutheran or Congregational. I don't know about Art. At one point Brenda had to play the organ in church.

Art worked as the production manager for *Newsweek* in the McCall printing plant. They were the largest printer in the United States and they printed sixty or seventy titles in Dayton. As a kid Brenda loved going with her dad to see the huge presses in action and smelling the printer's ink in the air. When she was older she even did pasteup for the foreign edition of *Newsweek*. All of which nurtured her high school ambition to be a journalist.

On graduation, she planned to go to college because she'd gotten a scholarship to Ohio Wesleyan, but her mother said no: women didn't go to college unless they wanted to be teachers. She should've said, "Okay, I'll be a teacher," and then switched to journalism when she got to Wesleyan. But she'd always been a sweet, obedient, over-achieving child and it didn't occur to her. And her mother was ada-mant. So Brenda never went to college. And she was very, very angry about that.

She'd been going with the guy next door for about three years. Like her, he was "a good kid"—they didn't fool around—but after the college episode Brenda was in a fuck-you mood and more or less forced the guy to sleep with her. That very first time, she got pregnant.

Again her mother was adamant: they had to get married. Again Brenda went along. Within a month she was walking down the aisle in a white dress her mother made (she was an expert dressmaker). Two weeks later, after the honeymoon, she had a miscarriage. She hadn't needed to get married at all. When she started to miscarry, she fainted in a downtown department store, but her mother wouldn't take her to the hospital. She had to miscarry in secret at home.

The poor slob on the other end of all this didn't like it any better than Brenda did, so as soon as she could she filed for divorce. That was the breaking point with her parents because she was the first person in their family who'd ever gotten a divorce. So from being a wonderful, overachieving, goody-two-shoes child, Brenda became overnight an alienated divorcée of twenty.

She went to work for a tool company as an executive secretary, which seemed like a good gig, until she found out the job involved the executives' tools as well as the ones they sold. She quit after hav-ing to organize call girls for visiting salesmen—and being made to watch them at work, so she could give head herself.

Today Dayton is just another struggling city in the Rust Belt. Back then, it had a tremendous industrial base: Frigidaire was there, National Cash Register, General Tire. When it still had jobs and factories, it was a major stop on the entertainment circuit. Comedy and music acts used it as a kind of test market. Showbiz wisdom was that if it went over in Dayton, it would go over anywhere.

One of the bigger venues in Dayton, out in a suburb called Kettering, was this place the Racquet Club. By day it was a swim and tennis club; at night it became a supper club with topflight entertainment.

Brenda heard on the grapevine that the maître d' had had a heart attack. She immediately drove out there and said, "I heard your maître d' had a heart attack. I want his job." (She always had balls, Brenda.) They said, "Where have you worked?" She said, "I haven't, but I'm really good with people." They were desperate for somebody to front the place so they gave her a temporary tryout.

She loved it and was really good at it. Her whole life began to center around the nightclub. Major acts came through all the time, including at one point in 1960 Lenny Bruce. He and Brenda became good friends—a platonic relationship according to Brenda; it was one of her friends he fucked—but they hung out, and had a great time.

Brenda used to pick up money every night for the club. Lenny was staying at a motel nearby, so she'd pick him up too and drive him to work. One evening they were passing a field full of flowers and Lenny yells, "Stop the car!" He jumps out and starts running across the field, leaping around in the flowers and rolling in them and yelling gibberish. Brenda thought he was insane; she didn't realize he was high and just wanted to roll around in some flowers like any other junkie. Then he got back in the car, and they went to the club.

The next Sunday he took things a step further: he sent her out to the airport to pick up a package. She drove out there, collected the package and drove back with it. He told her much later it was heroin. But what did she know? She was just doing stuff for her new friend. When he left, Lenny signed a picture for her: "You're going to have my baby. Love, Lenny."

Lenny recommended Burns and Carlin to the Racquet Club and we got a booking there for August 1960. It was only our second or third engagement after Chicago. When our publicity photos came in, apparently she and her roommate, Elaine, gave us the once-over. Brenda pointed at me and said, "He's mine." Elaine said, "Jack's mine." Fresh young meat they called us.

Our first night she caught my eye. And I caught hers: she told me later I reminded her a lot of Lenny—the same body language. After our first show I went over to her and asked: "What do you do in a town like this?" She said, "You can go out to breakfast. Or you can find someone with a stereo and hi-fi and go home with them." I said, "Do you have a stereo and hi-fi?" She said, "I do." So she took me home. For two weeks. We clicked immediately. Our minds clicked, our humor clicked. We both had the same thought: "This is going to be fun!"

Then the booking ended and it was time to leave. Brenda said she was in love. I didn't know if I was or not. But I knew it wasn't just another fling on the road. Which was what everyone at the club told Brenda after I'd gone: "You're never gonna see him again."

Burns and Carlin got busy and Brenda had to go into the hospital to have her appendix out so we were both pretty occupied for a while. I knew I did want to see her again but I couldn't take the plunge because I knew also that if I did, something decisive would happen. I was nervous about what that would be. So I did nothing. Meanwhile Brenda's pining away, thinking her friends in the club were right after all and she'll never see me again. Finally I called and we talked and it was so easy I couldn't figure out why the fuck I hadn't done it before. I was going to be in Chicago on New Year's so I asked her to come up. She couldn't. I had a couple of things to do around Chicago but after that I said I'd drive to Dayton. I gave her a day to expect me.

I got delayed for some reason for a couple of days, figuring I'd get there eventually. What I didn't know was that when I didn't show on the first day, Brenda cried all night. And when I didn't show the next day either, she cried all that night too. She was totally heartbroken, thought I was just screwing around with her.

By now she was working lunches at the club as well as nights. When I finally got to Dayton a few days late, in early January, it happened to be lunchtime.

I go in the door and she's seating people, giving them menus, taking orders and so on, when suddenly she turns around and sees me in the doorway. She drops the menus, runs the entire length of the dining room, jumps into my arms, we go to a motel and no one sees us for three days.

We lay in bed, we drank beer, I turned her on to grass for the first time. I asked her to marry me and she said, "Yes!"

We had to tell her parents, so we met them for lunch and her mother was sitting there with this pinched and Protestant face. Brenda and I both had the same thought, which was basically: "Aargh!" We couldn't do it. So when Art had to go to the bathroom I went with him. And there, pissing side by side in our urinals, I said: "I'd like to marry your daughter." He said: "Oh. Yeah. Okay."

Her dad liked me and felt he had a connection with me because of his own showbiz experience. Art also liked his beer, which was something we definitely had in common. So there was an affinity. But not with her mother. When I told her, "I'm going to marry your daughter," she looked like she'd gone into shock. I don't know if she disliked me. She was kind of reserved. Probably she was just very skeptical of me—a comedian who worked in nightclubs? Where would that lead? But she saw her daughter was happy with me and for once dropped the adamant thing.

At least she made Brenda's wedding dress.

Then it was off to New York. For two reasons: to introduce her to my neighborhood and to meet my mother. In that order: getting a good review from my old gang was the most important. The place I picked for her debut appearance was a terrific White Harlem bar called the Moylan Tavern.

The Moylan was on a street that's long gone called Moylan Place. Right under the El, off Broadway near 125th Street. They built a project over it.

It was the classic New York saloon. Being on the common border of several neighborhoods, it had great cross-cultural influences. There were blacks and Puerto Ricans of all trades, seminarians from the Jewish Theological Seminary and Union Theological Seminary, Irish construction workers, cops, firefighters, students and professors from the Juilliard School of Music, Columbia and Teachers College, retired pensioners and young Irish bucks trying to earn their wings, every type of New Yorker rubbing up against one another and most of the time in a peaceful manner.

It had much more than an insulated, ethnically pure bar in the middle of a neighborhood had. That was its attraction. It had always given me a familiar window on a largely unfamiliar world and by osmosis a certain tolerance, at odds with the neighborhood aggression I'd grown up with.

But now it was just another venue and another opening night. Brenda was nervous and so was I. I really wanted their approval. If they said, "Fuck, Georgie, what a dog!" I didn't know what I'd do.

The consensus seemed to be she was pretty cool. There were about fifteen guys in the Moylan when I took her in and they all liked what they saw. They liked that she sat at the bar and drank with them and not at a table like other women. She always was a bit of a chameleon, able to transplant herself anywhere she had to be. She made it seem the most natural thing in the world for a midwestern girl from Ohio to be drinking with these tough Irish dudes a couple of blocks from Harlem. There was one tense moment, though. Brenda was rather flat-chested and she used to wear little rubber falsies. We're playing pool and at least three or four guys are paying close attention to the game. Brenda lays in to shoot and one of her falsies falls out. Popped right out of her bra and hit the deck. I caught that sucker on the first bounce. I checked around. No one had noticed. Even Brenda hadn't noticed. When she finished shooting I slipped it to her: "Here, your falsie fell out."

As for Mary, Brenda liked her right away. She figured it was because they were both Geminis, so they were both hip to each other's female tricks. And Mary immediately adopted Brenda as her daughter. Mary had never had a daughter and in a way Brenda no longer had a mother.

We got married on June 3, 1961, in Dayton at her family's house, 4477 River Ridge Road, before a justice of the peace. My mother flew out from New York. Jack Burns was my best man, Murray Becker was there. Brenda's best friend, Elaine, was her maid of honor. We'd met in August of '60. In those ten months we'd been together for a total of five weeks. But Brenda was itching to get out of Dayton. She'd say: "I don't belong in that family. I don't belong in that town. I think I was probably raised by wolves."

So it was into my car with not much more than her clothes and back on the road with Burns and Carlin. But for us there was something different now. We were starting out on our own journey—one that would continue for almost thirty-six years. We had great adventures and a lot of them, both with Jack and later when I began working as a single. Many of them revolved around having to drive long distances to be somewhere for a show or opening night and barely making it, the obstacles to be overcome just to get there on time.

The best time was when Jack and I were arrested in Dallas for armed robbery. We had been booked at a place called the Gaslight, a great little folk and jazz club. Brenda and I drove down from Dayton. Jack was coming from Chicago to meet us there.

We're staying in this horrible motel, with no air-conditioning, and Dallas is hotter than hell. I drop off my shirt and Jack's at a laundry to have them laundered for the next night, when we open. The next day I go to pick them up. As I walk into the dry cleaner, I notice two guys just sitting in the laundry, in civilian clothes, ties, not doing their laundry, just sitting like it's a barbershop waiting room. Odd, but I think nothing of it and give the woman who runs the place my ticket and she nods very obviously to these men—poor concealment there—and ducks down behind the counter. I think, "What the fuck? Am I the millionth customer or something?"

Suddenly these two have guns out and are telling me to put my hands up. I'm thrown over the counter, handcuffed and they drag me outside. There are three or four more guys and they have all these shotguns. And they're all over our car—literally ripping things out of it. I didn't know what the fuck was going on and they wouldn't tell me a thing. They threw me into a squad car and headed for the motel.

I knew Brenda would be in panties and nothing else, because of the heat. So I pound on the door and the cops are pounding on the door and I'm yelling, "Get dressed, honey!" like some moron in a sitcom. Brenda throws something on and opens the door and there I am in handcuffs. The cops swarm into the room, ripping things out of the dresser drawers, the closets, luggage, everything. Now I see Jack being dragged out of the other room. He's thrown in one car, Brenda and me in another. They take us down to headquarters. It's crawling with detectives—like they've got the case of the year.

We'd only been married for about three months so Brenda didn't really know Jack. I knew she was thinking: "What the fuck have I gotten into?"

They separate us into three different rooms. One cop interrogates Brenda. "What are you doing traveling with two men?" She says: "George is my husband and the other guy is his partner. They're a comedy team. They're here to play whatever the club was." And the cop says, "Oh yeah? How often do they play the AAA Club?" She realizes he must be talking about the American Automobile Association. So she says—of course—how could they play the AAA? So now this cocksucker starts in with: "Do you sleep with them?" She says she sleeps with me. "You don't sleep with the other guy? What do you do for the other guy? Jerk him off?"

They play Mutt and Jeff with us, telling Jack I'd confessed and me that Jack had confessed. All this stupid fucking cop crap. But they can't get anything out of us because we have no fucking clue what's going on. Meanwhile it's the middle of the afternoon and we have to open a show that evening. And we haven't even got our shirts back from the laundry.

We gradually pieced together what it was all about. Jack wanted to do a routine about the European Common Market. So he'd clipped a story about it from a Chicago paper. On the other side, perfectly matching it, was another story about a big armed robbery at the Chicago Motor Club. Two men and a woman. The cops figured, here were two men and a woman. Jack had come from Chicago. The gunman had been keeping his reviews.

The way they got this vital clue was that the girl in the laundry had found the clipping in Jack's shirt pocket and called the police. This was gonna be her big day, taking down three interstate armed robbers.

It was clear that the cops had fucked up big-time, but they wouldn't let us go. They kept us until around six. And finally they released us. Never said, "We're sorry, we made a mistake, what can we do for you?" They put our car back together and we went to the motel and got to the club just in time to open—in dirty shirts.

It was bizarre. It was stupid. It was Dallas.

The lead cop—the one who asked Brenda if she jerked Jack off—later turned up as the guy in charge of investigating the Kennedy assassination, Will Fritz. He interrogated Oswald after his arrest. The obvious conclusion: Oswald had as much to do with the assassination as the three of us did with the Motor Club robbery in Chicago.

Being on the road with Brenda wasn't all wonderful. Hard times were coming when I was a single. Our car was broken into once and we lost everything we had, which at the time, when we were living hand to mouth, was devastating. But we never let any of it defeat us. We'd say: Okay this is the way it is, we go from here.

That's what we did for those years—we went from here. We were a good team. A very good team.

8

THOSE FABULOUS SIXTIES

George, Kelly and Brenda Carlin
(Courtesy of Kelly Carlin-McCall)

At the Blue Dog in Baltimore I once did a show for no one. The owner insisted: "In case someone comes in, I want him to know there's a show."

The Colony Club in Omaha was just about completely silent the whole time I was there. The bonus was you could smell the shit from the stockyards. Right onstage.

At Oakton Manor in Wisconsin, they seemed to be wondering who and what I was. I could see the questioning in their faces. "Why is this man dressed like that? Why is he saying these things? What does it have to do with us?"

The Copa Club in Cleveland decreed that the comic stood behind the bar, slightly above the bottles. All you could see was the back of the bartender's head and people at the bar shouting, "Another beer here!" After two nights the owner said: "You're really not right for the room." I said, "You're really right about that."

The Lake Club in Springfield, Illinois, had a long, long bar and about an acre of tables. The tables and I were on the same level. None of the glory of being two feet higher than the audience. And if you ain't higher, you're lower. No—the lowest. Sometimes I can still see the hundreds of pairs of hostile, unblinking eyes out there in the darkness . . .

Only a couple months and it was kicking in just how hard this shit was. How few places there were where I felt secure. How many times I had to repeat to myself after the died-a-death nights: "Remember that terrific set three Fridays ago? Hang your hopes on that.

Last night was an aberration. They were noisy, they were drunk, it was the second show, they'd already seen some of it . . ." (There was always a reason why the bad night wasn't really.) But it could be very discouraging. And incredibly exciting when it was promising. The ratio of promise to discouragement was paper thin, but just enough to keep me going.

Chicago became a headquarters for a time because of its central location to midwestern cities and their hip, exciting nightclubs. Plus it wasn't far from Brenda's family in Dayton. Spending time around Chicago, I got familiar with the folk fringe and the nascent rock underground. These musicians were the people I felt most at home with.

When I was done being discouraged at the Playboy Club I'd go over to Wells Sreet on the Near North Side, the center of rock and folkie activity, for a dose of promise. Doing free sets at the Rising Moon and the Earl of Old Town, I got my first taste of the folk and underground milieu and the feelings that came with it. The freedom on the stage, the people with open-ended and -minded philosophies, who were more than ready for experimentation: they lived for it. You couldn't really fail in these places as badly as you could in a formal setting.

I had a dual life between 1962 and 1964. I worked in nightclubs to earn money and I spent most of my free time with the folkies, rock 'n' rollers, people from Second City. The outsider, the rebel in me was being fed by these associations. As a lifelong pot smoker I fit in that way too. I felt comfortable around them. Already by this time they were beginning to look a little like the hippies they would become. Beginning to affect the free-and-easy physical style that went with their philosophies.

I could do material in these places I didn't always trust to a nightclub: about integration, the John Birch Society, the Ku Klux Klan.

I did have certain routines with a political-social component that I'd been doing since Burns and Carlin broke up. There was my all-purpose Kennedy impression:

It's nice to return to Chicago, home of the adjustable voting machine. Our trip here was fine, though we did have trouble getting the yacht down the Saint Lawrence Seaway . . .

The boilerplate John Birch Society piece:

We won the mixed bowling league—that's the colored against the whites . . . We were going to have a guest from the KKK— the Grand Imperial Almighty Omnipotent Invincible Stomper, but his wife wouldn't let him out tonight . . .

Obligatory pieces about the South:

There's a textile mill in South Carolina where the lunchroom has been integrated but the restrooms are still segregated. That's like, "Hell, I'll break bread with 'em but not wind" . . . The textile industry moved south for one reason—there's a bigger demand for sheets . . .

Obviously this wasn't the kind of stuff that went over real big in, say, the fabulous Copa Club in Cleveland, or the lovely Lake Club in Springfield, Illinois.

I was being pulled in two directions: I wanted the widest audience I could get, as any artist does. At the same time, I was drawn to the "narrower" subject matter, wanting to be someone who spoke to and for these folkies and hippies-to-be.

But it was a tough time, very tough. Brenda and I had no home, no address. If we were out of work we stayed in Dayton at Brenda's folks', or with my mother in Manhattan. Once in a while in the backseat of the car. Then, in the fall of 1962, Brenda got pregnant.

We didn't plan it. We were in New Orleans for the World Series and the Yankees won. Celebrations followed and a few hours later Brenda got pregnant. (She was positive, she said.) We went back to Chicago, where I was working at the Playboy Club—appropriately enough—and took the bunny test. Sure enough, the rabbit died.

Brenda had a great pregnancy and in her seventh month went home to Dayton to have the baby. Her parents picked her up at the airport and her mother weighed about eighty pounds. Brenda freaked. Her dad said nothing and seemed to know nothing. So Brenda drove straight to the family doctor: "What the hell is happening with my mother?"

He said, "She's dying of cancer." He hadn't told anybody, not her father or her younger sister, nobody. And Brenda's mother was the sort of person who never shared anything with anyone. But she only had weeks to live. The poor woman really wanted to see our baby—she decorated a complete nursery for her, trimmed a bassinet and made a special bedspread and baby clothes. A little palace for the baby. But her dream was not to be. She slipped into a diabetic coma not long after and in a day was gone.

As Brenda's mother was dying, our child was born. A daughter. We named her Kelly.

Now we were three. And broke. And homeless. We moved back to 121st Street and I borrowed money from anyone I could, old friends from the neighborhood, Mort Sahl, my mother, anyone. I had a running debit balance with Doug, a pal from the old days. I remember sitting with him on a bench in the median of Broadway at 122nd Street once, relaxing with a six-pack and a couple of joints. I owed Doug six hundred dollars but I needed a sum in four figures. I made him an offer: you lend me X dollars to get to whatever the target sum was, I'll give you a percentage of my future earnings in perpetuity. He said okay—and never held me to it.

My mother, on the other hand, had a fucking list: "That telegram when I wired you fifty dollars in Chicago? The telegram was $2.50. So that's $52.50." I would say: "What about those sneakers you got me in fourth grade? Where does being a parent end and becoming a loan shark begin?"

March 1963—when Brenda was six months pregnant with Kelly—was a turning point. I'd just played a pot-and-coffee place called the House of Pegasus in Fort Lauderdale and run into a group of New Yorkers, some of whom later became the group Spanky and Our Gang. I'd smoked enough pot with them that I'd reached a resolve, a crossroads. The way I put it to Brenda was, "I have to take a stand. We've got to live or die in New York. I can't keep going out to nowhere places, playing to people who have nothing to do with where I ought to be heading. I've got to find somewhere I can work things out." Though it risked cutting us off from what little income we had, she supported me totally. And I began to have a powerful feeling of things inside me developing. Just like her, in fact. Perhaps it was creative couvade syndrome.

At the time, the only way for struggling comics to be seen was something called a hoot. "Hoot" was short for "hootenanny," originally an impromptu concert of folk music, but which had evolved into a version of amateur night where all kinds of aspiring entertainers could strut their stuff—not just singers, musicians and comics, but jugglers, dancers, magicians.

That March, I did my first hoot at the Cafe Wha?—a hole-in-the-wall off Bleecker—and another the next night at the Bitter End on Bleecker itself. Nothing. A few nights later I auditioned at the Village Vanguard, a venerable old jazz joint in the West Village. Still nothing. Next month I did the same circuit, and at the Bitter End hoot, Howie Solomon caught me. Howie owned a new, quite large coffeehouse-style club across Bleecker Street called the Cafe Au Go Go.

The Go Go was well on its way to becoming the epicenter of everything people now remember Bleecker Street—and by extension the Village—to have been in the sixties. Stan Getz recorded his *Au Go Go* album there, other jazz giants like MJQ and Nina Simone played it. Mort Sahl was a regular. Steve Stills got his start as a solo, as did many other folkies who later crossed over to rock. Howie covered the field and he offered me exactly the kind of deal I was looking for: an open-ended arrangement to be a regular when the mike was open, two nights here, four nights there, drop by of an evening if you're downtown. He'd offered the same deal to a number of young musicians but to only one other comic, a guy three years my junior named Richard Pryor.

The Go Go became my home-court advantage. I still took jobs outside New York—I wasn't turning down money—but I had made my stand. Now I had a place to stand as well, a laboratory in the very heart of what would soon be the counterculture. An audience not only open to material that contained some ideas, some risk, but outsiders by instinct or choice who didn't accept received values, who resisted convention, who felt alienation from the smug certainties of middle-class Middle America. And who in a few short months would add to this potent mix a smoldering rage . . .

When Kennedy came on the scene, I identified closely with the youthful Irish Catholic man of ideas. He wasn't my class but he was my tribe. A politician, yes; but like a lot of my contemporaries, I wasn't old enough yet to have been disappointed. With him a new beginning seemed possible, a chance for ideas to be advanced that took into account how people felt and lived, how the world treated them. A slow but sure march toward more concern about people and less about property. The black struggle was the most visible and emotional example of it, but Kennedy's promise included much else, explicitly and implicitly, about people who had been ignored or marginalized in the rush to the fifties' consumer paradise.

During the Kennedy years, I found my political values. Or rather I found political ideas that matched the feelings of an individual who was not organized politically.

My Kennedy impressions were affectionate. I continued to do JFK through these years but my ear gave me as much pleasure as satirizing him. Though I have this other alien creature inside that wants to get out, most of me is just pure hambone-entertainer child-showoff. And I had this favorite phrase of Kennedy's: "We will low-ur the quo-tah of sug-ah from Cu-ber." I loved that because in a nine-word sentence I got to use two intrusive *r*'s and leave off two final *r*'s. Flashy word shit. My claim to fame.

Like most people, I remember where I was when the assassination happened and what I was doing. I was walking my baby daughter on 110th and Broadway in the very fancy pram Mary had bought her. There was a blind man's news kiosk on the corner. I went to buy the newspaper but he didn't hand me one. He just said, "You hear about the president? The president has been shot down in Dallas."

I went into Rexall's or Liggett's or some drugstore and called Brenda. I said, "Turn on the television," and I realized I was crying. It came out as a cry. As a gasp. And yet I hadn't felt grief before I tried to speak the words to her. Saying the words caused the emotions . . .

That's all I consciously remember. Beyond that, I'm not sure what I felt. I was limited by being very self-absorbed in my career path. I've probably done some blocking in all the years. And there was always the marijuana.

But I was stunned. I don't know if I was depressed. As far as the Moylan—the community—was concerned, there was great shock that this kind of thing could even happen. In America or anywhere. But the sheer elemental shock of it blocked out or pushed away other, more nuanced emotional reactions that might've taken place in its absence. I knew guys who liked Kennedy, guys who didn't. Obviously there were cultural links: we were all Irish Catholics. But in general they were conservative and Kennedy was a liberal.

I was down in the Moylan when Oswald got shot, because there was a TV there, and we all saw it. Other than that, as far as I recall the bar functioned normally the weekend of the assassination. The feeling was, "Hey, we're drinking here and there's exciting stuff on TV."

There was another assassination going on at the time—a slower and more methodical one but in the end just as deadly. One that affected me far more deeply and directly.

Two years earlier, in 1961, Lenny Bruce had begun to be hit with a series of arrests for obscenity in San Francisco, Los Angeles (at three different clubs), Chicago and finally in New York (twice in two weeks) at . . . the Cafe Au Go Go. The British police also deported him from the UK when he tried to perform in London.

I guess it would be clinically paranoid to think these were coordinated, but because several ended in acquittal or mistrial (in one case he was illegally tried in absentia) and because he was often arrested while awaiting trial for a previous arrest, it certainly looked like there was some degree of consensus. As if by some kind of bush telegraph, law enforcers across America had agreed that this comic had to be made to shut the fuck up.

I was there when Lenny was busted in Chicago—in fact I went to jail with him. It was in December 1962 at the Gate of Horn. Bob Carey of the Tarriers, one of my folkie friends, and I were drinking beer upstairs and watching Lenny be his usual genius self. Suddenly a policeman stands up in the audience and says, just like they do on a street corner when someone gets shot or run down and a crowd gathers: "A'right, the show's over!" He actually said it, not as a metaphor, but as a literal piece of information being transmitted to the audience by someone in authority. "A'right, the show's over!" Wonderful.

They hauled Lenny away. Lenny had been busted so often that he always wore his coat during performances so he could leave immediately with the police. (He didn't want to get separated from that coat; it was a nice piece of cashmere.)

The cops bust the upstairs bartender too, because he's serving the people during sets, and they bust the owner, Alan Ribback. Carey and I stay upstairs. Downstairs the cops are trying to close the front door so they can check ID before people leave in case there are minors present. They really wanted to punish the club for having the balls to let Lenny speak free. Eventually they found a girl who was fifteen or sixteen and Alan later got into legal troubles for that. The Gate of Horn was never really the same afterward.

Carey and I were still drinking—we were pretty juiced—and purposely I arranged to be almost the last going out. The policeman said, "I wanna see your ID." I said, "I don't believe in identification. Sorry." And I tried to give some kind of fucking stupid drunk speech.

The cop grabbed me by the collar and pants in the old buncheroo fashion and hustled me down the stairs and through the lobby to the front door. As I was passing the bar area, I yelled out: "Brenda, I'm going to jail!" Then it's out the door with my hands cuffed behind me and into this paddy wagon where Lenny was.

I knew Lenny not just because he gave Jack and me our break, but because he was a friend of Brenda's. Whenever we were in the same city on the road, we'd check in with him and he'd always welcome us, especially Brenda "the shiksa." He was an affectionate and lovable man—even to cops. He always called them "peace officers."

He said, "Why you here, man?" I said, "I told them I don't believe in this shit." I omitted to mention that it wasn't a principled First Amendment stand so much as a smart-ass joke.

Lenny showed me how to work my arms down under my ass and my feet so the handcuffs were in front of me. Somehow that worked. Much better. And off I went to jail with Lenny in a paddy wagon. And even though it began as a drunken joke, the whole affair had a radicalizing effect on me.

It was only reinforced when Lenny was busted at the Go Go. Not once but twice. I was out of town at the time because when the Go Go had major headliners, the regulars had no opportunity to appear.

By now it was becoming pretty clear that Lenny wasn't being arrested for obscenity. He was being arrested for being funny about religion and in particular Catholicism. A lot of big city cops—not just in New York but in Philly, San Fran, Chicago—tend to be Irish Catholic. In addition Lenny's persecutors had names like Ryan (the judge who tried him in absentia in Chicago), Hogan (the DA who went after him in New York) and Murtagh (the trial judge in New York). Lenny's Chicago trial began on Ash Wednesday, 1963. In court, judge and jury having just come from Mass, everyone had ash crosses on their foreheads.

So it probably shouldn't have blown my mind that the vice squad cop who busted Lenny at the Go Go—the one who wore the wire—grew up in my neighborhood. But it did when I found out in the Moylan a couple weeks later. He was a guy named Randy. I'm immediately thinking, why would Randy do that? He must know what great stuff Lenny's doing, knocking down this bullshit, seeing through that. Surely any of the guys I grew up with would agree. We were so outside the law, so inconsonant with authority.

A few days later Randy comes into the Moylan and he has a transcript from the wire he wore. He's showing it around to the guys: "You gotta see this. Lookit what that foulmouth had to say . . . A nun's tit, fecal matter on a crucifix, Pope this, Cardinal that." And there are universal reactions of outrage. I try to mount a feeble defense of Lenny and they get even more outraged. Now I am truly

blown away. Because these are disrespectful guys. They stopped going to Mass when they were twelve, thirteen. Nothing was sacred to
them.

It was the most dramatic evidence I'd had to date that these lines
were sharply drawn, the legacy of that Catholic upbringing, that
clannish Irish working-class neighborhood ethic was a rigid demar-
cation. Just because you grew up with a guy and shared A, B, C, D
and E with him didn't mean that on F through Z you wouldn't be
diametrically opposed to each other.

Twelve days before Lenny died in 1966 Brenda and I went up
to his house in Hollywood. We'd just moved there and we wanted
to check in just like the old days. He had a beard by then and he
was completely immersed in his legal battle; he knew the law incredibly well on the specifics of his cases. He didn't appear in clubs
anymore—the Irish cops and judges had indeed shut him the fuck
up. He was just about bankrupt, having spent all his income and
intellect trying to vindicate himself. We visited for a while and he
was as affectionate and lovable as ever. That was the last time we saw
him alive.

Lenny was one of the very few comics—perhaps the only one—I
sought out and felt comfortable hanging with. I never had a circle
of friends in the comedy biz. I never went to the delis or coffeeshops
after late shows, where people would sit around eating breakfast and
riffing till dawn. I always felt alien, not a part of them. Not that I
was different or better, I was just apart. They had some common
bond that didn't include or interest me. A competitiveness that I was
very uncomfortable with. I wasn't a compulsive entertainer. I could
always think on my feet, but I never was quick around the kind of
people who dominate a table. I was a product of ideas, not ad-libs.
Later I came to realize the curiousness of choosing to be, and feeling, apart from people and at the same time dying to be accepted.
Longing to be accepted, to be asked in. But on my terms.

I rubbed elbows with some comics—like Richard—but it was
rock musicians who shaped my development. John Sebastian, Cass
Elliot, Zal Yanovsky, Phil Ochs—all the people in the Village in

the midsixties who were forming and reforming into groups like the Mugwumps and Poco. Having had that initiation on Wells Street I felt at ease with them. They were companions, not competitors.

In the end I was a loner. A loner happy to be alone. I worked alone, I wrote alone. I was sticking to my plan, which I'd nurtured for years. Stage One: radio as a way into show business. Stage Two: become a comedian, like the comedians I'd listened to on the radio as a boy. Stage Three: achieve fame as a comedian and take possession of the ultimate dream: movie stardom. To be Danny Kaye—or Danny Kaye the Second. (Though by now this had shifted in the direction of Jack Lemmon the Second.)

Stage One of this plan had already worked; there seemed no reason to believe that Stage Two wouldn't someday succeed also, leading, as inevitably as night follows day, to Stage Three: all Hollywood, helpless with laughter, at my feet.

But Stage Two was turning out to be a long, hard and lonely row to hoe. There was a deeper problem: I didn't feel free onstage. I was constricted, a very Protestant-Catholic comedian. Even on pot, which I was on every day, I was still in that Playboy Club, in that Playboy tie, talking about Bart Starr and a stupid Vitalis commercial and how he could throw the football and grab someone's ass. That I knew intellectually there was an anal, uptight world out there I didn't feel part of didn't erase the fact that I was a living, breathing example of it.

And for all the comfort I felt in the Village with its outsider-Left-liberal-pot-smoking audience, this wasn't the direction I was going in at the Go Go. As much as I might want to say I had a risky, edgy side that wanted to experiment with material that had social significance, and this was the right audience and Greenwich Village was the right place, I'd be full of shit. What I was trying to do was to develop a TV act.

Or rather that one solid five- or six-minute piece that would open the doors to TV.

And I had it now. It was called "The Indian Sergeant." The premise grew out of all the Westerns I'd seen as a kid. If the U.S. Army or the pioneers or cowpokes always had a weather-beaten, battle-hardened sergeant or trail boss who pumped up his men before the climactic battle, the Indians must have had the same NCO type who did the same for them. My Indian sergeant was my well-worn Irish guy from the Upper West Side . . .

All right, tall guys over by the trees, fat guys down behind the rocks and you with the beads—get outta line! Boy, there's one in every village.

All right, youse've all been given a piece of birch bark and a feather dipped in eagle's blood. We want youse to write on the birch bark—with the feather—in the upper right-hand corner. The upper RIGHT HAND corner. That's your ARROW hand. You write your name. Last name first, first name last. If your name is "Running Bear" you write, "Bear, Running." Under-neath your name we want your age. In summers. If you've been alive for eighteen summers, you put "18 summers." Yeah, Trot-ting Bear? (pause) If you were born in the winter, just put that down. Next, you write down your date of enlistment. That's the day we came around and took you from your parents and made you sleep on the hot coals.

Now, a lot of youse guys have been asking me about promotions. You'd like to make Brave second class. Get another scar up on your arm. Well, the results of your tests have come in and youse doin' beautifully. "Burning Settlers' Homes," everybody passed. "Imitating a Coyote," everybody passed. "Sneaking Quietly Through the Woods," everybody passed, except Limping Ox. However, Limping Ox is being fitted with a pair of corrective moccasins . . .

I received a smoke signal from headquarters today. Actually I didn't receive the signal. They smoke-signaled me but I was out, so I returned their signal later. The smoke signal is: there'll be a massacre tonight at nine o'clock. We meet down by the bonfire, dance around a little, and move out. This'll be the fourth straight night we've attacked the fort. However, tonight it will not be as easy as before: tonight there will be SOLDIERS in the fort!

Okay, uniform. This is a FORMAL massacre. You want your Class A summer loincloth. Two green stripes over the eye, no feather. Arms are blue, legs are red, chest is optional. What's that, Prancing Antelope? No, you can't put any purple on your eyelids. Hey, ain't you the one with the beads? I told youse—get outta line!

I can't say it was edgy, socially significant, daring, risky or anything else that the pot-smoking rebel outsider aspired to. But it worked.

The Merv Griffin Show was different from other network shows in that it was syndicated, so while it wasn't fundamentally "freer" than any other variety-style TV show, the burden of approval of things didn't weigh entirely on the producer and production staff—it was also on a group of stations that wouldn't receive it until two weeks later. There was less panic and pressure. The staff were more relaxed. Merv wasn't as much an overlord of his domain as Paar or Carson were of theirs. And the Little Theater on West 44th Street where it was shot for its first few years was very congenial; all those friendly vibes of live performance had survived. A warmer atmosphere than the cold, technical ambience of a TV studio, a warmth which could be perceived as freedom. At least the freedom to fail a little or screw up in some way that could be turned back into comedy.

Everyone was vying for the *Griffin* "interview"—the first step in getting on the show, when you'd go in and tell the producer or the booker (like the legendary Tom O'Malley) what you wanted to do if you got it.

Richard Pryor and I were pretty much contemporaneous at the Go Go. But Richard got his *Griffin* interview first, in early '65. I hadn't been seen yet. After Richie's interview, Tom O'Malley came in to see me and I got an interview scheduled. By the time I did the interview, Richard had done his first *Merv*. By the time I did mine, Richard had done two. And so on. I always had this lag time with Richie—a week or a month or some unit of time behind his professional development. It went on for years, through albums and Grammys and specials until I finally overtook him in the Heart Attack 500.

The Merv Griffin Show was my big breakthrough, that odd little syndicated talk show whose host everyone discounted or made fun of. All that happened afterward flowed from that one appearance. It was in July '65. I did "The Indian Sergeant." And it killed. I didn't win the big prize: being invited to sit on the couch with Merv. But that would come in due course. Needless to say, Richie had already made it to the couch.

Right after the show they told me that they wanted me to do three more. I didn't have anything else prepared. Fragmentary media spoofs were rambling around in my act, none of them five to six minutes long. I was going to have my work cut out. Just as with school assignments when I was a kid, I put it off and put it off. Invariably I wound up the day before a show going down from our sixth-floor apartment—which we'd finally escaped to the year before—to my mother's second-floor apartment. I'd sit at the kitchen table where I'd done my homework a few years before and write the next day's piece. I would take the two minutes I already had and build it up into five or six. It was nerve-racking because there was no chance to test this new stuff on anybody, outside of myself. I did always trust myself to know the difference between something that would work for me and something that wouldn't. I was wrong a lot but my average was pretty good.

One media piece I'd been fooling with was a takeoff of a Top 40 deejay. It got to be a comedy cliché later but at the time no one had really done it. And it came from my own experience. I did it on my second *Merv* and it wasn't hard to expand, because all I had to do was add a few more stupid names for bands and more stupid song titles . . . Here's Willie West on Wonderful WINO, all this of course done at breakneck speed:

Hi there, kids. Welcome to the Willie West Show *here on* W-W-W-W-W-W-W-W-W-I-I-I-I-I-N-N-N-N-N-O-O-O-O-

O-O-O-O! Wonderful WINO RADIO-O-O-O-O! Welcome-to-the-Willie-West-Show-here-in-the-wonderful-West-If-it's-a weird-one-it's-best-Willie-West-with-the-hundred-and-one-wild-and-woolly-wedges-of-WAX! Right here on Wonderful WINO-O-O!

1750 on your dial! Just above the police calls, kids! We got stacks and stacks of wax and wax, we're gonna pick and click the oldies-but-goldies, the newies-but-gooeys. We got the Top 700 records right here on Wonderful WINO-O-O-O!!!!

Now the big rockin' sound of that great new group from England—The KANSAS CITY BOYS! With—"MY BABY'S DEAD"!!!!

"Brrrding-ding Brrrding-ding-ding-ding-ding . . . My baby's DEAD!! DE-EH-EH-AAAAUD! Got hit by a TRAIN! Big 'ol train, diddle-do-do-do. I'm gonna GIT that train diddle-do-do-do!!!"

Another big romantic ballad and ya heard it right here on Wonderful WI—bulletin-bulletin-bulletin-bulletin-bulletin-bulletin-bulletin-bulletin -bulletin-bulletin-bulletin-bulletin . . .
The SUN *did not* COME UP *this morning!!* HUGE CRACKS *have appeared in the* EARTH'S SURFACE!! BIG ROCKS *are falling out of the* SKY!! *Details later on* Action Central News!

Hey, kids, TWO IN A ROW, *a big double play here on the* Weird Willie West Show. *This is brand new, hasn't even been released yet but it's* NUMBER ONE *on the charts this week and moving higher all the time . . . Next week it'll be a* GOLDEN OLDIE! *We got some dedications! This goes out to . . . Red Louie, Spike Choochoo, Spanish Annan, Dirty Mary, Baby Carlos, Peewee, Junior, Toots, Baboo Spot, Greasy Creep and Woozie Mush, our pick to make you sick . . . JENNY!*

Eeeee-eeeee-eeeee-eeeee-doe-doe-eeeee-eeeee-eeeee-bum bada loop-bum-badda boop dada-doot bum-badaloop-badaloop-badaloop badaloop blip-blip-blip-blip-blip-blip-blip-blip blip-blip-blip-blip-blip-blip-blip-blip-blip —JENNY!!!

After the fourth show, the *Griffin* people were sufficiently impressed that they said, "We'd like you to do a cycle of thirteen." A nice ring to that; almost like the thirteen-show cycle of a series. A mixed blessing, though. The first four were hard enough to find material for—what the fuck will I do for thirteen?

On the other hand it was a great opportunity. The first thing I did was repeat "The Indian Sergeant." Merv really loved that. Then I was able to repeat a couple of others. I took a bunch of TV commercials and made a whole TV commercials routine. Then I rewrote "Wonderful WINO" with different jokes, same character, and added News, Sports and Weather. Somewhere in here Al Sleet, the Hippy-Dippy Weatherman, made his debut. But "The Indian Sergeant" was a mother lode: I eventually came up with a Columbus Sergeant, a Sergeant on the *Pinta*, a Robin Hood Sergeant, a Santa Claus Sergeant. I was learning early a basic rule of television: repeat, repeat, repeat. Find variations, but stick to the successful format.

There was a certain secret tension. Now I had to forget all of those pieces with some adventure and risk to them: the stuff I'd been showing off to my coffeehouse friends. Mr. Anal hated to let things go. But for now and the foreseeable future they had to be abandoned. They weren't going to work where I was going.

My fondest memories of sixties television are the *Griffin* shows. Although it was a television show like any other, it had a little something more. The thrilling thing about Merv's show was that it was on Broadway, 44th Street between Broadway and Eighth no less, in the heart of the theater district, when that heart still beat strong and steady. The Little Theater was right next to Sardi's, where I was happy to find Hirschfelds of my heroes Danny Kaye and Jack Lemmon, whom I would one day join on those beige walls. More important they served great creamed spinach. Just like the good old Automat.

When you grow up in New York and you collect autographs as a boy, you know where all the stage doors are. Broadway is the center, the mecca, true magnetic north. Though I didn't aspire to be a Broadway actor, Broadway was the symbolic pinnacle of what I wanted to be and belong to. Broadway was where I first found out that guys actually stood up in front of people to make them laugh. (In this case between features at the Capitol Theatre or the Strand.) Wonderful to be back downtown in those same streets I'd once haunted, running from stage door to stage door searching for autographs, but now with some level of acceptance, invited to be, however briefly, on the inside looking out.

Hello, Dolly! with Carol Channing was next door. (The first time around when she was a mere forty-three.) Sammy Davis Jr. was across the street, in *Golden Boy*. On Broadway.

After fighting against it for so long, I felt the wind at my back and the road rising to meet me.

9

INSIDE EVERY SILVER LINING THERE'S A DARK CLOUD

George, right, with Mike Douglas

(Photo of *The Mike Douglas Show* courtesy of CBS Television Distribution)

'm sitting in a brightly lit pink and white gazebo in a drab medium-sized studio in Philadelphia. It's much too early in the day. Mike Douglas is also sitting in the gazebo, watching his guests the Andrews Sisters, musical (and sexual) icons of World War II, belting out one of their close-harmony boogie-woogie hits. Not the kind of thing you want to hear at eleven in the morning, but for the audience of plump, blue-haired matrons this shit is sacred.

Sitting next to Mike is Jimmy Dean, himself an icon of white-bread wholesomeness and down-home values, and next to him, Mike's cohost, George Carlin.

As middle sister, Maxene, hits a high note, Jimmy leans over to me and says under his breath: "I bet that old Maxene's cooze hangs down like a sock."

The Mike Douglas Show in Philadelphia was a kind of extra added bonus to *Merv*. If you did *Merv* you did *Mike*. *Mike Douglas* was one of the top-rated daytime shows. Both were syndicated by Westinghouse: both had staggered play dates that might be a week later in one city and a week earlier in another. So both were pretty good exposure.

Mike was a nice enough guy: like Merv an ex-big-band singer. And because the ladies who came in from the suburbs to catch the show before lunch loved him so much, anyone he brought out had to be okay. If you were reasonably affable and clever and got through your stuff, you could get them to go: "Oh, he's a nice boy too."

Even so the show's central emotion was fear. I'd like to think it was bred by Mike's producer—a fat, loud, brash twentysomething named Roger Ailes who laughed at anything you said, funny or not—but, as I was learning fast, fear was the driving force of TV. Especially variety TV.

I'd take the train from New York to Philadelphia, and the whole way down, I'd be second-guessing myself over the piece I planned to do, wondering if this should come before that, trying to think of new jokes. Fearful of the constant threat: going into the sewer.

I did eight *Mervs* before I sat down at the panel. On *Mike Douglas*, you sat in the gazebo—his version of the panel—from the very first show. Right from the beginning I hated the scripted sociability of people sitting together, pretending to know stuff about one another, the fraudulent showbiz chitchat that went on in these conversations.

For comics it was especially hard. It was your job to keep people chuckling along. But you had no control over the phony setups. You had jokes ready and the host was supposed to ask you the right question, so you'd come back with your joke and bring the house down. But it was always nerve-racking, because you knew he'd get the setup wrong, which more often than not he did. And your hard work would go in the sewer.

Mike Douglas was daytime TV, which multiplied the opportunities for embarrassment. There'd be some activity you had to get physically involved in: an exercise lady or a juggler or a cooking segment. Once when I was cohost, Ailes sprang on me: "For tomorrow's cooking thing, we want you to have a recipe. We'll have all of the ingredients for it. You show Mike how to cook it."

I come up with—a jelly bean omelet. I'm thinking: "Boy, there's two things that don't go together. This will be REALLY humorous."

Next day I'm cooking and the egg mixture's half done and Mike's nodding along, pretending to be real serious. And I say: "Now in goes our filling: JELLY BEANS!" I'm expecting a nice laugh and then wing it from there. But Mike's still nodding, concentrating on the jelly bean omelet. Committing the details to memory so he can make one himself. Into the sewer again.

I hated that—being compromised, embarrassed, humiliated.

This loss of dignity and control. But hey, it's still only Stage Two: grin and bear it.

With all the exposure, things began to happen fast. In October '65 I was booked into Basin Street East, a place I could only have dreamed about six months earlier: my first big-time nightclub as a single with real momentum. I opened for the Tijuana Brass, who were white-hot, just beginning to crest. It was thrilling to discover that even though the place was packed with people who'd come to see Herb Alpert and his Brass, I could get them quiet and get their attention and even pull some laughs out of them. I did a really good job. I had a good act. I could handle a room of people who hadn't come to see me.

Bob Banner caught me at Basin Street. Banner was a long, lanky country-boy type from Texas who'd been cleaning up in New York as a producer. Among other things, he'd produced *Candid Camera* and discovered Carol Burnett and Dom DeLuise. He put me on *The Jimmy Dean Show,* an ABC primetime show he also produced. I did it in January '66 and they liked it so much they immediately had me back for another.

Next up was the Drake Hotel in Chicago, the far end of the spectrum from the Wells Street, folkie-hippie Chicago I knew. Very chichi, very snooty room where the comics had to wear tuxedos. My opening night I was standing behind a pillar in the middle of the room waiting for my announcement to go on and some large woman with far too many diamonds tapped my arm and told me to bring her some water. I said: "I will, as soon as I finish my act."

Bob Banner was soon back with an offer to be a regular and a writer on the *Kraft Summer Music Hall,* a summer replacement series in the *Andy Williams* slot. It was to star the new white-bread heartthrob singing sensation John Davidson. Since it started taping in April, I was needed in March 1966. In L.A. We closed down our tiny sixth-floor apartment, gave my mother the key and the three of us headed to California. Where we would stay for more than thirty years.

On *Kraft Summer Music Hall* I was the "house comic." I appeared on every show. Other regulars included the King Cousins, who were an offshoot of the King Family, and a singing duo: Jackie and Gayle from the New Christy Minstrels. Jackie eventually married John Davidson. It was a "young" show and the guests included Richie Pryor and Flip Wilson, singers like Nancy Sinatra, Noel Harrison (Rex's son), the Everlys, Chad & Jeremy.

John Davidson himself was bland as hell but easy to please; the son of a Baptist minister. Nothing seemed to upset him. One reason could've been, as he told me years later, that he'd fucked every girl on the show. I was always impressed with that. At the time I would never have thought it possible.

I did my spot and I wrote the chatter. The chatter was easy, because it was always, "Thank you, Gayle, thank you, John." I had those two lines and I worked from there. With the exception of the white pants, yellow shirts, striped blazers and boaters—that Andy Williams touch of Iowa in the summer of 1890—the show was very pleasant. It seemed as though this shit would lead somewhere.

Still, the Jimmy Dean and John Davidson shows, my first extended network exposure, were also the first taste I got of all the blocking and sitting around empty TV studios for long hours while whatever went on went on around you. Which you didn't understand a word of nor wanted to. Occasionally a voice up in the lights would tell somebody on the stage, "Do that again." "This time come in from the right." "Now stand over there . . ." All this boredom—the other driving force of television.

That didn't mean the fear was gone. However pleasant the people were, fear kicked back in with the endless fucking run-throughs. These were nerve-racking because you had to succeed for everyone present, the cast, the guests, the execs, the staff. Then you had to succeed again at dress rehearsal for the same people (who'd now heard your material at least once) plus the technicians and cameramen. And you still had air ahead. You'd dissipated your edge and energy and you hadn't even done yet what you'd come to do. Fear and boredom. Boredom and fear.

There were some private compensations. *Kraft Summer Music Hall* was where Al Pouch, the Hippy-Dippy Mailman, made his debut until he became Al Sleet, the Hippy-Dippy Weatherman.

What was great about having Al on this harmless, pleasant, white-bread show was that to my way of thinking—after all, I *was* Al—Al was a pothead. Like me, he was permanently stoned. That's where his misperceptions came from. Sure, he was a bit ignorant too. But he was fueled by cannabis.

I don't know where the John Davidson staff and the great middle-American viewing audience thought Al's weirdness came from, whether he sipped a little wine or whether they just thought Al was dumb as a brick, an early version of Forrest Gump.

But *I* knew Al's jokes were written from a pot mentality. By someone who smoked pot all day, every day. That felt wonderfully subversive. I've never been a full-blown radical. I wasn't cut out to man the barricades. But any time the subversive part of me is satisfied, it delights me. Thank God I'm nurturing this little animal over here.

'EYYYYYYYYYYYYYYYYYYYYYYY, baby, was' happenin'? Que paso? Al Sleet your Hippy-Dippy Weatherman here with all the hippy-dippy weather, man! First of all the pollen count from Long Island Jewish Hospital, onetwothreefourfive haha-haha. Present temperature is sixty-eight degrees at the airport, which is stupid 'cos I don't know anyone who lives at the airport. Downtown it's much hotter. Downtown's ON FIRE, man.

Now, I imagine some of you were a little surprised at the weather over the weekend. Especially if you watched my show on Friday. I'd like to personally apologize to the former residents of Rogers, Illinois. Caught them cats nappin', man! . . .

Now we take a look at the radar. Hey, the radar's pickin' up Mitch Miller! Sing along with Mitch, man! (sings) Baby . . . Gimme your answer do, I'm half crazy, all . . . Where was I, man . . . ? Oh yeah, the radar's picking up a line of thundershowers extending from a point nine miles north-northeast of Secaucus, New Jersey, to a line six miles on either side of a line somewhere south-southwest of Fond du Lac. However the radar is also picking up a squadron of incoming Russian ICBMs so I wouldn't sweat the thundershowers!

Tonight's forecast: DARK! Continued mostly dark tonight turning to widely scattered LIGHT in the morning, man!

That's it from Al Sleet. Don't forget, folks: inside every silver lining there's a DARK CLOUD!

As I did more and more television—*The Hollywood Palace, The Tonight Show,* Perry Como, Jimmie Rodgers, Roger Miller, more Douglases, other variety crap I've mercifully forgotten—I began to realize that there was a price you paid for the chance to do your stuff. You had to make believe you really cared about and belonged to the larger community of show business. That you were really interested in their small talk and shared whatever their values were.

The two-track life was there all the time. I clung to the respectability and mainstreamness, yet I had no respect for the things stars did and talked about and seemed to glorify and find glory in. I'd watch other people do the show after I had: the same junk talk, the same empty chatter, all this stupid fawning and caring that wasn't really there.

But then along came the main chance. What all this dumb shit was leading to, my ultimate goal, the Holy Grail. Stage Three: my first shot at real acting!

I decided to start modestly with a small role in *That Girl.* No need to overreach. Take it nice and easy. I was cast as Marlo's agent. I knew I could do well at this. I was a natural onstage. Acting was just the next step in other kinds of performance I had mastered. Doing a character voice was an extension of what I did in my act. You memorize your lines and speak them, moving when needed. In the end it was all television. Piece of cake.

There were a few other considerations, like real direction. (Variety TV directors direct cameras and not much else.) On the set, Marlo's producers, Bill Persky and Sam Denoff, successful TV writers who were moving fast up the food chain and knew what they wanted, gave me some direction:

"Okay, remember now, you'd like to handle this account. You've had trouble with this type of person in the past, so you're a little leery, but at the same time you have to pay the bills and your wife has just left you. The phone upstairs is ringing but you're not going to answer that because you know the maid is going to get it. And there's a fire in the basement. By the way, you're originally Romanian, so you have an Eastern European attitude to everything . . ."

You absorb that and walk through it and now there's blocking:

"Okay. Try to come down and cut a little to the left, then come all the way down, cheat a bit toward the light, but stay out of her light and this time get closer to the window. Okay? Let's do it again."

And . . . action!

I try to remember the words, while putting something behind the words that smacks of authenticity—motivation, character, something, and also while following the direction and blocking, wondering if I should use one of my own characters, although then I'll be putting alien words into my guy's mouth and bang goes all his naturalness, because they're someone else's words which I have to somehow interpret . . .

In short: *Acting.*

And I was NOT ABLE to do that! I was absolutely at sea, completely lost. Whatever competence I might have had going in had vanished. I floundered. I fluffed lines. I tried to do everything I'd been told at the same time. I was failing! And failing feeds on itself. There's a constant diminution of confidence. On top of failing, your brain is whirring: "They hired me! They are thinking about that RIGHT NOW! About the three more days they have to go through! They must be very dissatisfied! I SUCK! I will CONTINUE TO SUCK! And it WILL BE ON NETWORK TELEVISION!"

I'd lobbied my manager hard for auditions and they came in thick and fast.

There was a screen test for a series called *Manly and the Mob.* Anthony Caruso, who'd played a million mobsters, whose face you would know in a minute, was the Mob. Great casting. I was Manly, the inept private detective—an American Clouseau. Easy enough comic character to play. Not that complex a task. This was my series to have or not have. This was my pilot. My ticket to stardom.

I couldn't do that either! Or any of the others. They were all absolute, total failures, every one a humiliation. *That Girl* hadn't just been first-time-out nerves. I was devastatingly inept! There were no Oscars in sight. No Hollywood helpless with laughter at my feet. Danny Kaye the Second? Jack Lemmon the Second? Forget it. It was all beyond my reach.

I felt like I'd lost both legs in a car crash. My dream, this thing I'd wanted since I was a little kid sitting transfixed in a funky, dark movie house on the edge of Harlem, this future I believed was my birthright, had dissolved into thin air like the morning mist.

Meanwhile Stage Two, which was to have been phased out, having served its purpose, the booster rocket designed to fall back to earth as I shot to movie stardom, continued to barrel upward, getting bigger and stronger all the time. To the outside world I was a comic on the fast track, hitting all the professional heights. But inside I was full of fear and confusion. I was beginning to feel the discontent that became intolerable later on.

Objectively 1967 was full of success. In February my first album, *Take-Offs and Put-Ons*, came out and went gold. It was nominated for a Grammy and lost by a squeaker to Bill Cosby, a very worthy opponent. I was playing the biggest nightclubs in the country. I was starting to play Vegas. That summer, I did another replacement series called *Away We Go*, fourteen episodes, this time in the *Jackie Gleason Show* slot. (Hence the title, "Away we go!" being one of Gleason's catchphrases. "To the moon, Alice!" didn't seem to work so well.) But this summer I was a star of the show. Along with Buddy Rich and Buddy Greco.

My schizophrenia was beginning to show. I would come to the studio every day with a single strand of Indian beads and a different button. One day the button said, "The Marine Corps Builds Oswalds," and Buddy Greco took great exception to that. (He later became a very different person, completely relaxed with the human race, but he used to be a very difficult, very conservative guy.)

The kind of stuff I did on *Away We Go* was singing a trio with my two Buddies of "It Was a Very Good Year." It was creaky sketches with creaky premises, it was trivial numbers in bunny suits. It began boring in on me how untrue I was being to myself. These dreary variety shows with uninteresting people who were just walking through their lives. Doing bland, middle-American showbiz-as-usual material. The more that feeling piled up, the more my acting failures weighed on my mind, the more I was becoming aware that something was seriously wrong. That I was in the wrong place with the wrong people for the wrong reasons.

Then there was *The Ed Sullivan Show.* The horrible, horrible *Sullivan Show*, torture chamber of comedians. I'd resisted doing it for a long time, but the offers kept improving and they agreed not to hack up my material, like they did with every other comic, however big. So in '67 I finally went on *Sullivan*. On what I thought were my terms.

The Ed Sullivan Show's worst weapon of torture was that it was live. There were no second takes on *Sullivan*. If you fucked up, all America saw it. If Mr. Pastry dropped his plates or Jackie Mason gave Ed the finger there were no do-overs, no cutaways, no edits. No apologies were accepted.

There was additional pressure: the studio audience knew the show was live too. They knew there was a chance they might be on television, sitting in front of the picture of Joe Louis or Jimmy Cagney or some other celebrity Ed wrote about in his stupid column. Half the audience had special invitations. It was a perk. If you were a Lincoln Mercury dealer on Long Island you got ten tickets and you brought people you wanted to impress. Everybody had their best things on. The audience was on display as much as you were.

When an audience is potentially on display, they're very inhibited. They're reluctant to let go. So laughter, which is a natural, spontaneous thing, must be avoided. They think: "I'll wait and make sure that if I laugh, it's something everyone's laughing at. That

I'm right in with the crowd. Because if I start roaring, 'Hahaha-ohhhhahaaahaaaa-God-oh-fuck-that's-funny,' and no one else does, I'll embarrass the shit out of myself." Not good for comedy.

The final turn of the screw: Sullivan himself. During your set, Ed would stand onstage over to stage right. Out of camera range but *onstage*. So the entire audience never watched the comic. They were watching Sullivan to see if he would laugh. And he never did.

Add all this up and you have the graveyard of laughter. Playing comedy to the *Sullivan* audience was agony. You'd get more laughs in a mausoleum.

I've always been an ordered and left-brained person about performance, worried to the point of obsession that every detail has been taken care of, is precisely in place. But I don't get nervous. On *Sullivan* I was always incredibly nervous. At first I thought it was the unpredictability, the lack of control, but I soon figured out it was because the show cultivated, it seemed almost deliberately, that driving force of network television—fear.

I'd stay at the Americana Hotel (now the Sheraton) on Seventh at 52nd. I'd take that walk—the Last Mile—across to Broadway and up to the stage door on 53rd Street. There was a deli right at the stage door; I'd get my two cans of Rheingold, because I knew I could handle two cans. It wouldn't show and it might help a little. But the nervousness never went away.

These days *Letterman* is taped in the same place, the Ed Sullivan Theater. Once in a while when I'm in New York I purposely walk the Last Mile across those same streets and up to that stage door on 53rd. Forty years later I still reexperience all the fear and vomiting nervousness.

It got even worse. *Sullivan* was on Sunday nights at eight. Because the dress rehearsal began around one to two p.m., you had to be there fairly early in the morning, right around the time normal people were in church. That was the choice: church or *Sullivan*. So you had ten to twelve hours to sit around getting absolutely fucking terrified before you went on live in front of 50 million belching, farting, comatose Americans who'd just eaten a big Sunday dinner. The boredom part of fear and boredom.

There was one tiny ray of sunlight. Ed found out that I was an Irish Catholic from New York. It didn't help with any of the physical horrors of the show, but it did mean I got preferential treatment when it came to having my material butchered, or simply being cut from the show after dress, both of which could happen even to the biggest names in comedy. The *Sullivan* people told my manager—whether it was true or not who knows—that I was Ed's favorite comic.

On one show he called me over after my set to where he stood, stage right. This was supposed to be a big honor. We had some inane exchange and then he said out of the blue, "You're a Catholic!" and then gestured to the audience with that weird insect thing he did with his arms: "Give him a big hand! He's a Catholic!"

Ed was partial to this form of intro. He once introduced my friend the Hispanic singer José Feliciano (another of the Au Go Go gang) as follows: "Want you to give the next act, José Feliciano, a big hand! He's blind—and he's Puerto Rican!"

But the real milestone of my *Sullivan* career was the show where I followed the skating chimpanzees. There's something I can say for the rest of my days: "I once followed the skating chimpanzees."

Terrified I always was, but I did do some ballsy and reckless things on *Sullivan*. It was traditional for comedians to try out a bit in clubs to see if it worked and then do it on *Sullivan*. I tried out things on *Sullivan* and if they worked, I'd do them in clubs.

Some of them didn't. Once I brought my brother on. Pat had never been in front of an audience in his life. Very verbal man, lots of laughs in private, but no experience whatsoever being funny in public for money. I wrote a piece using an old character from the Burns and Carlin days, a corrupt senator called Frebish. Pat was a newsman, interviewing me. We sat at a desk so that if he dried up, he could read the questions.

The plan was, Ed would do an intro, Ray Block, leader of the orchestra, would play a short sting, Pat would say, "Good evening, this is (whatever the funny show name was) and I'm here with Senator Frebish . . ."

Ed does his intro and . . . Ray Block forgets to play the music sting. So Pat and I sit there live in front of 50 million people for what seems like two months. I hiss: "Go ahead! Start!" Pat looks blank—where's the music? Eventually, after another month, he starts and of course the piece just went totally in the sewer. And it wasn't that funny to start with.

Vegas, on the other hand, was a cinch. I had this act—which was essentially my 1967 album—that I wasn't really *in*, so it was easy. All I had to do was turn it on and let it run. I was a cute, clever, presentable guy and I had a nice double-breasted jacket. I was good-looking without being overpoweringly handsome, neat hair, slim figure. And articulate. I said what I said well. I knew how to do those characters and those voices and those radio announcers and those ladies on TV. I was a nicely packaged commodity, slick, entertaining. I could give them what they wanted for how long they wanted.

Well, perhaps not quite. When I first played Vegas at the Flamingo in 1966, opening for Jack Jones, my contract laid out very specifically the time I was to do: nineteen minutes. I thought: "Fuck nineteen minutes! This is my first night ever in Vegas. This is an important moment. If I'm going good I'm going till I'm done!"

The audience is fantastic and I end up doing twenty-two minutes—three minutes over the contract. I come back to the dressing room and there waiting for me is a male mountain with a conspicuous bulge in his jacket. He very calmly and slowly tells me that my three extra minutes have cost the owner of the Flamingo, Mr. X (I've blanked on the name), some fucking staggering amount of money in the high six figures (which now would be ten to fifteen times that). They calibrated exactly how much the casino was earning every single minute of the day. The man-mountain lets me know that in the future I do not want Mr. X to be "disappointed." And I have no illusion as to what this means. Part of this woolly mammoth's job description is rubbing out opening acts who do more than nineteen minutes and dumping them in the desert. Despite growing up on some pretty mean streets, it was the scariest fucking moment of my life. From then on I never did a nanosecond over nineteen minutes.

The real point being: I could do exactly nineteen minutes or exactly twenty-nine or thirty-nine. I was by now a consummate pro. I could do whatever you wanted. Piece of cake.

A random scan of my bookings for '66/'67 shows names like: the Flamingo, the Cocoanut Grove, *The Hollywood Palace*, *The Perry Como Show*, *The Jackie Gleason Show*, Lake Tahoe, *The Dean Martin Show* and on and on. Next stop on this track I change my name to Jackie Carlin, buy some white shoes, gold chains and pinkie rings and I'm set for life.

What was happening to me internally was that I'd got not just seeds of doubt, but *saplings* of doubt sprouting inside me. About my acting of course, but about all my goals, about being on this rigid track, about being rewarded more and more for being cute and clever and funny.

But not for being George Carlin.

And there was something else too that I could see happening, but didn't know how to change, that was just as related to the track I was speeding along on and to the doubt and discontent it caused me.

After Burns and Carlin broke up, Brenda and I were together all the time. She devoted herself to me and my comedy. She helped me with the details and logistics, booked travel, kept the books, made suggestions, she was my sounding board, she sat in every club I played every night, whether there was one person or it was packed. She celebrated when I did well, she was there to hold my hand when things sucked. We did a lot of holding hands.

On the road our days didn't vary much. We wouldn't get up till eleven or twelve; eat breakfast, hang around and watch TV. If we were in a city we wanted to see, we'd get out a bit and walk around. We were confined somewhat because we didn't have much money to spend. But we were carefree, we did crazy stuff, we kept on clicking as we had at first.

I couldn't be there when Brenda was in Dayton getting ready to have Kelly. I did fly in when she was actually born and I was up on a ladder taking pictures when she was just a few minutes old. I felt bad that I had to leave and go back on the road. I could tell Brenda wasn't happy.

But she didn't let that get in her way. When Kelly was just two and half months old—they were back in New York by then—she packed her up and they came down to meet me in Florida. That was Kelly's first road trip. From then on for the next three years, it was just like before, except there were three of us now. We were together all the time, on the road or back in New York. And just like before, Brenda was my manager and bookkeeper, collaborator and comforter.

Then the day after we got to L.A. in March 1966, I had to go to work on preproduction for *Kraft Summer Music Hall*. Brenda was left alone with Kelly, who was not yet three. Suddenly she had nothing to do. She knew no one. She had nowhere to go. So she got drunk.

She started getting terrible migraine headaches—a pretty good indicator of stress and tension. But I missed the marker. And she wasn't inactive. She volunteered at a hospital and she did one big thing in L.A. that she'd always wanted to try but we couldn't afford till then: take flying lessons. She passed her tests, she became proficient. But she was used to sharing her accomplishments with me, and I wasn't there for her to share it. I was too busy. Instead of boosting her confidence it became a source of resentment. So she got drunk.

There was a woman in our first apartment house who was a model, so she was home a lot between calls. She began to come over and hang with Brenda and they drank in the afternoon. I didn't find out about that until later; there was a lot I didn't know at the time or realize. I was getting too busy too quickly. Or perhaps I didn't want to know or realize. Marijuana can do that to you.

Brenda was used to being out on the road with me, doing everything with me and for me. Now I had agents and a manager and people who handled booking and flights and money. They'd taken her place. She told me later that there was a point in '67 when she literally couldn't sign her own name. She just couldn't write the words "Brenda Carlin." She was losing her identity. So she got drunk.

With me on the road, or sitting around some fucking TV studio for days on end, she had to be mother and father to Kelly. Then I'd come home with an armful of presents and it would be: "Daddy's home! Fun time!" Which cast her as the domestic tyrant, the one who said No. Time for bed. Time for school. She hated being that. So she got drunk.

I don't remember when Brenda's drinking became something more than Brenda drinking something. But I do know we began to fight. She would say she felt like a piece of furniture. That I was just walking around her as if she weren't there. I didn't know what she meant. I just swallowed everything. You have to be aware of feelings before you can deny them and push them down. In a lot of ways, for a lot of reasons, I wasn't even aware of my own feelings. The ones that would manage to break through, I would immediately say: "That can't be."

We'd notice odd things about Kelly. We'd find her sleeping on the floor in the morning, instead of in the bed. We never understood why at the time. And Kelly couldn't watch me on television. She'd put her head down so she couldn't see me on the screen. She couldn't handle it for some reason. We didn't understand that either.

There was something about me and Brenda's chemistry that we didn't have to consciously say, "We'll stick this out for our child, we have to make this work." We felt bound together. In spite of all that was going on there was an inevitability about that. I never had a thought of leaving Brenda. There was a feeling that the good times were still good enough. And often, when she was sober, which was in the morning of course, she'd sound really sensible. She'd say, "Yeah, I'm going to watch that." It was still just the beginning of things. And I was smoking a lot of pot. I could hardly blame her for drinking to keep up.

So there we were: a successful young couple with plenty of money, a nice house in Beverly Hills. With a mountain of grass. And a lake of booze. And a beautiful daughter who couldn't watch her daddy do what he did for a living.

I always said Kelly has an old soul. Perhaps even then, in the wisdom of her four years on earth, she sensed that I was on a treadmill to nowhere. Without a clue how to get off.

10

THE LONG EPIPHANY

George performing at the Kiel Opera House, 1973
(Copyright G. Robert Bishop)

On June 5, 1968, just after midnight, while I was working at Bimbo's 365 Club in San Francisco with Lana Cantrell, Robert Kennedy was shot dead at the Ambassador Hotel down in L.A. I told them I wasn't going on for the second show. They— whoever They were, Bimbo I guess—insisted that I go on. No way. In fact I decided as I watched the coverage through the night that I wasn't going back the next night either. Fuck Bimbo.

Then the Chicago convention police riot happened and that brought people down on one side or the other with more firmness than they might've had before. I was no exception.

It's funny but I never find myself responding very much to events of great magnitude. There's a part of me that knows that's exactly what's supposed to happen. I will sometimes marvel at the timing or circumstances or setting or the individuals involved. "Weird" is the word that occurs to me most often. "That's fucking weird." Weird— but never unexpected.

I didn't respond with rage to any of what was happening in 1968. Dr. King's murder in April was depressingly predictable. There was a sinking feeling: that something good was ebbing away and being encouraged in that direction by the usual forces. The establishment was winning—its war, its assassins, its secret government—and that fact overpowered and debilitated me more than it enraged me.

I've always been the kind of person—whether it comes from being half shanty, half lace-curtain Irish I don't know—who needs to be changed, rather than instigating change myself. I could never make life-changing decisions in a split-second. I'm always open to change but I need to have it happen in a natural, organic, timely fashion.

I always say that everything in nature works very, very slowly. Okay, what about a volcano? Well, an eruption may seem like split-second drama, but it's actually the end result of a long process that's gone on for years far below the earth's surface. My change when it came was like that, drawn out over several years, then exploding in a series of eruptions.

By now—1968 and '69—everything about my comedy seemed rote. On the *Smothers Brothers*, where I remember feeling at home, feeling we'd taken over, where even the things about the show that were the same, such as blocking and standing around like a dick for hours, had a different flavor . . . even there, on the only comedy show that was actually taking a stand against the war, I did . . . "The Indian Sergeant."

Why the fuck didn't I sit down a month before and write something daring for Tommy Smothers?

One time I did do something revolutionary and subversive—without even realizing it. For *The Jackie Gleason Show* I'd written a piece, which aired in January 1969, called "The J. Edgar Hoover Show."

> . . . *with Ramsey Clark and the Orchestra and the Joe Valachi Singers and, special guest, Joe Bananas' sister Chiquita!*

Naturally, I played host J. Edgar Hoover:

> *I just came from a stakeout. It was backyard barbecue. Ha ha ha! Laugh it up or we'll lock you up! Time to meet the guys who really make the show possible—the rotten, vicious criminals . . . Let's take a look at Pretty Boy Cliff. (holds up a picture of a gorilla) Cliff is four foot eight and weighs 350 pounds. Other than that he has no distinguishing features. Cliff is wanted for stealing a circus train and attempting to drive it to Havana. He fancies himself a lady-killer—and so do the police . . . They've*

*got the lady to prove it . . . Join us again tomorrow night when
our guest might be someone hiding out near you. If he is tune us
in, turn him in, and drop out . . . of sight!*

Apart from that mildest of dope references in the last line, about
as harmless a piece of TV fluff as you could imagine. Nonetheless,
as I discovered thirty years later, thanks to the Freedom of Information Act, it got my FBI file started. Apparently a week after the airing
the director himself received a copy of a letter which a Mr. (NAME
BLACKED OUT), a former special agent, had sent to Jackie Gleason in Miami. Mr. (NAME BLACKED OUT) had "commented
on appearance of one George Carlin, an alleged comedian . . . and
that the subject of Carlin's material was the FBI and Mr. Hoover and
that his treatment of both was shoddy and in shockingly bad taste."

BuFiles, it appeared, contained "no information identifiable with
Carlin." But the best part of the covering letter was the kicker: "The
[Miami] Office advised that from their prior contacts with Jackie
Gleason and specifically with Mr. Hank Meyers, Gleason's Public
Relations Director, who is also an SAC Contact [i.e., an FBI stoolie],
they are of the opinion that Gleason holds the Director and the FBI
in the highest esteem and that Gleason himself thinks that the Di-
rector is one of the greatest men who has ever lived."

How different my life might've been if I'd known the FBI considered me the satirical equivalent of Huey Newton. As it was, the most
revolutionary thing I did at the time was fly to London to do . . . *This
Is Tom Jones*.

It was a particularly low point. Like all other guests we had a suite
in the Dorchester. So Brenda and I decided to have a party. In the
suite that night were Jim Brown, a bunch of musicians, including
Mama Cass—and Mia Farrow. (Nobody knew it was Mia Farrow,
because she didn't say anything—just sat there under a big hat. After
she left, somebody said: "Wasn't that Mia Farrow?") Mama Cass
had her aide-de-camp with her, which I thought was a really cool
thing to call your assistant. And Jim Brown was very angry about a
lot of shit. Which I certainly understood.

I was wearing a suit. I was awkward and goofy. It was my party but I felt really out of place. I was living with a lot of private misery. All these fucking stupid TV shows with all that lighting shit, meaningless banter, all that garbage, all that wasted time and energy. My brilliant act, which was doing so well, had nowhere to go. I was writing and performing material that went around in circles, media material taking off on media form, television about television. And while I was powerfully attracted to the life my rock and folkie friends led—as a comedian, how did I go about leading that? There were very few counterculture comedy centers—one terrific group in San Francisco called the Committee, who'd been on *Smothers* with me, but that was about it. I felt inadequate compared to an outfit like the Committee. I felt I'd somehow stained myself with this middle-class show-business shit.

And however much kinship I had with the counterculture, it brought up again the eternal dilemma: of longing to belong but not liking to belong—even though the group I wanted to belong to now were non-belongers.

Maybe it wasn't belonging that I longed for so much as being able to fulfill my proper role. I wasn't doing my job. I wasn't using my mind to produce the external evidence of my inner state. I was superficially skimming off the top these mild and passable parodies. The very fact that they were parodies is telling. There was nothing of me in them.

I looked at what my friends were doing, the music they were making, the doors they were opening, the stands they were taking, the changes they were acknowledging and instigating. Then I looked at the people in TV studios and nightclubs where I did my superficially skimming act, mostly for the parents of the people I admired. I felt like a traitor to my generation.

George Carlin has become a showbiz mystery. One of the very best young contemporary clowns, he had a splendid comic spirit, a fresh new outlook on comedy, got the top TV bookings, has been considered for several terribly remunerative TV-talk-show chairmanships, his material was attractive to teenagers, college kids and mature marrieds; his records sold friskily and all seemed right in his straight future . . . Carlin now seems an artistic drop-out. His clothes, incensed hangdog demeanor, long pony-tail-style hairdo, grubby pants, a totally unwashed, shambling, savagely apologetic aspect as if speaking straight from a hobo jungle, combine in his new "style," essentially no style at all beyond a belligerent, truculent "statement."

Thus spake Jack O'Brian, the self-described "Voice of Broadway," in 1973, following a rowdy concert I'd done at the Westbury Music Fair in Long Island. I couldn't have been happier with his words if I'd written them myself. Yes, Jack, you dopey old bigot, you hit the nail right on the head.

How had I become an unwashed, shambling, savagely apologetic hobo with grubby pants and an incensed, hangdog demeanor? Well, it hadn't been easy. I think it all began with that long, pony-tail-style hairdo.

I once said, I always had long hair—only I used to keep it inside my head. But letting it come out where people could see it was a drawn-out process. Looking back on it I'm not even sure where and when it began. It was a barely conscious decision—almost as if the hair decided to come out of its own accord. My hair had a mind of its own.

Terrible things were happening to me. But because of them, my life began to change. In the fall of 1969 I was fired from the Frontier Hotel in Vegas—where I had an extremely lucrative two-year deal—for saying the word "ass."

I had been working into my act a little short thing about, "I got no ass. You might notice, I go right from the shoulders to the heels, like most Irish guys. No ass. When I was in the service, black guys used to see me in the showers and say, 'Hey, man, where yo' ass at? Stud got no ass.' "

That was it. They fired me. Closed me after the very first show. Here's what happened. The show had been reserved exclusively for players in the Howard Hughes Invitational (golf tournament) and their guests. These people, who had been at the Hole No. 19 or whatever they call that bar thing at golf courses, show up fucking half drunk. The Frontier starts the show about an hour late to accommodate them. I come out and they're really unruly. They're not a good audience. And just as a matter of principle I'm not happy with these golf cocksuckers anyway.

I do the ass routine and I'm told in between shows that Robert Maheu, the Mormon who ran the place and was Howard Hughes's keeper, had gotten complaints from the audience: "The people didn't appreciate what you said. Don't bother with the second show. You'll get your money for the rest of the week."

Being fired from the Frontier for saying "ass." A harbinger—don't you love that word?—of all that was to come.

Then there was acid. I know exactly when I first did acid—it was in October 1969 while I was playing a major, now long-defunct jazz club in Chicago called Mister Kelly's. Next to my record of that booking, which was otherwise uneventful, is written in a trembling hand the word "acid." Actually in the course of a two-week gig I did acid multiple times, maybe five, maybe ten. (After the first couple of trips your numeracy tends to decline.)

Fuck the drug war. Dropping acid was a profound turning point for me, a seminal experience. I make no apologies for it. More people should do acid. It should be sold over the counter. Acid finally moved me from one place to the other; allowed change to take place—change that had been rumbling underground all this time, but which I still needed to have happen to me rather than initiate. (I suppose I did initiate it by dropping the stuff but I couldn't know what would transpire; at least I had the illusion that change had happened to me rather than through me.) Suddenly all the conflict that had been tormenting me between the alternative values and straight values began to resolve.

But. This radically different, utterly changed, reimprinted, reprogrammed person had to now go play the Copacabana in New York. The Copa was the quintessential place I did not belong. I'd only agreed to do it (long before the acid) when management said: "It's Christmas. Oliver is headlining (Oliver was a pseudo-folkie who'd had a number one song). There'll be a lot of people who don't normally go to a place like the Copacabana. So you'll get a younger, TV-audience crowd. You'll be okay."

The Copa was owned by Jules Podell, an old-line, semi-gangster type with this big pinkie ring that he would tap loudly on the table when he didn't like something.

So I did my act: "Indian Sergeant," "Hippy-Dippy Weatherman," "Wonderful WINO," all the standard stuff, but less convincingly than ever. Sometimes midway through the show, not having my heart in it, with Podell sitting out there, I'd start in on the Copa itself: "These dumps went out of style in the 1940s and they forgot to close."

Tap tap tap tap.

Some nights I'd lie down on the floor under the piano and describe its underside: "There are vertical and diagonal pieces of wood with little nails in them and one of them says, 'New York City 00-601.' " Or still lying on the floor I'd describe the ceiling of the club—unfavorably. Another time, I brought the Yellow Pages onstage: "I'm now going to read from 'Upholsterers.' " Which I did. There'd be a few embarrassed, unbelieving laughs. Perhaps there were some people in the audience who'd heard of Dada surrealism and thought it was Dada. But not a lot. And always from the table out there in the darkness: tap, tap, tap, tap, tap!

This went on for three entire weeks, the tirades and Dada shit alternating with the not even halfhearted performances. Every night I would ask to be fired onstage. I would say, "Please fire me." Podell wouldn't do it. Just the tapping.

Then, on my next-to-last night, during the first show, in the final minutes of my final piece . . . they slowly turned down the lights on me. Ever so slowly, as if the sun were setting. Then, just as slowly, they turned my volume off. At the end I was standing onstage, in the dark, in total silence. In a way it was kind of perfect. The lights had gone down on that part of my life.

It was January 6, 1970—the Feast of the Epiphany. A great start to a watershed year. I'd now been fired from two of the supposedly more prestigious and certainly more high-visibility mainstream locations in the country. And while the Frontier could be written off as a temporary lapse, a minor infraction, I'd flaunted my disgust and conflict and unhappiness every night for three weeks in the media capital of the world.

I got at least one good review from a very unexpected source: my mother. She wrote me a letter, enclosing reviews of a Samuel Beckett play she'd just seen. This is what devout-Catholic-Eisenhower-Republican Mary had to say to her wayward son about his latest developments:

Dear George:

I should be on the check-out line at the supermarket but I must say these words to you. Please read these reviews. You will someday be a Beckett or a Joyce or maybe a Bernard Shaw. You seem to have their kind of disturbance . . . Some day you will release what you have down inside of you and it will be listened to and heard.

They condemn you for idolizing Lenny Bruce—how little they really know what you see in his courage, sincerity and daring. Please George insist on being yourself. Don't let anyone change you or silence you. I am so hungry for a heart-to-heart with you . . . Why have I got this restlessness—this groping for answers which I sometimes feel I have passed on to you? Do you follow me George? Why can't I quiet this undisciplined questioning of what goes on around us? Why am I caught up by it?

Wow—had Mary been dropping a little acid too?

There was no turning back. Of its own volition hair was sprouting all over me. Two weeks later—newly bearded—I did the Radio and Television Correspondents' Dinner in Washington. Nixon was there. His reaction to my new beard is unrecorded.

On the talk shows that I did, Steve Allen, for example, or Della Reese, I began to be quite open about my changes and new values and what I saw as the government's omissions and inconsistencies. Virginia Graham had a terrific show, which I guested four or five times. She was a great character. Didn't give a shit about what people thought and loved to stir things up. She was always saying sweetly, "Let's you two fight"—in other words: "Why don't you two guests of mine rip each other to shreds?"

I did once. I ripped up Representative Bob Dornan, the red-headed maniac from Orange County, when he'd just become a congressman. He talked about "these hippies desecrating the flag" and "the violence of people who are blowing up math buildings" and protested about protesters getting violent. So I called him on it: "Wait a minute. A flag is supposed to represent everything that a country does. It doesn't only represent the good things. If you burn the flag, you're burning the flag for what you perceive to be the bad things the country has done. It's only a symbol. It's only a piece of cloth." And "The violence of the Left is symbolic, the injuries are not intended. The violence of the Right is real—directed at people, designed to cause injuries. Vietnam, nuclear weapons, police out of control are intentional forms of violence. The violence from the Right is aimed directly at people and the violence from the Left is aimed at institutions and symbols." I got him mad as hell. It was a nice turning around of his own words. Which was great: "Take that, you cocksucker."

David Frost was great too. I did two of those. First time, John Lennon was on and I got bumped because Lennon went long. Backstage I got to talking to Lennon, and I guess I wanted to tell him something because I ended up asking: "How can I call you?" So he gave me his number. I still have it in his own handwriting, "John Lennon and Yoko," someplace on Bank Street. I'm really proud of that. That goes along with my Charlie Parker autograph. Second time I did a whole show. And Frost was good—he gave you questions so you could take off and wail for a while.

The other change that took place was my starting to play coffeehouses and folk clubs. There wasn't yet much new material, but what I did was simply talk about the changes and make the point that I had to stop working from the surface of my brain and get into the middle of my gut. Talk about who I was and how I felt. The coffeehouse ethos lent itself to that first-person, quasi-confessional approach. And this was a crucial difference, because talking directly to the audience rather than performing for them in character as I always had would soon evolve into a completely new kind of material.

But mainly I had to explain myself to me. What had been pulling at me all this time, dragging me away from the old approach and toward the new, was the lack of my voice in my work. The absence of me in my act. I would say, "I wasn't in my act. I was all these other people." And I would introduce them all, the old familiar characters, one by one, to make the point.

I was stumbling across the difference between being an entertainer and being an artist. Even more basically I needed to authenticate myself by hearing what I was thinking said out loud. The best way I know to clarify my thinking is to hear and see what I think I'm thinking. Because however clear it may seem to you internally, it's never clear exactly what it is, until you speak and hear the words. You are your own first-night audience.

More disasters—at least in the conventional sense—were ahead. At the end of August I was to return to the scene of my former crimes at the Frontier Hotel in Vegas. I gave a pretty cocky interview to the *Los Angeles Herald-Examiner*: "The way my act is growing the censorship [of the word "ass" the previous year] has given it direction instead of it being vanilla custard. It gives me many more chances to test the willingness of an audience . . . I've always felt a comic is a potential social critic; a philosopher or evangelist."

I didn't test the willingness of the audience for several weeks (I was playing with the Supremes), but then came a night when I threw in a thought about the double meanings of that fine little word "shit," and by extension about my own previous problems with the Frontier. This time it wasn't golf assholes who did me in, but business assholes—Chrysler salesmen.

I said, "I don't say shit. Down the street Buddy Hackett says shit, Redd Foxx says shit. I don't say shit. I smoke a little of it, but I don't say it." And I'm off onto something else. When I leave the stage, I'm informed that I've been relieved of my duties. A spokesman for the hotel later told the papers that I had "apparently been unsatisfied [*sic*] with the reaction of the audience and began belaboring them with four-letter words . . . We estimate that at least 70% of the show was offensive." They closed me down five days early, paid me pro rata (I was making $12,500 a week at the time), and canceled me forever. That was it for the foreseeable future for George Carlin and Las Vegas.

But what was in conventional terms a third major professional disaster was in fact another turning point. The experience became the first line in the routine that kicked off the "FM" side of my next album and was in many ways its trademark—the shit routine which went by the name of "Shoot":

> *I got fired last year in Las Vegas for saying shit. In a town where the big game is called craps. That's some kind of a double standard. I'm sure there was some Texan standing out in the casino yelling, "Oh SHIT! I CRAPPED!" And they fly those guys in free. Fired me. Shit.*

> *Get into as much trouble saying shit as you can smoking it down there. Shit's a nice word, friendly happy word. Handy word. The middle class has never really been into shit as a word. Not really comfortable. You'll hear it around the kitchen if someone drops a casserole. "Oh shit! Look at the noodles. Oh shit!! Don't say that, Johnny—just hear it." Sometimes they say shoot. But they can't kid me. Shoot is shit with two o's.*

> *The use of shit is always figurative speech: "Get that shit outta-here, willya? Move that shit. I don't wanna hear that shit. Don't gimme that shit. I don't have to take that shit. YOU'RE fulla shit! Think I'm a shithead or something?" Always figurative. You never hear anyone say: "Lookit the little piles of shit in the street, Martha!" They don't say that. They have other words for that: doo-doo, ka-ka, poo-poo. And good old Number Two. Could never figure that one out, man. How did they arrive at that? Out of all the numbers, TWO gotta mean shit! My dog does Number Five. That's three Ones and a Two . . .*

There is a clear line of evolution between "Shoot" and "Seven Words." The piece grew out of a desire to talk about language standards and the inconsistency in them. So by being authentic about what had happened to me I found a way into a new comedy that was accurate and natural.

The hair and the beard—which had to have been a factor in the firing, a clear signal in divided times that I had come down on one side of the Kulturkampf—were getting longer. As hair emerged from my head, material did too. I'd already written the "Hair" poem, which was my way of telling straight, parent-aged people that "You should discount my hair as a reason to discount my material." This too became a cut on the "FM" side of the next album:

> *I'm aware some stare at my hair*
> *In fact to be fair*
> *Some really despair of my hair*
> *But I don't care, 'cos they're not aware*
> *Nor are they debonair*
> *In fact they're just square*
>
> *They see hair down to there, say, "Beware!"*
> *And go off on a tear*
> *I say, "No fair!"*
> *A head that's bare is really nowhere*
> *So be like a bear, be fair with your hair*
> *Show it you care*
> *Wear it there . . . or to there . . .*
> *Or to THERE if you dare!*

Then there was the beard:

> *Here's my beard*
> *Ain't it weird?*
> *Don't be skeered*
> *Just a beard!*

The word "beard" shakes a lot of people up. Not AMERICAN-sounding. BEE-AR-D! Lenin had a BEE-ARR-D! Gabby Hayes had . . . WHISKERS!

The hair was certainly part of the next and final disaster. *Daily Variety* for Monday, November 30, 1970, carried the bare bones of the story:

> Comic George Carlin was cancelled and asked to leave Lake Geneva (Wis.) Playboy Club after the audience got ugly during his second show Saturday night. Management said it feared for his safety. It was his shtick about materialism in American society, press censorship, poverty, Nixon-Agnew and the Vietnam War that apparently incensed the late-night crowd. Club manager said Carlin "insulted the audience directly and used offensive language and material . . ." Reacting to his statements about poverty, one woman heckled "You don't know anything about poverty. We don't have any in this country!" A comment about going through Cambodia to get out of Vietnam brought the retort: "How do you know? You've never been shot at!" Club manager said comic would have been in danger "if he'd gone anywhere the audience could have got to him."

The booking at Lake Geneva was scary. When the guy heckled me about never having been shot at, the only thing that went through my head was, "Does he have a gun?" People were yelling things like, "Where's the old George Carlin?" Soon it became the entire audience, maybe two hundred straight, tight, asshole-looking Wisconsin-Saturday-night-out people, getting up, walking out, fingers being waved at me—it was something out of a movie. I finished whatever time I felt they had to pay me for, and in a ridiculous act of bravado walked out through the audience, although there was clearly a wing onstage.

The Lake Geneva Playboy Club was a self-contained resort. I would have to spend the night in a hotel room in the compound, alongside many of the people from that disgusted, hostile audience. Management not only sent me a telegram canceling me but said, "We cannot guarantee your safety if you remain on the premises. We're asking you to leave." Apparently people had been going to the front desk and asking for my room number. So I thought, "Fine, I'm only ninety miles from Chicago and Hugh Hefner's mansion. Hef is probably home. Freedom of speech is involved. Hef says he cares about that. Hef will back me up and I'll get my fucking money." I drive down to Chicago, go to the mansion and Hef is there with Bill Cosby, playing pinball. I tell Hef the whole story. And he says: "Well, there are two Hefs, George. One of them sitting in that audience would have loved that material. The other Hef [and here he was paraphrasing Lenny], 'Ya gotta do business with these assholes.' "

So I was finally finished with that fairy tale too.

I began to do sets at a folk club called the Ice House in Pasadena. The very first night I was there, I parked my Trans Am alongside the curb instead of in the parking lot. And when I came out someone had sideswiped it and the whole driver's side was just demolished and fucked up. I remember thinking: "This is the price I'm paying. This is a message that this material thing, this symbol of what I'm philosophically rejecting, is behind me. It's irrelevant. This affirms why I'm here. I must follow through on this."

There was another side to this time of discovery: acting on principle costs money. In spite of all the things that had been going on in my head throughout 1970, Brenda and I had arranged to buy a house in Calabasas. Our first home ever, in suburban Los Angeles. The deal was proceeding, in fact at the time the Frontier canceled my deal it was already in escrow. Ironically, my manager and I had calculated that when the Frontier contract expired at the end of that run, we would then be free to negotiate with any hotel in Las Vegas and get a much better deal. So the house would have been no great financial burden.

All that stuff ran away. The house, that dream just disappeared. It was a wrenching thing for Brenda. We had to leave the house in Beverly Hills we were renting from a CBS executive and move back to the apartment complex we lived in when we first came to L.A. We moved back down in the world. From there we went to Venice, which back then, long before gentrification, was a very run-down, hippie-ridden neighborhood. We took a little apartment on Pacific Avenue, as a conscious way of entering the counterculture.

I think Brenda was afraid of how I was—of the things I now

believed and where I was going. I remember a resistance in her, whether it was just body language or facial expressions or some retort, even when I was just reacting to something on TV. It produced a lot of fear and apprehension in her. When I got angry with her I would attack her for being a middle-class, midwestern, Protestant, conventional thinker. Trapped and bound by those values.

And there was always my pot smoking. It left her out. She never smoked pot, and the few times she did, she didn't like it. And pot is a club. When the pot smokers are off laughing in the corner and you're sitting there drinking your Cutty mist, that's devastating.

This wasn't a political clash so much as a behavioral one. What I was saying was identified in her mind with unstable and dangerous people. There wasn't a chasm between us at this time but certainly a good-sized crevice.

I felt trapped by my commitment to things I wanted for Brenda and Kelly versus the things I wanted for myself. I never felt, "Gee, if I could only get away from this woman." I do remember thinking, "Gee, if I could just get her to stop drinking, some of this could begin to change." But that was selfish, because here I was full of pot and my own intake of alcohol.

Right in the midst of this, as my hair and beard began to sprout and the break was becoming irreversible, Brenda found out she was pregnant again. We had no money. This time I said, "We can't do it." And very reluctantly Brenda agreed. It was 1970, well before *Roe v. Wade.*

We had about seven hundred dollars in the bank. I took it out. I drove Brenda to Burbank, to the parking lot of a bank. A woman met her, blindfolded her and drove her to an apartment house somewhere else in Burbank. She said there was just a room with a table and a bucket. They did the abortion. Then she was blindfolded again, driven back to the lot and I took her home. I can't begin to imagine now what she went through because of that.

In addition, I was so focused on what was happening to me and where it would lead that I never actually sat down with her and explained myself, the physical and mental changes I was going through. Eventually she asked me what the fuck was going on. I said, "I'm going to be the person on the outside that I've been on the inside my whole life." And she looked at me as if she were looking at another guy. As if she no longer knew who this man was.

But I couldn't change course now. I'd begun in earnest to drive toward a new way of doing material, in which I would authenticate what I thought and felt by talking directly to the audience. I had a set of beliefs and values that gave me all the ironic contrast I needed to create art. I was rediscovering the Us-versus-Them dynamic from my old neighborhood and the underdog attitudes I grew up with. My sense of Us versus Them had been alive and well on the streets around Columbia; and in the air force, where I rejected everything they put on me. But it had been submerged when I got into the nightclubs and the smothering chatter of television. The only thing that had kept it alive had been pot, which gave me an internal playground where the rebel in me had a place to look at society and disagree. Now I had to redirect that energy outward to the real world, rediscover why They were Our enemies.

I had ways of stating this cleverly. The key, it seemed to me, was simply to tell the truth about where I came from, what had shaped me, made me a class clown, how I had become what I was now. There was an autobiographical part to this that went along with that new first-person approach: "Have you noticed . . . ?" "Know what I think . . . ?" "Do you remember . . . ?"

I would no longer deal with subjects that were expected of me, in ways which had been determined by others. I would determine the ways. My own experiences would be the subject. I went into myself, I discovered my own voice and I found it authentic. So, apparently, did the audiences in the coffeehouses I was now playing. And while I was back to making no money, when they laughed now it felt great. I was getting votes of confidence for the path I had taken. They were reaffirming something that I felt and now was able to think through as well as feel. It meant I was right. Which strengthened my resolve to carry this through.

The means was my new album, *FM & AM*, the premise being that there had been an old AM George Carlin I no longer was, from whom a new FM George Carlin was emerging. (FM radio representing the underground and counterculture and AM the old-fashioned and square.) Not that the material on the AM side was old-fashioned and square—actually I thought it was too good to waste. But it clearly demonstrated where I had once been and defined where I was now going.

I also felt an obligation to explain myself. Not just that I had made this change but that it was genuine. I knew the progressive part of the audience would be suspicious of me: "Is he just cashing in on the times?" ("Ripping off the counterculture" was the prevailing cliché.) The clear contrast between the AM and the FM side was my way of saying, "If you think that, you'll have to deal with the material. The material disproves that."

There was a lot more than just the success of the material riding on this album.

So it was really disturbing when the time came to record *FM & AM* in June 1971 and somehow a lot of my confidence had vanished. It was in Washington, D.C. I was opening for the Dillards at the Cellar Door. I had two shows to do my stuff, but I was convinced I didn't get it on tape the way it should've been. I was really disappointed, certain that with this golden opportunity to make a coherent statement, after all this sacrifice, conflict and risk, I'd blown it.

I walked around Georgetown, crying all night. I'd had my chance; the sound truck wouldn't be back the next night. And the album wasn't to be released for another six months. So these were dark and uncertain times.

There were dire financial consequences to the path I'd taken. And as of June 1971 I had no idea where it led, or where I would end up. No guarantees, nothing.

But far underground, the volcano began to rumble.

11

WURDS, WERDS, WORDS

A contemplative moment on stage
(Copyright Susan Ragan)

I do love words.

One time when I was about twelve, I was coming out of Muller's Ice Cream Parlor on Broadway, and across the street outside the University Bar and Grill, my pal Mickey was kicking the shit out of a Juilliard student. The kid was a classical musician with long hair. In 1950 that was the only long hair there was. And Mickey's yelling: "You longhair fucking music prick."

Longhair fucking music prick. Great. I wrote it down. Another time I heard this guy Chris calling Mrs. Kohler a "Kraut cunt." Kraut cunt. Also great! I wrote that down.

Some guy came home from the service and I asked him what it was like being in the army. His reply: "Fine if you don't mind waking up at five in the morning with some burly, loudmouthed cocksucker yelling at you." Burly, loudmouthed cocksucker. Great rhythm to that. Loud burly cocksucker: not the same at all. I wrote that down. Soon I had a list of about ten of these.

Sure enough, my mother found the list—with dire results: she threatened me with psychiatry. But twenty years later the list bore fruit. It contained all of the "Seven Words You Can Never Say on Television," aka the "Seven Dirty Words," arguably the best-known cut from my breakout album, *Class Clown*. Which in turn spawned all the pieces on the ways we use, misuse and abuse words I've done in the thirty-odd years since.

I needn't have worried myself sick all those months after I recorded *FM & AM*. It came out in January '72 and was an immediate hit.

It quickly went gold. The AM-to-FM premise seemed to click with people. In the early seventies, the feeling that something freer and fresher was emerging from the violence and confusion of the sixties was pervasive.

That feeling was mirrored by the cover art. Not the usual self-consciously goofy comedy-album shot, but serious and thoughtful. It conveyed that I had more than a merely mimic side. I was more than what I had been up to that point: a string of words that skated over real meaning and then disappeared into the night.

By the time *FM & AM* came out I was already hot to do another album. The FM part of me was bubbling over with truly authentic material: autobiographical stuff, school memories, first-person, outward-directed commentary like "Seven Words." All in my voice. George Carlin was finally front and center in my act.

FM & AM by then felt like something I'd needed to get out of the way, so that I could go ahead to the next generation. I felt good, knowing that although this album was selling so well, I could put it on the shelf.

On other people's shelves too, but especially my own. I've always liked the idea of having a shelf for my stuff. Tangible proofs of the things I've done. All those videos and CDs stacked neatly together. If I get a nice big massive stroke and all I can do is watch TV for the rest of my life, I'll always be able to look over at that shelf and say to myself: "Good job. Well done. Task completed."

Just four months after *FM & AM* came out I recorded *Class Clown*. I realized that these pieces had been incubating and building for a long time, held back by my own uncertainty; now they were bursting out of me, full-blown:

I used to be Irish Catholic. Now I'm an American. You know— you GROW. I was from one of those Irish neighborhoods in New York. A parish school. Corpus Christi was the name, but it could have been any Catholic Church: Our Lady of Great Agony. St. Rita Moreno. Our Lady of Perpetual Motion. The school wasn't one of those prison schools with a lot of corpo-ral punishment—Sister Mary Discipline with the steel ruler:

WHEESH! "AAAAAAARRRRRGGGHHH!! My HAND!!"
You'd fall two years behind in penmanship, right?

"He's behind in penmanship, Mrs. Carlin. I don't know why."
He's CRIPPLED—THAT'S WHY! He's trying to learn to write
with his LEFT HAND!

We didn't have that. The pastor was into John Dewey and he'd
talked the diocese into experimenting with progressive education. And whipping the religion on us anyway and seeing what
would happen. There was a lot of classroom freedom. No grades,
no uniforms, no sexual segregation . . . In fact, there was so
much freedom that by eighth grade many of us had lost the faith!
They made questioners out of us. And they really didn't have any
answers for us: they'd fall back on, "Well, it's a MYSTERY . . ."
"A mystery? Oh. Thank you, Fadder!"

I used to imitate the priests, which was right on the verge of blas-
phemy. I did Father Byrne the best. He did the children's Mass
and told parables about Dusty and Buddy. Dusty was a Catholic. And Buddy—WAS NOT. And Buddy was always trying to
talk Dusty into having a hotdog on Friday.

I could do Father Byrne so well that I wanted to do him in confession. Get into Father Byrne's confessional one Saturday and
hear a few confessions. Because I knew, according to my faith,
that if anyone really thought I was Father Byrne and really
wanted to be forgiven—and PERFORMED THE PENANCE
I had assigned—they would've been FORGIVEN, man! That's
what they taught us—it's your intention that counts. What you
want to do. Mortal sin had to be a grievous offense, sufficient
reflection and full consent of the will. YA HADDA WANNA!

In fact, WANNA was a sin all by itself! Thou shalt not WANNA!
It was a sin for you to WANNA feel up Ellen. It was a sin for you
to PLAN to feel up Ellen. It was a sin for you to FIGURE OUT

A PLACE to feel up Ellen. It was a sin to TAKE Ellen to the place to feel her up. It was a sin to try to feel her up and it was a sin to feel her up! There were SIX SINS in one FEEL! . . .

(With an Irish priest at confession) . . . First of all, he recognized your voice, because you'd grown up there. He knew everyone. "What'd you do that for, George?" "Oh God! He KNOWS!" And the Irish priests were always heavily into penance and punishment. They'd give you a couple of novenas, nine First Fridays, five First Saturdays, the Stations of the Cross, a trip to Lourdes. That was one of things that bothered me about my religion. That conflict between pain and pleasure. They were always PUSH-ING for pain. You were always PULLING for PLEASURE!

There were other things that bothered me. My church would keep changing rules. "That law is eternal—except for THIS WEEK-END!" Special dispensation! Eating meat on a Friday is definitely a SIN—except for the people in Philadelphia—THEY WERE NUMBER ONE IN THE SCRAP IRON DRIVE!

I've been gone a long time now. It's not even a sin anymore to eat meat on Friday. But I'll bet you there are still some guys in hell doing time on a MEAT RAP!

Once a week Father Russell would come for Heavy Mystery Time. And you'd save all your weird questions for Father Russell. You'd take a whole week thinking up trick questions. "Ey, Fadder: If God is all-powerful, can he make a rock so big he himself can't lift it? AHAHAHAHAHA! We GOT 'IM NOW!"

Or you'd take a simple sin and surround it with the most bizarre circumstances to relieve the guilt. Example: you had to perform your Easter Duty—receiving communion at Eastertime—once between Ash Wednesday and Pentecost Sunday. So you'd ask the priest: "Ey, Fadder: Suppose that you didn't make your EAS-TER DUTY. And it's PENTECOST SUNDAY. And you're on *a SHIP AT SEA. And the chaplain GOES INTO A COMA. But you wanted to receive. And then it's MONDAY, TOO LATE! But then . . . you CROSS THE INTERNATIONAL DATE LINE! . . .*

With *Class Clown* and *Occupation: Foole* in 1973 (which was really part two of *Class Clown*), I had a sense of coming alive, of experiencing myself fully, of great potential for further exploration. Each time I shone light into a new corner I discovered new passageways. What I had been doing before had been limited and closed: a cul-de-sac. This new approach had an open end. It stretched off into the distance and the future.

As long as you have observations to make, as long as you can see things and let them register against your template, as long as you're able to take impressions and compare them with the old ones, you will always have material. People have always asked me: "Don't you ever think you might run out of ideas? Don't you ever worry about not having anything to say anymore?" Occasionally that does flash through your mind, because it's a natural human impulse to think in terms of beginnings and endings. The truth is, I can't run out of ideas—not as long as I keep getting new information and I can keep processing it.

I had skills and gifts that I hadn't suspected. Originally, stand-up had been intended only as a means to an end. But now that it had become its own end, now that it was starting to be the thing I did, all the walls came down. "Jesus, I am good at this. Here I am just talking about something and suddenly I've attached two minutes to it that's funny in itself." I was taking my life and putting it out to the world—me, the artist, the writer, the performer, creating something out of nothing or perhaps out of something I already knew without knowing that I knew it. Making something greater out of something smaller.

All three of these albums eventually went gold, and *FM & AM* won me my first Grammy. They also benefited from being on the leading edge of a new boom in comedy albums. Albums had been the medium of choice for rock and the counterculture, which both rejected and was rejected by television. It was natural for our new humor to use albums too as our medium. That's at the heart of "Seven Words You Can Never Say on Television." Even though it's been possible for a while to say *some* of them *sometimes* on television, it's still one of my favorite pieces, if for no other reason than the grief it caused people who deserve to have grief caused to them.

There are four hundred thousand words in the English language and there are seven of them you can't say on television. What a ratio that is! Three hundred ninety-nine thousand nine hundred and ninety-three . . . to seven! They must really be bad. They'd have to be outrageous to be separated from a group that large. "All of you over here . . . You seven, you bad words."

That's what they told us, you remember? "That's a bad word." What? There are no bad words. Bad thoughts, bad intentions, but no bad words.

You know the seven, don't you, that you can't say on television? Shit, piss, fuck, cunt, cocksucker, motherfucker and tits. Those are the Heavy Seven. Those are the ones that'll infect your soul, curve your spine, and keep the country from winning the war. Shit, piss, fuck, cunt, cocksucker, motherfucker and tits.

Tits doesn't even belong on the list. Such a friendly-sounding word. Sounds like a nickname, right? "Hey, Tits, c'mere, man!" "Hey, Tits, meet Toots. Toots, Tits, Tits, Toots." Sounds like a snack, doesn't it?

Yes I know, it IS!

But I don't mean your sexist snack. I mean new NABISCO TITS! The new cheese tits. Corn tits, and pizza tits, and sesame tits, onion tits. Tater tits. Yeah. Bet you can't eat just one, right? I usually switch off. But that word does not belong on the list.

Actually, none of the words belong on the list but you can un-derstand why some of them are there. I mean, I'm not completely insensitive to people's feelings. I can dig why some of those words got on the list. Like cocksucker and motherfucker. Those are heavyweight words. There's a lot going on there, man. Besides the literal translation and the emotional feeling, they're just busy words. A lot of syllables to contend with. Those k's are aggressive sounds, they jump out at you. Cocksucker, Motherfucker, Cock-sucker, Motherfucker. It's like an assault on you.

Two of the other four-letter Anglo-Saxon words are piss and cunt, which go together of course but forget that. A little accidental humor I threw in. Piss and cunt. The reason that piss and cunt are on the list is that a long time ago certain ladies said, "Those are the two I'm not going to say. I don't mind fuck and shit, but P and C are out! P and C are out!" Which led to such stupid sentences as: "Okay, you fuckers, I'm going to tinkle now."

And of course, the word fuck. I don't really—here's some more accidental humor—I don't really want to get into that now! Be-cause it takes too long. But the word fuck is a very important word. It's the beginning of life and yet it's a word we use to hurt one another. People much wiser than I have said, "I'd rather have my son watch a film with two people making love than two people trying to kill one another." And I can agree. It's a great sentiment, I wish I knew who said it first. But I'd like to take it a step further. I'd like to substitute the word fuck for the word kill in all those movie clichés we grew up with:

"Okay, sheriff, we're going to fuck you now. But we're gonna fuck you slow."

Those are the seven you can never say on television under any circumstances, you just cannot say them ever, not even clinically, you cannot weave them in on the panel with Doc and Ed and Johnny, I mean it's just impossible. Forget those seven, they're out. There are, however, some two-way words. Like prick. It's okay to prick your finger. But don't FINGER YOUR PRICK! . . .

Another part of the excitement of doing albums came from them being distributed by Atlantic Records. I had a corporate push behind me and also the music business. Going to their offices was exciting! Record offices were full of stickers and posters and shit on the walls. The people all dressed the way they wanted to. The women looked terrific. As if a bunch of high school kids had said, "Let's play office."

You felt connected to all the other acts on the label—rock and folk superstars. You got the feeling vividly when the person whose office you were visiting or doing business in took a phone call and mentioned some of these artists in the conversation. "Hey, I'm on the same roster as the Rolling Stones!"

Then there's something everyone with an album does. You go into the record store and see about ten of your records displayed. Or you look in the comedy rack and see your name on the separators. You have your own section! And I did this more than once: if there was a bunch of comedy albums not organized, I would take mine out and put them in the front. Absolutely!

So suddenly there was money. The college dates I'd wanted began to come in, not huge yet, $3,000 or $4,000 a pop, but some of them the kind where you got a guarantee versus a percentage of the gross. If you packed them in, those could be big.

I had money. I felt terrific. So why not get more cocaine? To do *Class Clown*, which I recorded on May 27, 1972, I had to say to myself, "I want to be sharp and clean and clear tonight. No cocaine." My diction on it is remarkably lucid. In other words, I was already using enough cocaine that I had to think consciously about not using it to record an album.

But it was a great time. I felt so free. So flush. It was such a catharsis, such a coming to terms, such a reward. It was proof that I was right—fuck you people, look at this! Not only are they going for it—it's GOOD too! I needn't have been worried about success. Lily Tomlin once said, "I worry about being a success in a mediocre world," and I'd always been fearful that if I had mass appeal I wouldn't have substance. So I was happy that I had substance and yet was getting all this attention, approval, applause, approbation, affirmation—all those A's I never got in school.

Throughout '72 and early '73 the excitement built and built. It was a time of First Times. There was the first time of selling out a theater or a club. I still have the handwritten sign from the Main Point, a little folkie room, near Bryn Mawr, west of Philadelphia. About four hundred people had shown up, and they had to put up a sign on the door: "SOLD OUT." The first time this ever happened in my life!

There was the first time I got caught in my own traffic jam. The first time you're driving to the theater and you're stuck in theater traffic you have created! (This also happened in Philadelphia, at the Academy of Music.) Just a fabulous feeling: "I did this! I've created a fucking traffic jam!" To stand there and see them all walking in and think: "Each one of these people has left his or her home and paid money and come here just to hear me and this stuff I'm doing." It's so affirming—it fires your imagination about the rest of your future.

There was another, deeper level of fulfillment too, about playing at colleges to college students.

I had a deferred adolescence. In my actual adolescence I was already thinking like an adult and making adult decisions. I was planning my career at eleven, getting engaged at fifteen, getting my mother if not out of my life certainly out of my heart in advance of any normal differentiation that a child goes through with his parents. And I joined the air force at seventeen.

So my late childhood was postponed, or rather not experienced. Then, in 1967, as I'm entering my thirties, along comes a youth-oriented culture that attracts me for political reasons, but for other hidden reasons too. "Oh, there's something I didn't do when I was that age. *They're burning a car!*" When I make the identity full and complete and it includes what I do for a living and as an art form, I say, "Let me tell you about when I was a kid. I'm just like you!" I finally found a way to live that deferred adolescence.

Generationally—for what generations are worth—I'm at the midpoint between the Boomer generation and the GI generation. I had no biological identification with one side or the other of the generational conflict of the time. Which was good, because it gave me a feeling for both. Though technically I was past the magic age of thirty, beyond which there was no trust and no hope and no life.

My rejection of the older generation's notions of values and authority were by now complete. In my mind and heart, I was saying, "Your values suck, I reject your inherent authority, I don't buy that authority comes on a direct line from God to my parents, to my appointed church people, or to the police or to anyone else." For me, all authority comes from within. All my power comes from within me.

But the other side of me—the side that respected much about the GI generation and had nostalgia for it—could find fulfillment too. In the summer of 1972, I played Carnegie Hall. It not only meant validation but arrival at a certain level. You may not really be on the same level as others who played there before you, but you now have something in common with them. Lenny worked Carnegie Hall. Stokowski worked Carnegie Hall. I worked Carnegie Hall. Fabulous. And it was an acknowledgment that I did accept certain kinds of authoritative wisdom: for example, that Carnegie was a prestigious place to appear.

A simpler pleasure was standing over on the northwest corner of 57th and Seventh and watching people milling around outside the stage door. Summer night, and I'm thinking, "Gee, here I am, where I used to stand waiting to get Gene Krupa's autograph." And now I'm going to come out the same doors where I once got his autograph, twenty years before.

Gene Krupa was my hero. I have had very few heroes in my life—mostly they're people who've been arrested. But when Gene Krupa came out those doors, he had on a fucking camel's-hair, wraparound overcoat, he had the forelock hanging down in all its marvelous arranged casualness and he had a terrific-looking blonde on each arm. With a big smile and chewing gum. I got his autograph and all the other guys'. Jazz at the Philharmonic. I still look at those autographs and play the music from that night.

I yelled out during the show because I knew they were recording—there was a sound van outside the stage door. My pal

Doug and I were there and we were loaded. It was the midnight show during a slow ballad medley and Charlie Shavers was taking a really romantic solo. Right in the middle, at the top of my lungs, I yell, "Make me cream, Charlie." That way I figured I'll be on the record.

Later, when I'd be recording, it was done to me. Many times.

Carnegie was a completion of a loop, a coming back to a beginning. It was also something of a trauma for my mother. This was Carnegie Hall, after all—just as much a pinnacle for her as it was for me. And here I was at my very hottest, doing "Seven Dirty Words" and all the other stuff, making light of the Church and God and of the business world she loved. And they gave me a standing ovation. She was profoundly shocked that in a place like that what I was saying would be so rewarded by approval. When she came backstage after the show, she was ashen. Brenda and I often used that word about her face that night. Ashen.

But she soon had the approval of Holy Mother Church, thanks to the Corpus Christi nuns who loved what I was doing, and roses returned to the cheeks of the Rose of Tralee.

As usual, a price had to be paid for all this pleasure. I discovered in July of '72 that not only could you not say the Heavy Seven on television, you couldn't say them in Milwaukee either. Here's how the AP reported it:

> Comedian George Carlin was taken into custody Friday night and charged with disorderly conduct after he allegedly used profanity during a performance at Summerfest, a ten-day festival on the city's lakefront. Henry Jordan, executive director of Summerfest, said, "Carlin got up on stage and . . . he used a lot of profanity. The police went up on stage after he had finished his act and arrested him." Jordan said he supported the police, adding that many in the crowd of 70,000 were children.

According to the arresting officer and complainant, Patrolman Elmer G. Lenz, about forty of the many thousands of children were "youths in wheelchairs who were physically unable to leave the showgrounds even if they found the show was in bad taste." Of course, wheelchairs are so named because they include wheels with which their occupants can propel themselves wherever they wish to go, but that wasn't foremost in Patrolman Lenz's mind in bringing their presence up. When it came to words, he knew right from wrong.

What Lenz didn't know was how close he came to really nailing me. While I was out onstage at Summerfest, Brenda came on under the pretense of bringing me a glass of water. She says: "There's police backstage, and when you come off they're going to grab you and arrest you." Now, I have a lot of cocaine in my jacket pocket. I have at least a full vial, probably a vial I'm working from and whatever else I have in a little bag. It's all on me out there onstage. I can't give it to her, so off she goes. She comes back on a little later and says: "We'll all make like you're coming off one side. Then you come off the other side and Corky or Jim (two of the musicians from the band who were opening for me) will be over there and take your jacket." So I come off the side where the police weren't and handed my jacket to these guys. I'm clean and they're happy as hell. They have all my drugs.

Throughout the trial I was represented by the distinguished civil-rights attorney William Coffey—who had also represented the Milwaukee activist Father Groppi. Five months later, one Judge Gieringer threw out the complaint, saying that while he had no doubt indecent language was used, he didn't believe anyone was violently aroused. Interesting, because at the concert, I had been talking about "fuck" meaning loving and at some point I'd told all these people that I'd like to fuck them. You'd think that would have aroused at least one or two Milwaukeeans in a crowd of seventy thousand. I'm a nice-looking guy. And I had more hair then.

Actually, it wasn't a recording of the concert that was played in court for the judge but the cut from *Class Clown*. "During the recording," wrote the *Milwaukee Journal*, "Judge Gieringer grinned and laughed softly, though self-consciously." Patrolman Lenz was incensed by the judge's ruling and said the hearing was a "railroad job"—although the only person who could've been railroaded was me, and I hadn't been.

Judge Gieringer's decision sidestepped the little matter of the First Amendment and its pesky guarantee of free speech. That wasn't the case in my second "bust." By now what I used to refer to as the Milwaukee Seven had spawned an equally mind-rotting, spine-curving, peace-without-honor sequel called "Filthy Words," which first appeared on *Occupation: Foole*:

The list is open to amendment. Lots of people pointed things out to me, and I noticed some myself. The first thing that we noticed was that the word fuck was really repeated in there because the word motherfucker is a compound word; it's another form of the word fuck. If you want to be a purist, it can't be on the list of basic words. Also, cocksucker is a compound word, and neither half is really dirty. The word sucker is merely suggestive. And the word cock is a halfway dirty word; fifty percent dirty, dirty half the time, depending on what you mean by it. Remember when you first heard it in sixth grade, you used to giggle, "And the cock crowed three times! Heyyy! It's in the Bible! Cock is in the Bible!" And the first time you heard about a cockfight, remember? "What!" "Nooo! Are you kidding?" "It's chickens, man."

Then you had the four-letter words of old Anglo-Saxon fame—shit and fuck. Shit is an interesting word because for the middle class it's still a rude, dirty, gooshy kinda word. But the word shit is okay for the man at work—he can say it like crazy:

"Get that shit outta here, will ya?" "I don't wanna see that shit anymore." "I can't cut that shit, buddy." "I've had that shit up to here." "I think you're full of shit myself, man." "He don't know shit from Shinola." (I always wondered how the Shinola people felt about that. "Hi! I'm the new man from Shinola!" "Hi, how are ya? Nice to see ya.") "I don't know whether to shit or wind my watch. Guess I'll shit on my watch." "Boy, the shit is gonna hit the fan!" "Built like a brick shithouse." "He's up shit creek." Hot

shit, holy shit, tough shit, eat shit. Shit-eating grin. (Whoever thought of that was ill.) "Shit on a stick." "Shit in a handbag"—I always liked that—"He ain't worth shit in a handbag." Shitty. "He acted real shitty, you know what I mean? I got the money back, but a real shitty attitude." "Yeah, he had a shitfit! Wow! Glad I wasn't there!" And all the animals: bullshit, horseshit, cowshit, ratshit. Batshit! First time I heard batshit I really came apart. Guy in Oklahoma said it, man. "Awww, batshit!" Snakeshit. "Slicker than owlshit." "Get your shit together." "Shit or get off the pot." "I gotta shitload fulla them." "I got a shitpot full, right?" Shithead, shitheel, shit in your heart, shit for brains, shitfaced—heyyy! Always try to think of how that could have originated . . . the first guy to say that. Somebody got drunk and fell in some shit, you know? "Hey . . . I'm shitfaced! Shitfaced today!" Anyway, enough of that shit.

The big one, the word fuck. That's the one that hangs them up the most. 'Course, in a lot of cases that's the very act that hangs them up the most. So it's natural that the word would have the same effect. It's a great word, fuck. Nice word, easy word, cute word. Easy word to say: one syllable, short u . . . Fuck! Starts with a nice soft sound, "fffff," ends with a "KKK"! Right? It has something for everyone: fffucKKKKK! Good word. Kind of a proud word too. "Who are you?" "I am FUCK! FUCK of the MOUNTAINS!" "Tune in again next week to Fuck of the Mountains!"

I've also found three more words that you could never say on television, and they are fart, turd and twat. Those three. Fart we talked about, it's harmless, it's like tits, it's a cutesy word, no problem. Turd . . . you can't say, but who WANTS to? The subject never comes up on the panel, so I don't worry about that one. But the word twat is an interesting one. Twat! "Right in the twat!" Twat is the only slang word applying to a part of the sexual anatomy that doesn't have another meaning to it. Like snatch, box and pussy, all have other meanings, man. Even in a

Walt Disney movie you can say, "We're gonna snatch that pussy and put 'im in a box." But twat stands alone.

On October 30, 1973, WBAI in New York broadcast this cut during a program called *Lunchpail,* in the course of a discussion about society's double standards toward language. The host warned the audience in advance that, "If you don't like this sort of thing, don't listen."

"A New York man," said a subsequent U.S. Supreme Court summary, "who, while driving with his young son, heard the WBAI broadcast, wrote a letter to the FCC complaining about the use of such language on the air." After some back-and-forth between the FCC and WBAI, the FCC released in 1975 a declaratory order concerning the broadcast of "indecent" language, defining "indecent" as words that describe "in terms patently offensive as measured by contemporary community standards sexual or excretory activities and organs at times of the day when there is a reasonable risk that children may be in the audience." The FCC found my routine to be indecent by that standard and put what amounted to a warning in WBAI's license file. WBAI—actually the Pacifica Foundation, which owns WBAI—fought it, won in the U.S. Court of Appeals, the FCC appealed to the Supreme Court, and in 1978 the Supreme Court—surprise, surprise—found in favor of the FCC, 5–4.

The *Los Angeles Times* ran the news as its front-page lead on July 3, 1978—"Court Bans 7 Dirty Words," blared the headline.

Justice John Paul Stevens wrote the majority decision, saying: "The broadcast media have established a uniquely pervasive presence in the lives of all Americans. Patently offensive, indecent material presented over the airwaves confronts the citizen . . . in the privacy of the home, where the individual's right to be left alone plainly outweighs the First Amendment rights of an intruder." Why can't the individual reach out his or her hand and turn that little knob? "To say that one may avoid further offense by turning off the radio when he hears indecent language is like saying that the remedy for an assault is to run away after the first blow."

I'm no lawyer, but this guy seems to be saying that anyone whose language he finds indecent is like a burglar coming into his house with a gun or a mugger hitting him in the head with a pipe. Which is a pretty paranoid view of free speech.

Justice William Brennan wrote the dissent: "In our land of cultural pluralism there are many who think, act, and talk differently from the members of the Court and who do not share their fragile sensibilities. It is only an acute ethnocentric myopia that enables the Court to approve censorship of the communications solely because of the words they contain . . . The Court's decision . . . is another of the dominant culture's efforts to force those groups who do not share its mores to conform to its own way of thinking, acting, and speaking."

All right, Bill Brennan! We Irish stick together. And he got it right. Words were the issue. The Court was banning not just words, but ways of thinking, acting, speaking, communicating with one another. There was plenty more hypocrisy at work. The original— and sole—complainant wasn't some average Joe who conceivably might have been speaking for contemporary community standards, if there are such things. He was a character named John Douglas, a member of the board of a big-time right-wing watchdog group called Morality in Media. John Douglas was, in Nat Hentoff's words, "a professional offendee." Of course he couldn't turn off the radio, because that would've meant taking his right hand from its ten-to-two-o'clock position on the steering wheel and committing the hideous sin of reckless driving.

But he could have told his "young son" to change the station. His young son was actually fifteen, several years older than I was when I made my original longhair-fucking-music-prick-Kraut-cunt-burly-loudmouthed-cocksucker list, way back in 1950, in a simpler, more innocent time. Was John Douglas really claiming this angelic mid-seventies teenager had never heard the word "shit" or "fuck"? Of course not. Other than turning out another fucked-up, tight-assed clone of himself, John Douglas's complaint showed not the slightest interest in his son's welfare, poor kid.

Kids are always the giveaway. "Young sons." "Youths in wheelchairs." The main reason to outlaw indecency, wrote Justice Stevens in his majority opinion, is that "broadcasting is uniquely accessible to children, even those too young to read." Which in turn means that the only thing you can safely broadcast anytime, anywhere, in any medium, is material that's suitable for kids. Could this be why our society shows so many signs of arrested development?

FCC v. Pacifica Foundation has become a standard case to teach in communications classes and many law schools. I take perverse pride in that. I'm actually a footnote to the judicial history of America.

The one part of this I really love is that all nine members of the Berger Court had to sit around listening to the "Filthy Words" cut from *Occupation: Foole.* I've often wondered if, during the presentation of the evidence against me, any of them grinned and laughed softly, though self-consciously.

12

HIGH ON THE HILL

George and Mary Carlin, circa 1974
(Courtesy of Kelly Carlin-McCall)

I used to mark my really severe drug use by the years I couldn't remember who won the World Series. There were three or four years in there, mid to late seventies. *Cincinnati Reds? Twice in a row?* When the fuck did that happen? *How* the fuck did that happen?

I've always been scrupulous—overscrupulous—about keeping records of every appearance I made anywhere. But during the break-out success after my changes, roughly 1972 to 1975, the record keeping broke down. Anal became cocainal.

As the period kicked in, we were still living the good hippie life down in Venice. But when the money began to flow we decided to move back into a house—in Pacific Palisades, way at the top of a hill. An area of the Palisades which was at that time almost entirely populated by executives from the RAND Corporation and their families. I was the town hippie—a rebellious weird longhair with a weird family who screamed at one another all night long and had strange people coming in and out at odd hours carrying small packages.

One night, Kelly and I sauntered outside at twilight in front of the house. Across the way, there was an outdoor cocktail party going on, a gathering of suits. They had obviously come from the RAND Corporation and were having a little meeting-with-barbecue. They were drinking, and definitely within earshot. I don't know how loaded I was but I said, quite loud enough for them to hear, "Hey, Kelly, look at those assholes over there!" A useful life-lesson for an eight-year-old girl.

I did tend to direct my hostility at the square world and businessmen. Disturbing, because it seemed to control me: I couldn't turn it on and off. I embarrassed myself a lot and probably Brenda just as much. At times it was a component of the drug taking, but it also existed independent of drugs. When I became successful as an outsider and could be physically identified as such, the famous outsider, "the one who's saying all those things," I became very defensive.

Despite my self-discovery and self-fulfillment and excitement about them, I was frustrated at the way the things I was saying in my work—my only artistic way of expressing my feelings—were being received. I really believed that the way these suits ran the world was seriously wrong. Not only were they wrong, they were ignoring people over property and profit. But I wasn't being fully understood: the people on the other side of the fence—or the street—saw me as a simplistic slogan-monger, a left-wing poseur. I resented that. But my artistic role—comedian—made it impossible to explain how carefully structured it was, how it sprang from profound changes that had occurred in my head as well as my heart. I felt misunderstood and self-conscious. In other words, hostile.

One convenience of our new house was that right up there on the hill lived an actor who became my most reliable source of cocaine—an actor who later cleaned up and became quite successful. I spent a lot of time up there; it was so easy to go up and score. The only celebrity I ever ran into was Peter Lawford. We did a lot of lines together.

I had other, less memorable sources, and Brenda would soon develop her own independent ones. It was during this period—in '73 and '74—that things really began to unravel. On top of the liquor, Brenda was now doing coke, plus the pills—like Valium—she took to balance the coke. At least she never got involved with heavy downers like reds and Tuinal.

I'd always used Ritalin. My Ritalin habit didn't make me crazy. I used to take half a Ritalin, or at most one and a half. (I had a doctor's prescription for the stuff.) That was my speed during my so-called straight years: the groundwork was laid early on for my attraction to cocaine.

The timetable on this downward path is not exact—it never is, I guess—except that it began to happen with the success of my first three records. In that context, Brenda's pain and problems were understandable. She'd been my partner during my changes, helping me—again—with the press kit, travel, support, whatever her misgivings, while others were firing me and bitching about my new direction. Once I began to make money again and there were managers and agents and record execs handling things, these jobs went away. Again. She had nothing left to do.

The money didn't help because she felt she was losing me. She didn't have a husband. She had a man who was out there for everybody else, but was hardly ever there for her. Or Kelly. I don't remember this—there's a lot I don't remember—but she said that once an interviewer asked me how old Kelly was, and I didn't know.

So she'd sit around and drink. And snort cocaine. She went out to lunch. She went shopping. No life at all. She used to say she felt not just replaced by my managers, but patronized. As if she were a houseplant. Stick her over there. Water her from time to time. Keep her in the shade.

She was already like Jekyll and Hyde on alcohol. Add in the coke, and the mix became toxic. And while she wouldn't be mean to anyone else, she was incredibly mean to me. There was a lot of hitting. I'd try to move her from one place to another when she was drunk on top of cocaine, or at least restrain her. But it was hard, very hard. At least with a person who's fucked up on cocaine you can get through to some extent. There's a vestige of linear thought. But alcohol changes everything, rationality, personality. I lived for years with, "No, you're not going out. Give me the car keys. You're not going out." She would hit me, and then I would not punch her, exactly—I never did that—but I probably slapped her. I'm sure I pushed her a lot. And she kicked me in the balls a lot.

By '74 she was having hallucinations. One time when I was on the road she saw many, many people on the roof. She kept calling the security service to drive by and see what they were doing up there. Or she'd see mobs of people outside in our deserted suburban street. One night I came home late, unexpectedly, without calling. Brenda tried to stab me with a sword she had and just missed skewering me. She didn't know who I was.

I wasn't a lot better. Once I had a long conversation in my room with five people who weren't there. I came out to find Brenda: "Brenda, Pat's in there and Doug and Jimmy Mellon and a couple of the other guys. Could you call the liquor store? We need some beers." She said, "What are you talking about?" I said, "For the guys. We're in my room. We're listening to records and shit." And she said, "There's nobody in the house. Nobody's come here all day." We go back, look around and the place is empty. And yet, I'd sat there seeing all these people for hours. Answered their questions. Asked them things. Got replies, apparently.

In 1973, on a trip we took to Hawaii with Kelly, the craziness hit new heights. We stayed in a hotel called the Napili Kai in Maui. I was buying eighths or quarters from a chef in a local restaurant and doing them in the hotel. It was one of those hotels where everyone had their own little cottage or condo, but of course everybody was also right next door. And here were these Carlin people, fighting and yelling and threatening one another, creating this terrible fucking aura, all this horrible, out-of-control, pathetic drug use and abuse of one another.

Kelly often ended up being the arbitrator between us. She was the one who said what we never did: "Let's save the marriage." At the Napili Kai, in the depths of this cocaine madness, she attempted an actual intervention. At ten years old she was going to solve everything.

The trigger of it was that Brenda and I had taken knives to each other. We hadn't stuck them in each other's flesh yet but we were wielding them. Probably not intending to use them but making dramatic, dangerous gestures. That's when Kelly sat us down and said, "This has got to stop." She was crying and sobbing: "I have to tell you about how I feel about all this . . . It's my turn to talk!"

Then and there she wrote a contract for us, which read: "You/I will not drink or snort coke or smoke pot for the next X days of our vacation. We're going to have a family vacation and we're going to have a good time." She made us sign it.

It lasted all of thirty minutes. For some reason I went in the bathroom and shut the door. Brenda accused me of doing drugs—which for once I wasn't—and went back down to the bar. So then I did have to do some. And that seemed like it for Kelly's contract.

Except it wasn't. What she'd written and done was like a round-house punch to the solar plexus. Even if it didn't have immediate results, it had a dramatic long-term impact. From then on I tried harder to do right. It had a more lingering effect on Brenda that she wasn't immediately conscious of. But before very long she'd hit bottom and was getting sober.

One great hallucination story—which demonstrates where your head goes on this stuff—happened right after we got back from Hawaii. The air is very clear in Hawaii and the sun stands out as a disc. Not a perfect disc, because of the brilliance around it, but still there's the sun, bright and clear. But in Pacific Palisades, where there's a constant marine layer of clouds, sometimes you're above the clouds and sometimes in the midst of them. Since the sky is amorphous and hazy, the sun is only detectable if the cloud cover is thin enough.

I wake up the morning after returning from Hawaii, where I've grown accustomed to seeing the sun this certain way, and I'm still full of cocaine. I get up. My mother is sleeping in the room we have for her. Brenda is asleep. I look up and I see what looks like the sun through the cloud layer, but far bigger and more diffuse than I'm used to seeing it. I decide it has exploded.

I shake Brenda awake: "Get Kelly up! The sun has exploded! We have eight minutes to live!" Not understanding that if I was able to detect the explosion, the radiant energy would have reached earth by now. No, I was certain it had exploded and we had eight minutes for the shock wave to get here, which would then be the end of the world. I wake up my mother and Kelly and get them all outside and they're still groggy and agreeing with me: "Okay, this is the end of the world. The sun has exploded. We should go inside."

Then Brenda said, "Wait, maybe you're not right." I accept that remote possibility and call a friend of mine in Sacramento, Joe Balladino, a drummer and a good friend, a big Italian pothead. He'd given up drumming and had been out with me on the road as my road manager. We wore the same kind of hats and we called ourselves the Blip Brothers.

I said: "Hey, Joe, would you go outside and take a look at the sun? Tell me if it has exploded, will ya?" He said: "Sure, man—hold on a minute." There's a short silence and he came back and said, "No, looks okay up here." So I said, "Okay, maybe I'm wrong about this. Maybe it's not the end of the world."

A lot, a lot, a lot of cocaine. We would each have some—separate stashes—another of those deceptive practices you think will keep the peace, but which actually leads to more conflict. I would use all of mine up and I would want some of hers. So she would hide hers, or if I knew she'd finished hers, I would hide mine. Then we'd start looking for each other's stash. Then we would forget where we had hidden our own. We'd kiss and make up: "Look, you have some and I have some, so we'll pool and we'll both have some. Let's look together." We'd take every book from the bookcase because we thought we'd hidden it there. Hundreds of books. We'd look in every page of every book. Look behind the books. Try to put the books back. Leave the books stacked up.

Or I'd decide it was time to sort out all the nuts and bolts and nails in the house. I wasn't a homey, do-it-yourself guy at all, but I had thousands of nuts and bolts and nails and washers that the anal me hadn't thrown away over the years. Brenda would find me hours later with every nut and bolt and screw and washer and nail carefully laid out on the carpet. I was putting the ones that matched each other together. Very important work. Must be done now—even though it's four-thirty in the morning. If I'd thought of it, I would have scrubbed the lawn, each blade of grass with a toothbrush, separately. Get it nice and clean. Clean and green.

Hallucinations could come not just from the drug alone, but from starving for days on end. I'd stay up as much as six days and not eat, or eat only morsels of food. Fasting, in fact. Now, as we know, mystics often have visions purely from lack of food. I was right up there with those medieval saints the good sisters introduced me to. Never did see Jesus though. Many guys from the old neighborhood. No Jesus.

Even without visions, there was the deadly treadmill of staying awake and taking more drugs to try to put off the time when you would finally have to go to sleep and running out and going through the rigamarole of getting more and taking it and putting off sleeptime and then realizing that you couldn't go any further. It would all just come crashing down and you'd go into this deep, deep sleep.

They'd have to cancel dates. I'd miss whole strings of dates. Then I'd go to the cocaine-doctor in Westwood, Dr. von Leden. He'd write me physician notes that excused me from the concerts so we wouldn't get sued. Usually the excuse was that I had laryngitis, which I often did, as I'd sing for six days straight at the top of my voice to the music I was playing. Or I would talk, talk, talk, whether I had company or not. Then I'd try to do a two-and-a-half-hour concert and I would lose my voice. Part of it was the numbing from the sheer bulk of cocaine; part the things it was cut with, which anesthetized vocal cords and mucous membranes, making speech mechanically impossible.

Dr. von Leden had an Austrian accent and a slight speech impediment. He'd say, "Ja, you see, this cocaine you shouldn't take, because it makes you wap. And when you wap you lose your voice. You must stop wapping." I'd always agree to stop wapping but a month later I'd be back again, all wapped out.

Early on in this lunacy, I bought a jet. An Aero Commander 1121 Jet Commander. I flew everywhere in it, usually with my pal the singer Kenny Rankin. Kenny was an ex–speed freak, who'd gone through Phoenix House and got clean. That didn't last. Traveling with me and being around all the coke brought him solidly back. So I'm zipping around the country high on cocaine, in my own jet. With my own pilot, my own copilot. Sheer fucking madness.

There was one wonderful moment with the plane. We flew into LaGuardia from Cleveland to do some New York dates. They parked the jet on a ramp out near Butler Aviation: the executive-jet area. I didn't have to work anywhere that night, so after we'd checked in, I went back out to LaGuardia. I brought my Sony jam box (an early incarnation of the ghetto blaster), my music tapes, two six-packs, an ounce of pot and several grams of cocaine. I sat in my own jet plane, playing the music as loud as it would go, alone on the ramp at La-Guardia, and had myself a one-man party.

LaGuardia had special meaning for me. When we were kids, we'd steal these crappy bikes in the neighborhood and ride them across 125th Street, over the Triborough Bridge and along the Grand Central Parkway all the way out to LaGuardia. At LaGuardia there were bike racks, where nice kids would leave their nice, expensive bikes. We'd leave our crappy, stolen bikes in the racks, steal the nice bikes and ride them home.

There was a nostalgic contrast between the bicycle of my boyhood—the lowest, slowest mode of transportation—and the supersonic jet—the highest and fastest. Where I used to come to steal a bicycle, now I was sitting in my own jet, soaking up the music and cocaine. A wonderful symbol of success and speed and seventies drug madness.

We leased it out occasionally; once to Jeff Wald and his wife, Helen Reddy. They were flying around doing a series of dates, and somewhere the plane suddenly lost fifteen thousand feet of altitude. They were sure they were going to die. For some reason, they never leased it again.

Her near-death experience wasn't the only brush I had with Ms. Reddy. On another occasion she was at a party at Monte Kay's house, where Brenda got blind, falling-down drunk but wouldn't come home. Just refused, point-blank. I forced her out of the place physically, pushing, jostling, shoving, picking her up, trying to carry her.

Helen was a fierce women's libber, having had a huge hit with one of the anthems of the women's movement ("I Am Woman"). She took great exception to the combination of physical things I had to do to get Brenda out of Monte's house to the driveway and into the car. Having no prior knowledge of the actual situation, this appeared to Helen as violent physical abuse of a woman by a man and she reacted accordingly. She was woman, I heard her roar.

In the end it was yet another of the endless examples of how out of control we both were, and as '75 proceeded, things really began to fall apart. A big part of the problem was my mother. She had come out for some birthday early in the year and never went home. The woman who came to dinner.

I knew how corrosive she could be. This time she had become Brenda's drinking buddy. Though my mother didn't drink most of her life, as she got on in years—she was seventy-eight by now—she'd have a sip of this and a sip of that. It took away the aches and pains. But now she was pouring drinks for them both while feeding Brenda's unhappiness and paranoia and pushing her further into that toxic liquor-cocaine-Valium-liquor cycle.

Brenda was discreet about the cocaine—she'd do it in the bathroom. But I'm sure Mary knew she was doing it, even if in a way she didn't know. She was the kind of woman who wouldn't see something if she didn't want to, even looking right at it. And she was pumping all her own poison into poor Brenda: "He doesn't love you. You know he's no good. He's never been any good. If you ever leave him, come with me and I'll take care of you." In the shape she was in, Brenda had no defenses against malice like this.

She sank lower and lower. By 1975 she was reduced to sitting around the house drinking wine: Mateus Rosé, which she'd order—or Kelly would order—by phone from the liquor store down the hill, six or seven bottles at a time. Whenever she did actually sleep—she was terrified of dying in her sleep—she would sleep on the couch, then get up in the morning and immediately crawl to the kitchen to get booze. She couldn't walk because she shook so badly. She weighed less than ninety pounds.

I was taking cocaine fitfully, though when I did, I still did a good long run. But I would have relatively coherent periods and realize what a fucking mess my family was.

Inevitably, Brenda hit bottom. One night in August of 1975 we had a fight and she got in my little white BMW 3.0 CS and took my mother down the hill to the Santa Ynez Inn. They had drinks in the bar and left to head back. Brenda remembered waiting for the car at the main entrance, but after that nothing.

The next thing she knows, she's sitting in my car, having backed it into and through the lobby of the San Ynez Inn. The fire truck's there. My car is an accordion. They bring my mother home. The Santa Monica police lock Brenda up.

I went down to get her and I was able to get her out. I said: "I'm not doing this anymore. I'm not having Kelly see this anymore." I didn't yet know about "bottoming out" and all those other AA phrases. She said: "Fine. Help me." Which was what this was all about—begging me to help her as I should have long before.

I got a lawyer. She was up for DWI and she'd had a DWI before. Chances were she was going to have to go to Sybil Brand Institute, which was this real shitty women's jail in L.A. County, with a horrible reputation. Peter Pitchess, the L.A. County sheriff, was a cartoon Nazi who'd make sure Mrs. George Carlin did some time. We had to operate on the assumption that she wasn't going to walk this time.

I asked a friend at Atlantic Records to find me a lawyer. He went one better. What I wanted was simply to get Brenda off. Instead all records of her arrest and case just disappeared from the court system. They could never call her case up for adjudication, because it no longer existed. I paid for having that done. Believe me, it's by far the best way to stay out of jail.

She went to Saint John's Hospital in Santa Monica, which was just beginning its CDC—Chemical Dependency Center. She met a great sponsor—Tristram Colket III, a Main Line Philadelphia neurosurgeon, who had fucked up his own life by having a horrendous accident when he drove fucked-up drunk. He devoted his life to helping people get sober and staying sober himself in the process, which is the basic sobriety technique. By helping others you keep your own sobriety alive.

When she went to the hospital she packed every pill she had. There were thirty-two bottles of medication in her suitcase—and a nightgown. And in 1975, they did not yet have detox. The next morning, they woke her at six o'clock, made her make her bed, get dressed and go sit in lectures. She didn't know where she was. She couldn't walk. It took two people to hold her up and they didn't know if she was going to make it. They were giving her anticonvulsant drugs. She had chronic malnutrition and was anemic. All she'd done for months was drink. Everything in her body was screwed up: she was diagnosed with chronic active hepatitis and given only two years to live.

But she started to turn around, and the first thing she told me was, "I cannot have your mother in the house." Obviously I was in one of my coherent moods because I went right home, packed Mary up and put her on a plane back to New York. Later I found an entry in her diary for that day—a typical self-pitying Mary line: "George kicks me out today. He drove me to the airport."

Brenda started going to three meetings a day for the first year. When she got out of the hospital she started doing a 12-step work-day, where she would go down to skid row and rescue people and put them into facilities. She really practiced the AA thing for a long time until she realized the AA people were all sick in a different way. That they were just living out their sickness and not doing anything about their lives.

But she did, and never looked back. And the CDC couldn't have been more wrong about that "only two years to live."

All this happened in August '75. I was never happier in my life. I never had a greater feeling of relief than to know—although I didn't have solid proof yet—that I'd never again have to race out and take the car keys out of her hand, that I would never have to carry her out of any place, that I would never have to endure this terrible tension that went with her drinking.

The three things—my cocaine and pot, her drinking—were hard to separate. Talking about any one of them in isolation implied the others weren't there. I knew I was to blame too. It had been a mutual dance of death. But more than anything I was simply glad it was over.

A few years later, the Santa Ynez Inn became the Center for Enlightenment. Brenda always said that perhaps in some small way we helped that come about.

Two months after this, in October '75, I hosted the first *Saturday Night Live*. One of the original ideas had been that the show would have rotating hosts, Richie Pryor, Lily Tomlin and me, but somewhere along the line that got dropped and Lily and Richie didn't host till shows 6 and 7. Perhaps I poisoned the well a little: I certainly was full of cocaine. (Though I was far from the only one.) To me this counted as one of those times when "I'm away from home, I can party."

Bob Woodward, who wrote *Wired*, said that they had to break my hotel room door down, I was so coked up. Which I don't remember. It may be true. Maybe I went missing the day before or after the show, crashed after being up all week. One thing I do remember is that I refused to be in any sketches. I was still hesitant about acting and I told Lorne Michaels, the producer, "I'll just fuck it up. Instead of hanging around throughout the show in sketches, give me a series of monologues of a few minutes each." Which Lorne agreed to. I think I'm the only host who's ever done that. I also wore a suit, which Woodward definitely got wrong. He claimed the network insisted that I wear a suit. Actually I wanted to wear a nice three-piece suit, but with a Wallace Beery dirty tee underneath. They wouldn't let me do that. Too nervous. T-shirt had to be clean.

Everybody was very tentative. And the tension was intense. My role became to balance between the young radicals of the cast and writing staff and the old-guard stagehands and techies, a lot of whom were New York neighborhood guys I could relate to. I brought a little harmony between them by being able to communicate with both sides. At least that's my interpretation of how the week went.

Nervous or not, they did allow me to do the God material:

Maybe God is only a semi-supreme being. Everything He's ever made has died . . . When we put a statue of Jesus on the dash-board, instead of having him watch the traffic, which he should be doing, we got him watching us DRIVE! Watch this, Jesus— LEFT TURN! Are we so middle-class we have to perform for Jesus when we're driving?

It was fairly mild stuff, but before we were off the air the NBC switchboard had lit up and someone from Cardinal Cooke's office was on the phone with the official complaint. My second Cardinal Incident.

Somehow, despite the coke, over the course of the week I came to be acquainted with a woman prosecutor, an assistant DA in the New York DA's Office. I can't remember if I picked her up or if I got her phone number, but at the end of the taping I brought her to the big cast party. An assistant DA! That freaked out the fearless radicals!

13

SAY GOODBYE
TO GEORGE CARLIN

A more casual performance look

(Photograph by Joel Kornbluth)

My own drug use, post-Brenda-sober, fell off. Somewhat. I had longer periods of lucidity and a decreasing pattern of use. The length of a given period of drug use was getting shorter. The frequency of the periods was going down. Everything was in decline. Slow decline. I think. The cocaine anyway. Pot I still saw as benign. Beer I kept for work so I could function. One out of three ain't bad.

Brenda didn't say, "you can't do drugs anymore." She wasn't like that. She didn't try to cure me. Still I felt: "Gee, if she's going to stay sober, I can't be coming in wrecked and acting goofy." And of course when she cleaned up, I lost my drug partner. My drug playmate.

But there'd be times when I'd be gone for the weekend and get some—some of everything—and have my own little private party. Then be straightened out by the time I got home. So I was cleaner and soberer and possibly getting even cleaner and soberer. There are still large gaps in the record keeping. Anal George was still on an extended vacation. In this part of the story I have to keep telling myself that I'm quite sure my amounts of usage were really diminishing. But I'm not sure. Frankly the whole period is murky as shit.

What I am certain of is that the second half of the seventies was a period of uncertainty. A time of tentativeness, of groping around for what came next—and coming up mostly empty-handed. I wasn't quite running on fumes—my fifth album, *Toledo Window Box*, came out in '74 and eventually went gold, but it took a lot longer to get there than the previous three. Predictably there was quite a bit of drug material (the title referred to a bizarrely named brand of grass I'd once been offered):

Nursery rhymes are the first introduction children have—from zero through five—to bizarre behavior . . . I've thought about nursery rhymes. Quite a gang we had in there. All on various drug experiences. I got to thinking about this one night when the words "Snow White" passed through my mind.

I thought, Snow White, right? I didn't know whether it was smack or coke. Can't be smack—too much housework with those seven little devils around. More likely something to pep you up; something to make you wanna wash the garage.

The Seven Dwarfs were each on different trips. Happy was into grass and grass alone. Occasionally some hash—make a holiday for him. Sleepy was into reds. Grumpy . . . TOO MUCH SPEED. Sneezy was a full-blown coke freak. Doc was a connection. Dopey was into everything. Any old orifice will do for Dopey. Always got his arm out and his leg up. And then the one we always forget—Bashful. Bashful didn't use drugs: he was paranoid on his own . . .

> *Old King Cole was a merry old soul*
> *And a merry old soul was he*
> *He called for his pipe and he called for his bowl*
> *. . . I guess we all know about Old King Cole!*

Hansel and Gretel discovered the gingerbread house—about forty-five minutes after they discovered the mushrooms: "Yeah . . . I SEE IT TOO . . ."

> *Little Jack Horner sat in a corner*
> *Eating his Christmas pie*
> *Stuck in his thumb and pulled out a plum*
> *And said: "HOLY SHIT, AM I HIGH!"*

Mary had a little gram . . . no . . . Mary had a little lamb
Its stash was white as snow
And everywhere that Mary went
THEY BOTH ENJOYED A BLOW . . .

Monte Kay of Little David Records—who'd produced all of my gold albums—had become my manager. When I suggested he become my manager as well as my record producer, I asked him, "Is there a conflict of interest in there, Monte?" He looked me straight in the eye for a very long moment and said: "Nah." I believed him.

Monte saw—correctly—that the peak was past for the Hot-New-Guy-in-Town-with-the-Albums. We had to take a step somewhere else, somewhere new. The somewhere new turned out to be *The Tonight Show*, which I returned to in 1975. Sound odd considering my immediate past? That, in the absence of new vistas, I went right back to Johnny Carson? Well, I did. With a silk shirt, yet. One of those seventies deals with big, baggy sleeves. I thought, "I have to look decent." It was a joke. I looked horrible. (I don't know anything about clothes.) To complete the refurbished image I cut my hair.

I began appearing frequently on Carson; more frequently than I ever had in the sixties. Soon I was asked to host. (Technically "guest-host," a term I've never understood. How the fuck can you be a guest and a host?)

The hosting became frequent, then very frequent. There was one run of twelve shows where I did eight as a host and four as a guest. In the sixties I'd maybe reached double figures in *Tonight Show* appearances; later, in the eighties I did it regularly but sparingly. Somehow in this period I must have racked up the majority of my cumulative 130 *Tonight Shows*. I began thinking of it as a lifeline, something that would replace the albums as they faded.

In 1975, my fifth Little David album came out. Prior to this there'd been: *FM & AM*—clear concept; *Class Clown*—strong concept, ditto *Occupation: Foole. Toledo Window Box*—no concept, but still a catchy, snappy name that related to the counterculture. Now along comes . . .

An Evening with Wally Londo, Featuring Bill Slaszo.

No concept at all. And I'm putting two other people's names on my own album. Outnumbering me *TWO TO ONE!* And yet my head was the biggest it had ever been on an album cover. I was mortified when it came out that you could see all those little dirty pores—the ones you can never get the dirt out of, no matter what you do. Uncertainty. No focus. And with Wally and Bill, forget about the gold.

Soon I'm also back in Vegas—a financial decision, seemed an intelligent one at the time, of a piece with buying a new house in Brentwood, following the path that was most familiar and offered the least resistance, continuing the flow that supported the money machine.

Money now being handled—at Monte's suggestion—by a hotshot business management firm called Brown and Kraft, who also handled the affairs of my fellow celebrities Marlon Brando and Mary Tyler Moore. Going along with this was a nondecision that would haunt me for years to come, not because Brown and Kraft did anything illegal, but because, even though the whole idea was to take financial worries out of my hands, I had an irrational fear of looking at my accountants' monthly statement. I would get their statements out of my hands as fast as possible. I wouldn't even open them: just throw 'em on the pile with the others.

In 1976 it was back to Hawaii to appear on . . . *Perry Como's Hawaiian Holiday*. Produced by . . . Bob Banner. Perhaps the déjà vu was lost on me because I was still doing cocaine. I don't remember. I do remember that Monte controlled it out there so I couldn't get any from him until the end of the day's work. Which was groundbreaking stuff like paddling an outrigger canoe with Perry and Petula Clark while singing "One Paddle, Two Paddle." Or doing a piece about Captain Cook—Hawaii having been one of Captain Cook's landing places—in a superbly accurate reproduction of the Captain's captain clothes. I didn't play Captain Cook though—I played Captain Cook's First Mate. Yes, the Indian Sergeant is back in my life. A definite sign that I no longer know who the fuck I am. Or even which decade it is: the late seventies? Or the late sixties?

By the next summer I was appearing as a regular on *Tony Orlando and Dawn.* Not surprisingly, my sixth Little David album, *On the Road,* was directionless and unstructured: featuring the interminable "Death and Dying" routine, the longest piece I ever did. (On the album it only ran thirteen minutes but onstage it ran twenty-seven minutes.) Talking about dying for twenty-seven minutes should've given a seasoned comedian pause, but that hoary old metaphor for failure never occurred to me.

Another signal I missed was in '78, when I had a mild heart attack. It was in the septal branch artery. One morning when I was driving Kelly to school, my jaw felt tight. I knew that a tight jaw or pain in the jaw can be a symptom of a heart attack as well as the traditional pain in the chest. (The left arm, upper back and the jaw can all be locations where you feel angina.) Apparently each person's angina is slightly different. I had to spend two days in the hospital before they were able to find the enzyme in my blood that is the marker of an MI, or myocardial infarction. When muscle tissue dies an enzyme is released. If they find that enzyme, you had a heart attack. If they don't find it, you've had chest pain. So, they found it, and I'd had an MI. But it was so minor it didn't force me to change anything or reexamine anything. For a while I did eat margarine instead of butter.

One thing happened in that period which would be a major positive force in my life, although I didn't realize it until later. HBO came into the picture. I did two HBO one-hour specials in '77 and '78. These regular specials would soon take the place of my album career—eventually becoming one and the same thing. They didn't yet have as many subscribers as they would in the eighties, when they exploded, but it did give me access to a mass audience. At the time it just seemed like more TV. Not that different from *Perry Como* or *Tony Orlando* except I got to say "fuck."

The material I was doing tells the real story. After an explosion of self-revelation and self-discovery, and the revelation to others of my autobiographical self and past—together with a good strong dose of value judgments about the world around me—I'd become a person fascinated with his own navel. "Hey—look at my lint! You got lint? He's got lint! She's got lint! Everybody got lint!" I was turning to my bodily functions and extremities for inspiration, plundering the last few scraps of self-examination from them. It started on *Toledo Window Box* . . .

> *Snot is universal. There are some things that work in comedy because they're universal, but we don't talk about them. First of all, snot is the original rubber cement. Thumb and forefinger . . . ever try to toss one away? Won't go . . . You ever pick your nose and have a guy walk around the corner, "Hi, Bill! How are you?" and go to shake your hand? "Sorry, my right arm is paralyzed." "Oh, okay. Why don't you put that thing back in your nose and come in my office?"*

> *You CAN put it back in your nose. Lot of people stuck for a place to put one don't think of that. You CAN PUT IT BACK! They're viable for four hours after picking. Put it back in but don't jog it loose. Gotta sit still the first hour . . .*

> *Imagine if snot was FLUORESCENT! DAY-GLO MUCUS! There'd be no place to hide it. Where you gonna put a fluorescent snot? Gotta go down the head shop and wipe it on a poster.*

Urinals, pissing and farts were dealt with at some length on *Toledo Window Box*. On *Wally Londo* I really went to town. First snot made a comeback:

> *Have you ever been making out with someone and one of you has a snot that's whistling? Oo Oo Oo Oo Oo OoOoOoOoOoOo!! "I think we blew it out of tune on the climax, honey!"*

I moved on to the involuntary shake that happens when you piss—which I called the piss-shiver—and from there I transitioned to this important question:

Isn't it funny how we say take a shit and take a piss? You don't take 'em, YOU LEAVE 'EM! "I left a shit, Bill." "Jeez, where'd ya leave it this time? Last year the kids didn't find it till Easter!"

Then it was stomach noises, lots of those, and so to:

Did you ever belch and taste a hotdog you had two days ago? "'Ey, that was almost PUKE! A toss-up between puke and hot-dog there!"

Which brought me to the big finish—vomiting in the New York subway:

You ever notice that your whole sense of values changes when you're throwing up? I DON'T CARE ABOUT MY SHOES . . . BLEEEEUUUURRRRRRRRRRGGGGGHHHH!!!

When I'd finished scavenging my extremities, I turned to pets—the nearest thing to an extremity. Let me tell you about this little extension of me . . . my dog . . .

Example: *A dog appears on TV, and you try to get your dog to look at it. And he won't! He has no clue what that image is. His reflexes are triggered by your voice, which is screaming at him, and your hand, which is twisting his head off. He just thinks you're mad at him and is filled with doggie guilt.*

And when I'd done with that, my dog's extremities . . .

Example: *The neighbors are over for coffee, you're chatting away and there's Tippy on the floor, bent double like a fur donut, licking his own balls! Staggering! If you could do that you'd stay home perma-nently! But no one says a word . . .*

It was graced with the term "observational humor." I think I was even sometimes credited with inventing it. Later it would reemerge as what I call my micro-world material—but by then always bal-anced with macro-world material. Back in the seventies, it seemed a rich vein I could mine for a while.

The very fact that I didn't see what was happening—and I never have quite been able to untangle why I was behaving like this—is itself a sign of profound confusion. Yet I can't believe it was simply involuntary, that I was just passively letting it happen to me. I think I was also saying to myself, "Okay. I showed them I could be a success on my own terms. Now let's see what I can do from the place I've ended up."

In other words, given an opportunity to curve back to the middle, to become straight again, I took it. I got waylaid by that. Instead of taking a new leap into the dark—"I've got another place to go, another idea to show you!"—I said, "No, this is okay. Let's be safe."

I've always called these years of my life the Second Visitation of the Straights.

One other path I did consider, although it eventually led nowhere either. On *Toledo Window Box* there was a piece called "Water Sez." A stream of consciousness cut personifying water:

I'm gonna get some water. This is your H-two-O, my friend. I don't mind telling you. From the scientific community . . . Lookit that, huh? Just drops and drips. Water sez, "I don't care." Water sez, "Drink me, I don't give a shit." Water sez, "Put me on your ass, I don't care."

Water sez, "Leave me alone, I'm in the lake. Get the hell away from my water place!" Ice is water, some water is ice. Some water hasn't been water for a long time. It's ICE! At the North Pole. Long time no water! "Ice. What are you—I'm ice. I WAS water. I'm hopin' to be water again—after the Ice Age, hahahaha-haha!"

You could be two kinds of ice. You could be ice made in the machine at the Holiday Inn. OOO-ER! Or you could be a hunk of ice that comes across a Mail Pouch sign in Minnesota on January 21 . . .

Sometimes I just say shit I've never heard before, man.

There were a number of other little blips like this, bubbles of conceptual possibility that didn't get on the album. If I had been free of my middle-class entanglements, my family, my house, my debt structure, my obligations, this might have been the point where I veered off into conceptual art. Streams of consciousness harnessed into form, let loose again and harnessed back until finally you'd have something with form and structure that sprang purely from your improvisational side.

A fantasy, a what-if, a path not taken.

One thing I can be certain of: the old movie dream wasn't dead. It was just deferred. When my comedy exploded, I saw that by putting the movies aside, I'd make room for the comedy to become what it did. At the same time, the movie thing still had its appeal. Acting had a different set of rewards. For one thing, an outsider longing to be on the inside is the same as the soloist longing to work in an ensemble. I equate them because I get great satisfaction in being a part of the proper—for me—community. I'm uncomfortable with various social groupings and clusterings. But when I'm in the right group, doing the right thing, I get as much satisfaction out of that as anyone who does it all the time. Maybe more.

I had misgivings. There was no way a long-haired, bearded person with a hippie immediate past could just suddenly play a salesman or a clerk, let alone a leading man. I would be typecast immediately, and that's exactly what happened. Those were the kind of offers I got.

I did play a cabdriver in *Car Wash*. It was one day's work and they let me write the scene myself: I played a modified, lightened version of my old Upper West Side character. But I had no illusions—surprising, given how confused I was—that this would lead to a flood of offers from the studios, begging me to be in their movies.

Much better to pour my creative juices into producing, financing, writing and starring in my own movie. And along with the juices, all my savings. Yeah. That'll show the fucking mainstream and the studio system!

Among the quasi-gurus—charismatic people around the AA on the West Side that Brenda attended—was Artie Warner. Artie got into Brenda's circle and found out she was Mrs. George Carlin and Artie saw an opportunity.

Well before Richard Pryor came out with his great *Live in Concert* in '79 I thought it would be great to make a concert movie. Take the second HBO show, do it live in the round so it could be shot imaginatively, record it on tape. We'd use part of the concert for HBO, parts of it we'd transfer to film (which wasn't commonly done at the time), and we'd have our concert movie. Of course the themes I would be exploring were the mundane micro-world I was into at the time: teeth, fingernails, dogs and cats, how your sneakers smell when you get up, shit like that.

But . . . in the middle of talking about dogs or cats we cut to a live-action sketch that relates to the topic we're talking about on stage. We cut from George talking about training his dog to a vignette about a man training a dog. Some combination of concert footage, live-action vignettes. And, hey, why not throw in some animation? Good idea. (We actually commissioned the animation and as an independent piece it won awards in festivals like Tokyo.)

Artie Warner will become producer of all this, because he's a friend of Brenda's and he calls himself a producer and I want to stay outside of the mainstream. To make things more interesting I also make Artie my manager but without leaving Monte Kay or even informing him of his new shared duties. So now I'm paying two men management fees. The movie will be called *The Illustrated George Carlin*. (Because we're illustrating my monologues by showing vignettes of them.)

So this is my new departure, my novel approach, my step beyond stand-up. Something no one had done before (probably for good reasons). The movie dream part of me was being satisfied by these notions. I think this was why I was able to accept whatever fall from grace, whatever fall back into the mainstream, this whole period represented. I could accept that, because I saw myself as having taken an innovative step that was going to end-run the studio system and dazzle everybody with a new idea.

The plan was to sell the distribution rights, the TV, cable and airlines rights and so on. Whatever ancillary there was we'd raise enough money from to make the movie. That was the theory. The reality was that, having assembled a full preproduction staff with an impressive payroll, Artie took that crucial step all film producers must take on the first day of preproduction: he leased a new Cadillac.

For a while we looked like we were coming close. We had distributors. We had an office on Robertson Boulevard. I went around to advertising agencies that specialized in movies and interviewed them about their campaigns. I sat with casting ladies behind beat-up wooden tables and actors would come by to audition for the vignettes. We rented a theater to screen *Norman . . . Is That You?*, the Redd Foxx movie, because it had been shot on tape and transferred to film. We discussed the 525 lines of data on the screen as opposed to the 600 lines of data in the European format . . . All on my dime.

I had to walk away from *The Illustrated George Carlin*. I just ran out of money, although—because I never opened those monthly statements from Brown and Kraft—I had no clue just how much money I'd run out of. Years later I looked at the material. It was horrible! I'd been writing better ten years earlier for Buddy Greco. Some of the vignettes might have been improved by being performed. Most of it was just mortifying and empty. He may not exist, but God saved me from making *The Illustrated George Carlin*.

But then a new area of concern appeared on my radar which I was even less well equipped to deal with than how many Teamsters we'd need for the second unit. And from a totally unexpected quarter: Kelly.

It wasn't about drugs—the usual do-what-I-say-not-what-I-do-or-did hypocrisy Boomer parents grapple with. Kelly began smoking pot when she was thirteen, stealing roaches from my office. I figured it out after a while and rather than being Big Bad Dad—I did make a living being against all forms of authority—I let it go.

Brenda was aware of Kelly's smoking too. You might think it odd considering what we'd been through, but neither of us stopped her.

In fact I split ounces with her when I was home. I preferred the approach: "If it's in our house and you're not driving around, at least you're semisafe." What I didn't know was from that point on Kelly smoked almost continuously. She went to school stoned. She functioned throughout high school stoned. She got straight A's stoned. The bud doesn't fall far from the plant.

At fifteen she started attending Crossroads—an arts and science high school. Full of celebrity kids but a real brain factory. If you were smart you could really learn there. If you just wanted to take dope and float through, I guess you could do that too.

There were different cliques, a lot of kids who learned everything they could and stayed out of trouble. Then there were celebrity kids who did nothing but drugs. Kelly had a foot in both camps. Great grades, and a celebrity clique who smoked a lot of dope. Kelly's group eventually caused problems, but at the time I was completely star-struck. I loved it when Kelly would come home and say, "You know who I go to school with? Mahatma Gandhi!"

These kids would hang out at our house and occasionally steal things from me. (They told me about this later so it's not a blind accusation.) But what could I do? Like the drug situation, I could hardly bitch about it, having been a dedicated felon myself at their age.

They were okay kids. Core good. Different sets of problems at home or in themselves, but they weren't bad. But then Kelly got into a relationship with one of them, who began treating her bad. He beat her up as well as abusing her emotionally. She began to spiral out of control, cutting school, ramping up her drug use with cocaine and Quaaludes; there was depression, ulcers, even pregnancy.

I didn't know about any of this. We'd always kept our distance when it came to talking about her problems and her feelings. It was: "Kelly, I won't ask you any questions." "Dad, I won't volunteer any information to you." "Okay?" "Okay." Right or wrong, my understanding of life was if my daughter needs me she will come and tell me that there is something on her mind. It's not my place to be constantly saying to her: "Is everything all right? You don't look well. Are you okay?" I didn't want to be an intrusive parent. My own parent's fearsome need to control me scared me off any behavior like that. Don't be like Mary. The old, old story.

So I assumed there were no bad feelings. No bad stuff happening. We coexisted like that. What I never considered was the degree to which she'd been hurt from the drugs and drinking and fighting Brenda and I did when she was a kid.

When it came to Kelly's problems—especially pregnancy—I really abdicated my responsibilities. And yet it was all directed at me, all designed to get my attention. I just took an emotional walk on that. What I should have done was to be more aware; intervened, opened up. But I was afraid of what lay behind that door; afraid of what might come out. One of my biggest fears—the most difficult area of my existence—has always been unleashing my feelings.

I did come through in the end. Kind of. She finally told me about everything the kid was doing—his physical and verbal abuse of her, getting pregnant, everything. I went to his father: "First, you're footing the bill for all this. Second, I don't want him near her anymore."

To make sure the kid got the point, when he came around anyway, I got my baseball bat. I showed him the bat and said: "I don't play baseball. Neighborhood I come from, we use bats a different way. To change a person's behavior." Without actually threatening the kid, I made it clear that if I ever found him on my property again I'd beat his fucking head in.

He got the point. Never came near Kelly again. Later she told me it was the first time in her life she felt I'd done a real traditional fatherly thing. She was shocked, she said. And very proud.

At some point in 1980 I left Monte—Artie was already out of the picture—and drifted without management for a time. My career was really flat. I was out all the time on the road, and I was still drawing people, but there was no new, inventive, exciting direction, and the number of empty seats I saw over the footlights each night was growing.

To make matters worse, it was a time when there was an enormous amount of activity going on all around me in the world of comedy. *SNL* had gotten huge, a continuing hit and a cultural phenomenon; its cast members—Belushi, Chase, Aykroyd—were moving on to movie stardom, and other future comedy stars were taking their places. *Animal House*—the biggest-grossing comedy to date—was being imitated all over Hollywood. Monty Python had done *Holy Grail* and was about to release *Life of Brian*. Comedy was coming out of the walls.

Brick walls. Comedy clubs had been appearing everywhere for the last few years, like an infectious rash. A whole new generation of stand-ups were competing to appear in them. Some of them possibly inspired by my success. Some who might soon be competing with me. Most important, and closest to home, there was a new phenomenon sweeping comedy concerts nationwide. A wild and crazy guy who was doing unheard-of things for a comedian, packing fifteen- and twenty-thousand-seat arenas as if he were a rock supergroup. Steve Martin was not only white-hot, he was sucking up all the live-appearance comedy business there was.

And I was regressing, spinning my wheels, stagnating.

I began to get ominous signals. *National Lampoon* ran something in their letters column where it was done in their style—as a letter to the editors supposedly from me. It read: "Dear Editors, Hey man, like you guys, wow man, do you think man, like there is such a thing as, well, man, like self-parody?"

It stung, but I realized what they were talking about. They weren't wrong. There were other signs.

On the Road had a piece about peas (which happen to be my favorite vegetable). The ending was "Give peas a chance. I ask everybody, please, give peas a chance." Rick Moranis of *SCTV* used this to do a satire of me that went to devastating lengths. (I could make an intellectual argument that if you can take something as mundane as peas and turn it into a minor oratorio, that's not nothing.) But again I had to admit there was a certain truth to it. I did too much of that kind of shit. I was over some kind of limit.

In an article in *Rolling Stone*, Cheech Marin and Tommy Chong picked up on this. Cheech said, "George Carlin is irrelevant. George Carlin is obsolete. He's talking about peas now. If all you can talk about is peas, you're obsolete. What about the issues of the day?"

This from Cheech and Chong, masters of cutting-edge, state-of-the-art political and social satire.

Finally, in the last days of 1979, somebody wrote a column in a paper I admired (and when I say admired, it wasn't just some mainstream newspaper—on the other hand, I've completely blocked who it was). He wrote:

> Well, the '70s are over. Say goodbye to lava lamps. Say goodbye to wide lapels. Say goodbye to disco. Say goodbye to platform shoes with goldfish in them. Say goodbye to Studio 54. Say goodbye to CB radios . . .
>
> . . . And say goodbye to George Carlin.

14

DEATH AND TAXES

George onstage performing *It's Bad For Ya*
(Courtesy of Main Sequence, Ltd.)

I t's impossible to overestimate the importance of Jerry Hamza in my career and life. Without Jerry I don't think I would've escaped from the financial and creative swamp that bad choices and drugs had landed me in by the late seventies. Without his support and unerring instincts I would've never had the confidence to go beyond stand-up and begin to explore comedy as art. Along the way he also became something I'd never allowed myself before: my best friend.

Jerry's father was one of the biggest country music promoters in America. He worked out of Rochester, New York; from there he'd promote appearances all over the Northeast, the Midwest and Canada, and he'd been doing it since the Hank Williams days. Later it was with country superstars like Conway Twitty, Loretta Lynn, Tammy Wynette and Porter Wagoner. From a young age Jerry worked for his father, selling programs at the front or helping out backstage, gradually learning the business. By the time I met him, Jerry knew concert promotion inside out.

But he wasn't happy. His father was a tough man to work with, and Jerry wasn't wild about the lifestyle of country music stars— "road-rats" he called them—who thought nothing of clocking up hundreds of thousands of miles a year on the road, a lifestyle their promoters were expected to share. So he quit, and for a year or so, resisted his father's efforts to get him back into the business.

In 1977 I entered the picture. A friend of Jerry's father had promoted a couple of dates I'd done in Ohio, selling out both. (In 1977

I still had enough heat from the four gold albums to sell out in a market where I hadn't yet appeared.) Jerry's father was impressed that a comedian could sell out concerts and suggested to Jerry he promote some dates with me in Syracuse.

Jerry had no idea who I was and no familiarity at all with drugs or my on-the-road lifestyle, which basically consisted of trying to score coke from any local with a vague connection to show business and a beard. But there wasn't much driving involved—Syracuse is only eighty miles up the road from Rochester—and when he caught my show he liked what he saw. He thought I had something special. Just as important, I sold out four shows in two nights. From then on, Jerry promoted more and more of my concerts until by 1980 he was handling them all.

Of course, in promoting me, Jerry was making a break with his father, striking out on his own, establishing his independence. His father didn't get me at all. He told Jerry once: "I've been calling people cocksuckers all my life, and I never made a quarter with it!"

But by 1980 I was not only creatively at sea, I was no longer selling out two-thousand-seat houses. In venues I'd once sold out easily, we often saw only a few hundred faces. Sometimes we barely made expenses. And the audiences were showing definite signs of wear and tear. Aging hippie about covers it.

To stop the rot I needed new management. I checked out a couple of L.A. managers—in particular Bernie Brillstein, who managed Lorne Michaels and therefore several of the stars of *SNL*, like Belushi. I'd always liked Bernie, a funny guy in his own right, and he was hot. Bernie wasn't interested. He told me my problem was that I was too worried about managers stealing from me. Up front of him.

I mentioned my search to Jerry because the first thing a new manager would have to do would be to get people back into the concert seats. And he said: "What about me?"

I'd never thought about that; I had no idea he'd be interested. But he was, and he'd thought about it. His plan was to take over all aspects of my career. I would be his only act. He wasn't interested in managing talent and becoming a Hollywood schmuck. He was interested in an association with me based on friendship. He would move out to California, bringing his second family with him from Rochester. A major, life-changing move for him and, as things turned out, for me too. All it took was a handshake.

Jerry nursed me at first. He didn't tell me the awful truth. His perception of where my career was didn't match mine. He was more realistic. I still thought I was sustaining and maintaining myself at a certain place and forget about posterity: "Am I famous? Am I making any money? Am I at least out there? Do they know my name?" An awful lot of self-delusion, self-deception about how frightful the prospects were for anything further happening to me. I've always been good at seeing the brightest side of things; but I was bullshitting myself.

Jerry summed up his management strategy in two words: "hot" and "big." Hot meant getting me hot again, coming up with new projects, new departures, new material, news about George Carlin, that I was back, that I hadn't just faded away with disco and lava lamps. Big meant he believed I had the potential to achieve a permanent place in comedy. He wasn't in this for some quick commissions. He had long-range goals. He said that if we built things together, made certain moves and took certain steps—and if I was able to pull out the material—I could be one of the names that would be remembered from this era of the twentieth century.

That resonated. I knew deep down I had unfinished business. Things to be said, territories to be explored. I didn't know yet what they were or how to say them, but the negativity of the late seventies had given me an inner resolve to be terrific again, to go to a new level, to fucking show the world what was inside of me. It took Jerry to put his finger on it. And just in time.

Because now the bombshells began—major ones.

I had not only run out of money trying to fund *The Illustrated George Carlin*, Brown and Kraft had run out of money when the time came to pay my taxes. So they'd rolled over the taxes to the next year, gambling I guess that my earnings would increase enough that I'd be able to pay that year's taxes, plus the previous year's taxes, plus the penalties that had accrued for nonpayment. (If I'd bothered to open my monthly statements I might've had some inkling of what they were up to.) They'd rolled over taxes for at least two years: the delinquent back taxes plus accumulated penalties were now an astronomical amount and escalating every month. All this is in L.A., where the IRS has a definite "Let's go get the stars" approach.

Jerry decided to drop Brown and Kraft and go with his accountants in Rochester, Bonadio, Insero. He and his father had used them for years for all their real-estate dealings, their country music promotions and their vending business. They were accustomed to complex tax issues and it moved the case away from the L.A. IRS culture, lessening the likelihood that the media would find out about my problems or that the IRS would slap a lien on my house or my car. Jerry saw that even a tiny news item like that would be toxic to reviving my career.

To start fulfilling the "hot" goal, Jerry decided I needed a new album. I hadn't recorded an album in five years—after doing one almost every year—and it would be a talking point: "Check this out: George is on his way back."

But the album deal contained a second bombshell. I had a long-standing agreement with Atlantic Records that there'd be a large advance for my next album: $300,000. Jerry confirmed this with them: a welcome piece of good news. Later the same day, he got a call from the head of Atlantic, Sheldon Vogel: "Listen, we've been discussing George internally and going over his sales figures and it's not going to happen. We're offering him $100,000." It wasn't something you could argue with or take to court. They had the hammer.

To do something different and attention-getting, I needed to get back to a concept album. I made it half live, half in studio. It was called *A Place for My Stuff*. Overall I felt I didn't pull the concept off, although there's some good material on it. It was the first time I used the line: "Why is it that the people who are against abortion are people you wouldn't want to fuck in the first place?" The stand-up stuff was passable. The studio stuff really stunk. I had no experience in the studio and I wasn't about to let anybody help me. But it was something to talk about, and the "stuff" routine, which was the opening of the live portion, eventually became a signature piece for the next generation of material.

There's something in comedy called the Rule of Three. Three is the magic number. There are three ethnic types in the standard corny joke. History would've been very different with only Two Stooges. Repeating something three times is funny but four, five, eight, ten or sixteen times increasingly less so. I have a supplementary rule to go with the Rule of Three. Call it the Rule of Twenty-Three. After a certain number of repetitions, whatever it is starts being funny again.

The Rule of Twenty-Three is behind *A Place for My Stuff.* Stuff is a funny word and bears repetition. A lot of it. So although the piece was tightly written and disciplined, it sounded like a kind of incantation—or one of those litanies we used to have to say in church.

All you need is a place for your stuff . . . there's my stuff . . . there's her stuff . . . and that'll be his stuff . . . gotta take care of your stuff . . . a house is just stuff with a cover on it . . . a place to keep your stuff . . . you can get more stuff to add to your stuff . . . lock up your stuff . . . don't want people stealing your stuff . . . all kinds of ways to get rid of your stuff . . . and that's YOUR stuff . . . then there's other people's stuff . . . except other people's stuff isn't stuff, it's shit . . . where'd they get that shit . . . there's no room for my stuff . . .

In a way the album concept was an audio version of *The Illustrated George Carlin*—cutting away from live performance to recorded vignettes. Perhaps that's why Brenda and I decided to revive the movie at around the same time. Jerry went along, partly because he didn't want to come in like a new broom sweeping everything old away: "This stinks, that sucks." Partly he wanted me to go for the things I wanted (or thought I did).

He found two backers in Toronto: Ron Cohen, who was producing movies up there, and a director named Bob Schultz. But Bob was one of these guys who make a film frame with their thumbs and fingers and he started talking about "the thread" and "I see you on a beach. I see you on a beach at sunset . . ." I knew then that it was as hopeless as it had always been. The whole thing just collapsed in a heap.

I don't often cry, but I cried on the phone that night to Brenda: "It's not going to work! It's a rotten process! It sucks!" I went to a club called Yuk Yuk's, watched other guys being comedians and smoked a lot of pot in the stairwell. I called Brenda back (she was with her folks in Dayton) and said, "I'm driving down to Dayton."

I rented a car and drank a lot of beer on the way. A real lot: it's 360 miles. I was stopped twice but got out of it, because I was a celebrity. Finally I reached Dayton in the dead of night, got lost and crashed my car in the middle of nowhere into a huge fucking hole. Completely demolishing my nose. Which seemed to end any chance I might've had of ever being in the movies. No nose, no movies.

But God jumped in again. It's two in the morning when I crash. I'm bleeding profusely and I'm unconscious. The police who arrived—I found this out later from a good cop who saved my ass— were going to plant cocaine on me. I'd crashed in the black section and they were going to set up a comedian-in-the-black-section-scoring-drugs thing.

In fact, for once, I didn't have any drugs. Just a lot of empty beer bottles. The good cop told them they couldn't set me up, stopped them cold. Not only that, he wrote the crash up as strictly an accident. No DWI. Finally I get to a hospital. It's three in the morning— and on duty in the emergency room is a plastic surgeon! He was able to do the initial things that saved my nose. St. Elizabeth's Hospital, where Brenda was born. Catholic hospitals have always been good luck for me.

Slowly but surely Jerry was building things back up. He dealt with the Taxman on a weekly basis, keeping that off my back. He was making me more money from appearances than before. He did all the booking and promoting of the shows himself so there was no one to split with, no agency to pay, no promoter's fee and no promoter ripping us off on fifty or sixty seats. That automatically made things more profitable. He began to find little markets in between big markets, where you had a small theater of about 1,100 seats and could do two shows a night. Places like Club Bene in South Amboy,

New Jersey, that didn't affect the New York market or the Philadelphia market. He began loading me up and getting me out there.

Playboy came back into my life. They wanted to interview me. *Playboy* still had a huge circulation in the early eighties and their monthly interview was a big deal; a major indicator of media status. Jerry thought it was important, another talking point. Something else to send people: "See? George is on his way back."

Both of us knew what *Playboy* was really interested in: my drug problems. Still, Jerry figured it was worth the risk. It turned out in my favor: an opportunity to put the cocaine years behind me (which was true enough: all my coke money was going to the Taxman). It was pretty funny and fairly smart; a lot of personal history that underlined I'd been around for a while and wasn't about to leave the scene anytime soon. The cutline on the piece summed it up: "A candid conversation with the brilliant—and still rebellious— comedian about his new life after years of inactivity and a crippling cocaine habit."

Jerry wanted me to do another HBO special. We owed them one, actually: after the second one in 1978, Artie Warner had squeezed a $40,000 advance out of them to meet the movie payroll. HBO was growing fast and the whiz kid behind it, Michael Fuchs, had developed a winning strategy vis-à-vis network TV: that on cable you could say and do (but mostly say) things you'd never hear on NBC, CBS and ABC. That made me a natural for them.

Jerry wouldn't shoot it just anywhere: it had to be Carnegie Hall. He liked the alliteration of "Carlin at Carnegie," and it was in line with his "big" goal: not every comedian could play Carnegie. It would give me status, single me out. The only night he could book was a Sunday in the fall—he hated that because it would mean paying New York stagehands double golden time. But he took it, even though it would mean we could only shoot one show—there would be no "safety" show the following night to edit from and cover fuckups. Brenda's needs were met too—she would actually produce the show; Jerry, who'd never produced any television, would executive produce.

Then the third and biggest bombshell went off.

I happened to have a hatred for the Dodgers. (This has abated now, because I've realized where my real values lie. I've retreated from emotional sports involvement.) But at that time I was still rooted in the old patterns. I *hated* any Los Angeles team. I *wished them ill*. I still wish them ill from an intellectual standpoint.

I especially hate the Dodgers, because they deserted me when I was a boy. I was a Brooklyn Dodgers fan, and when they left New York, they left a hole in my heart. Then the Mets came along. I liked the Mets, because they represented what the Dodgers used to be—inept National League working-class stiffs. (At least they were in the beginning.) Back in '82, I was still totally in the Mets camp.

The Mets come to L.A. and Jerry and I get invited out to Dodger Stadium to watch the game from those moronic field-level boxes, where you really can't see the game. You only see the outfielders from the chest up, because of the crown of the field. But these fucking ignorant, cocksucking Dodger fans in the boxes think it's the hottest thing ever. Dodger fucks who know nothing about baseball, who arrive in the third inning and leave in the seventh (they're famous for that) and in between listen to the game on the radio so they can understand what the fuck's happening.

So there I am in the belly of the beast sitting in a field box with these privileged cocksuckers, drinking beers at a fierce clip and eating very fatty hotdogs, arguing with the Dodger fans and cursing at the Dodger players on the field. (I would've made a great soccer hooligan.)

We're in the sixth or seventh inning; the Mets are winning but Valenzuela is pitching. Fernando is at his peak and very popular out there. He's pitching a close, close game and the Dodgers look like they might pull it out. For once the Dodger fucks are watching every pitch, every swing.

Suddenly I get this bad tightness in my chest. It's not a pain. I don't collapse. The feeling is more like: "If I only just stretch enough, this will go away." But it wouldn't.

I said to Jerry, "Something's wrong with me. Let's go to the nurse.

We gotta go to the medical office." So I go to the medical office. Don't ever do that. A little tip for you readers out there who might be planning to have a heart attack at Dodger Stadium. Do *not* go to the nurse's office. Here is the extent of medical treatment for a heart attack at Dodger Stadium: 1. They have you lie down. 2. They ask you how you feel.

I said to Jerry, "I'm not having a heart attack, but let's get to a hospital and check." A friend of ours, John Battiste, a limo driver and an acting teacher, had driven us there. We'd said we'd meet up with him at the end of the game at a specific place. Meanwhile he was going to go and park somewhere else and hang out with the other limo drivers. So we had no idea where he might be.

So far all this had taken maybe half an hour. You have a couple of hours before the real damage sets in. I didn't know that, but then I didn't know I was having a heart attack either. But here the Carlin luck kicks in. Normally the Dodger fucks would have been repeating their usual pattern of leaving in the seventh inning. The aisles would've been clogged with thousands of fat cocksuckers on the hoof, slowing up egress. But for this game everyone was staying. So I guess while the Dodgers might've helped give me the heart attack, they also helped me beat it.

Jerry, who'd never been in Dodger Stadium in his life, found John instantly, right where we left him and next to the car. I lay down in the back and John drove like a maniac from downtown L.A. to Saint John's in Santa Monica. It's sixteen or seventeen miles, and he must have made it in ten minutes.

I get there and I'm in bad shape. I wasn't unconscious in the limo, but now I'm in and out. Or maybe they knocked me out or let me pass out. I have little recall of this part. They give you nitroglycerin, and then if you get a headache from the nitro they give you some morphine for the headache. They try to balance everything out and get you stable. All they want to do is stabilize you.

I come around long enough to see that Brenda and Kelly have arrived. Kelly is crying and crying. I say: "Don't worry, honey, I'll be okay." Which just makes her cry harder. What I don't know is that my pulse is down to 20 and Brenda's been told that I'm "going." There's not a lot left the medical team can do. The women in my life have been brought in to say goodbye. I pass out again.

Suddenly, at the last moment, someone came up with the idea to use streptokinase. Streptokinase, a highly effective clot-buster, is now standard cardiac therapy in emergency rooms, but at the time it had only just been developed and very few hospitals had it. It happened that Saint John's had been experimenting with it. They asked Brenda if they could use it. She said yes, absolutely! And it turned me around.

They wanted to go on and do open-heart surgery but Brenda said no. I don't know why. All they do is slice your chest open, crack your ribs, spread them back as if they're butterflying you, take your heart out, cut arteries from your leg, sew the new arteries back onto your heart, put your heart back and sew you up. What's the big deal? It's no worse than Aztec human sacrifice.

She said later she'd heard somewhere that a lot of men have real personality changes after open-heart surgery. That if this affected me to the point where I became afraid or withdrawn and couldn't work, it would destroy me.

She may have been right, but if I'd made the decision I would probably have said go ahead. I don't think I'd let surgery change my personality. First of all, I'm extremely optimistic and positive. Secondly, I hate to behave in clichés. I'd never go: "Now I'm compromised. I'm damaged. I'm crippled. I think I'll change my personality."

I realized I'd almost died. I didn't go: "Nothin' happened here! Gimme a beer." But I didn't dwell on it. I never had a Big Philosophical Moment. Although I will say this: I have looked death in the face. And found it wanting.

I'd like to keep you up to date on the Comedian's Health Sweepstakes. First Richard Pryor had a heart attack. Then I had a heart attack. Then Richard burned himself up. Fuck that shit! I'm going to have another heart attack. Current standings are . . . Heart Attacks: Carlin two, Pryor one. Burning Yourself Up: Richie one, Carlin zero.

Carlin at Carnegie in 1982 was the pivotal event in my career after the drift and confusion of the late seventies. The material wasn't stellar: with the exception of the heart attack sweepstakes and "Seven Dirty Words" (included by special request of Mr. Fuchs), it was mostly *A Place for My Stuff.*

As usual I was unhappy with my performance. So was Brenda. She'd been saying all along that Jerry was crazy to insist on Carnegie, where we could only do one show and no "safety." She actually reduced me to tears. But I thought she was right: I'd missed a giant opportunity.

Jerry wasn't so sure. He'd seen a performance that "wasn't bad." What he'd also seen, that I couldn't, was powerful symbolism. I was back at Carnegie Hall, where I'd been ten years earlier at the height of my first breakthrough. I'd shown I could bounce back from a near-fatal Big Ticker Event and joke about it. The lack of focus, the tentativeness, the hey-man looseness of the seventies had all vanished. I took the stage from the moment I came on and held it till I left. Sure, there were some fluffs and shot timing and nervousness, but the first hints of a new voice were emerging with an edge to it that hadn't been there before.

HBO's subscribers agreed with Jerry. When it came out in early '83 it was a ratings smash. Within weeks we were selling out double shows again and I was giving the wild and crazy guy a run for his money. *Carlin at Carnegie* was the real beginning of a relationship with HBO that over the next twenty-five years first incubated my artistic development and then set the seal on it. Without that anchor I don't know how exactly I would have evolved as a performer and an artist. You could say as HBO grew, I grew, but it wasn't just the size of the audience and the fact that it was self-selecting. The constant need for a new hour of material every couple of years kept me fresh and productive. And HBO's absolute lack of censorship was liberating. Whatever topic I chose, people I attacked, language

I used, views or opinions I expressed, I never heard: "We'd rather you didn't . . ." "We'd prefer if you'd . . ." "Could you change/tone down/leave out . . . ? " Even in the vicious, repressive atmosphere of the Bush years, they've never wavered.

HBO's *Carlin at Carnegie* special was the last time I ever recorded a version of "Seven Words You Can Never Say on Television." There was no need. For the first time, all seven were on television.

15

I GET PISSED, GODDAMIT!

George and Patrick Carlin
(Courtesy of Kelly Carlin-McCall)

'm in Pittsfield tonight. I go from there to Lexington and then to Winston-Salem for the two-a-nights . . . This weekend I'll be in Fort Myers and Corpus Christi . . . Then on to Pensacola, Birmingham, Raleigh . . . Work at full bore. Pressure, pressure.

Death and the Taxman looking over your shoulder makes life different.

There was a growing aggressiveness, a new confidence and coherence—and urgency. I didn't have the luxury of sitting around, smoking dope and thinking: "Boy, that was close." I had to get on with my life.

Throughout the eighties I had outbursts of anger. It kept building up and festering. Anger at myself for getting myself in this tax mess, for being such a cokehead I didn't have the sense to avoid the tax mess. Anger at myself for not getting Brenda help sooner and for the damage we did to Kelly.

But good stuff came from that anger. Gradually I learned to channel it where it really belonged—fueling the new voice that had made those brief appearances at Carnegie. A voice that slowly grew sharper, stronger, populating my whole personality; more authentically me, more authoritative.

All this can be linked to the confidence that came from being hooked up with Jerry. I was realizing that I hadn't just gotten a manager for his incredibly generous percentage. I also got an agent, a promoter, a road manager, a business adviser and financial backer; and as I've said, a best friend, a kindred spirit whose mind worked along the same diseased lines as mine. Who I could riff and free-associate with during the long road trips and wee hours in dreary motels. Over the years Jerry's sown the seeds of some of my best pieces.

Having such confidence in him, I could turn my attention internally to my work. Concentrate on how I expressed myself, how I could entertain them, make them like me, all the elements that make up what I do. When uncertainty and unreliability and financial pressure eat up a large percentage of your energy it's impossible to pay attention to that. And when it's relieved, all that energy is now yours.

Hamza's presence is so much larger than just a sentence that says: "And then I met Jerry."

The financial pressure was huge. I'd claimed two things in the seventies as major business losses. One was *The Illustrated George Carlin*—millions there, a money pit. The other was a piece of land up past Malibu, at Zuma Beach. Its official name was Meadow Creek Farms, but we called it the Funny Farm. We paid for the upkeep and the salary of the couple who ran it, Jill McAtee and her partner, Odie. Kelly kept horses at the Funny Farm and Brenda had a notion about eventually breeding horses up there.

Kelly had started riding in high school and it became kind of an obsession. She was really good—a hunter-jumper, English-style. In her senior year, when she was eighteen, she was third on the entire West Coast in junior jumpers. Competing is a form of performance and she had incredible performance anxiety: she threw up before and after events. But it was the one thing in our chaotic family environment that she could control. It gave her a sense of self and kept her anchored during her own problem years.

The Taxman hadn't allowed either of these as business losses—they would have to go to an arbitrator or tax court. (Eventually they allowed the movie.) For now we couldn't deduct them from our tax bill. Which was gigantic and always growing. Often they'd look at a year and say: "You owe another two hundred grand." When I couldn't pay it, the big run-up was interest and penalties, endless interest and penalties. Plus the years in question were at least

50 percent taxable. Some in the seventies were at the old 70 percent rate.

Say I owed a million. Not counting the running interest and penalties on the million dollars for every day they went unpaid, I had to earn two million at 50 percent tax rates to pay the back tax. Then I had to pay a million current taxes on the two million. I've earned two million dollars and I haven't even bought a hat!

Jerry shielded me from the worst implications of all of this. I'm sure he felt: "As long as we have to do this anyway, I'll relieve George of the worst news. Not tell him, boy, it looks fucking bleak and it's getting worse." But sometimes he would have to tell me: "They found another $525,000, they're looking at 1977 now as well as '78 and '79." Then we'd have to bite the bullet and get a loan or increase the mortgage or get a second mortgage. Sometimes the Taxman wanted money faster than I could make it. Jerry was a rock. Twice in the '80s, he reached into his own pocket and loaned me over a million dollars . . .

Brenda always said that I was being singled out because of what I did and said onstage. That's why it went on so long—almost twenty years in the end—without any attempt to settle it on the part of the IRS. And it's true that many people in showbiz have tax problems—worse than ours—but eventually there'd always be a settlement. Seventy cents on the dollar, fifty cents on the dollar, whatever. But that never happened for me. She was convinced the Taxman was really saying: "Shut the fuck up. Or suffer." I don't know if it was true but I loved her for thinking of it. She had a great line about the whole affair: Despite everything I said about the government, like not trusting anything they told me, I went out every night—and worked for them.

Abraham Maslow said that the fully realized person transcends his local group and identifies with the species. But the election of Ronald Reagan might've been the beginning of my giving up on my species. Because it was absurd. To this day it remains absurd. More than absurd, it was frightening: it represented the rise to supremacy of darkness, the ascendancy of ignorance.

All through the eighties I had a visceral reaction to those who supported him. Especially on planes. I lost count of how many times I sat up in first class with all these business suits, feeling a great welling anger in my gut. Livid at the conversations of these cocksuckers, with their smug body language, their little leather briefcases, their neatly folded *Wall Street Journals*, their aura of being in charge, running the show. I knew they were totally happy about what had happened and that they were in a position to gloat. It hastened new directions for me.

The osmosis from the prevailing political climate is very real in a person like myself. And so, all through those Reagan years, another process accelerated. Along with finding my authentic voice, I was finding an authentic position to speak from.

A decade earlier, when I'd done my gold albums, I didn't have any synthesized sets of feelings or information about politics. Beyond a few one-liners about racism or Vietnam I had no coherent point of view. It was more a question of: "Let's just get HIIIGGGHHH! Yeah, man, I'm against this and I'm against that, but who the fuck knows why?"

I was very unsophisticated. I certainly couldn't back up what political positions I had or argue them any with weight. I didn't have a political self. Yes, I'd thrown off the phony media me, rediscovered the authentic rebel child and clown, rejoined my own history, dug out my personal truth from misguided ambitions. All good. But after a certain point, I'd discovered not much remained to be rediscovered. I'd exhausted my personal history—right down to snot-as-rubber-cement and my old toenails. I'd never considered or explored the creative process in terms of the tension between the internal me and the external political environment. But now I could and would . . .

Death continued to keep an eye on the Carlin household. After the heart attack we decided I needed an angioplasty, which is a technique where a tiny balloon is inserted in a narrowed artery and inflated to increase blood flow. There were only a few places in the early eighties that had done the procedure enough times to have a good track record. The cardiologist at Saint John's sent my angiograms around to the short list of hospitals, including Emory University in Atlanta, where a surgeon named Andreas Gruentzig practiced. He was the Austrian doctor who'd invented angioplasty and was considered the best. He agreed to do my arteries, or as they say, my "vessel."

He did my right coronary vessel. The angiogram showed that two other vessels—my left anterior descending coronary artery and the diagonal off the LAD where they come together—were also narrowing. So the angioplasty is over and I'm in the recovery room with this sandbag on the wound to help close it. And I'm feeling chipper because the thing was a success. Gruentzig comes in and he's covered with blood. All over, even on those scrub things they wear on their feet.

Which I think is great. And he says, "Ja. You looking pink. Ja—much pinker." I said, "Yeah, I feel good. Let me ask you something. How come you didn't do those other two on the left?" He says, "We're not here to show off. We have sufficient blood flow from the right coronary artery now. If one of them would have closed down you would still have had enough collateral flow that you would be healthy and you would not lose much tissue." I thought that was pretty snotty—especially in his Austrian accent, but Jerry was laughing. Later I asked him why: "You're sitting there and this guy is covered in your blood and you're basically begging him to give you open-heart surgery!"

Then it was Brenda's turn. When we did *Carlin at Carnegie* in 1982 she'd found a little lump on her breast, but it was just a cyst so she let it go. After she finished editing—it took four months because we didn't have that safety show—she went in for a checkup, and the doctor looked at it and said yeah, it was a cyst, but he didn't want to aspirate it because of the implants she'd gotten in the seventies.

So she went in for minor surgery and when she woke up there were three doctors standing over her bed. Under the cyst they'd found a tumor that no mammogram had shown. Luckily it hadn't spread to the lymph nodes, but her options were either radiation and chemo or a modified mastectomy—taking a wedge of the breast out with the tumor. They gave her forty-eight hours to decide.

This was a rock and a hard place. After she got sober she was diagnosed with chronic active hepatitis (now called hepatitis C). Her liver was shot. They put her on prednisone and gave her a few weeks to live. She went through hell on these drugs, became psychotic and suicidal and diabetic. She pulled through, but when it was all over she still had hepatitis. But they did give her TWO YEARS to live. Nine years later she still had the hepatitis C so chemo and radiation weren't much of an option. They'd probably kill her.

But . . . a mastectomy? She was only forty-four. We called three different surgeons and asked them, "What would you tell your wife to do?" They all said get it out. So she had a modified mastectomy. And it worked.

Given that her mother died of breast cancer, Brenda obsessed about reliving that history: that she wouldn't make it past fifty (which was the age her mother died). But she didn't die and there was no recurrence, although given her compromised system her doctors had concerns about that. In 1985 she had reconstructive surgery, and that was a good move too. (The surgeon was Steven Hoffman, the one who did Michael Jackson.) But once you've had cancer you're always in the waiting room, and every time she went in for a mammogram she too felt Death was looking over her shoulder.

We kept Brenda for many more years but we did lose Mary. In the early eighties I'd relented about her banishment to New York. She came back to California and I set her up in Santa Monica at an assisted-living place on Ocean Avenue called the Georgian Hotel. It was a quiet place and a quiet neighborhood, overlooking the ocean, but she still had some tart comments left in her—she was in her mideighties by now—and a steady stream of complaints about how I ignored her and never had time for her. Same old Mary. But she seemed to have forgotten about the $52.50 I owed her.

In late '83 she had a massive stroke that left her nonambulatory, and we moved her to a more full-service assisted-living place across from Saint John's. She declined pretty quickly and died in June of 1984 at the age of eighty-seven.

In '86 I had to get a second angioplasty. An angiogram showed that one of the arteries Gruentzig hadn't done was now closing. The cardiologist from Saint John's who had taken me to Emory University decided to do the angioplasty himself right there in Santa Monica. Now, if you have an angioplasty and anything happens, if they split a vein or something, they do immediate bypass surgery, or that's it, you die. They always have a team standing by. I wasn't too worried—it's not invasive and I'd been through it before.

But Brenda was tense and she turned out to be right. During the procedure the wire went into the wrong artery and there was damage to it. So she and Kelly are sitting outside the OR and suddenly there are doctors and carts everywhere in the hall and they're figuring I'm going to die and it's déjà vu—Hi and Goodbye time again.

Anyway they work on me and I'm fine, though Brenda was certain I'd had another heart attack because of all the activity. They medicate me to keep the arteries open and I get through it. A few months later I got angina, which indicated a closing artery, and something had to be done. Brenda had got it into her head that I needed to go to San Francisco, where there was a doctor named Meyler, who'd been Gruentzig's original partner and developed the angioplasty technique with him. We had a big fight about this, because I couldn't see what was wrong with going back to Saint John's, and she was saying, "Why wouldn't you go to the man who was Gruentzig's partner?" Finally I had her make an appointment for me. We went up to San Francisco and Meyler did this wonderful variant of angioplasty called the kissing balloon technique, where they did the other two vessels at the same time. And that was angioplasty Number Three. And by no means the last.

I began to do something about my political ignorance. I subscribed to publications like *Anarchy* magazine, *Mother Jones*, *In These Times*, the *Nation*. I read a lot of sociology and social history. I sought out the most radical parts of the *Village Voice*, which I'd always kept a subscription to because I liked the New York edge. I knew I'd always find someone really far left. Not just *Village Voice*–left, but someone really wailing, like Alexander Cockburn. I discovered Noam Chomsky, Hunter Thompson, Gore Vidal, writers who said things in a daring manner, truly dissenting voices.

I had a left-wing, humanitarian, secular humanist, liberal inclination on the one hand, which implied positions on myriad issues. On the other I had prejudices and angers and hatreds toward various classes of people. None of which included skin color or ethnicity or religion. Well—religion, yes. I used to get angry at blue-collar right-wingers, but that passed, because I saw that in the end they were just a different sort of victim.

I felt discomfort at having received positions on issues, simply because of my preference for the left of center, for people's rights over property rights. I was beginning to find that a lot of my positions clashed. The habits of liberals, their automatic language, their knee-jerk responses to certain issues, deserved the epithets the right wing stuck them with. I'd see how true they often were. Here they were, banding together in packs, so that I could predict what they were going to say about some event or conflict and it wasn't even out of their mouths yet. I was very uncomfortable with that. Liberal orthodoxy was as repugnant to me as conservative orthodoxy.

That wasn't an entirely new feeling. I'd worked for Jesse Unruh in 1970 when he ran against Reagan, during Reagan's second run for governor. (My brief little brush with electoral politics.) One of the rally talks I gave for Unruh was at an Elks Lodge in Stockton. I pointed out to these democratic liberals that, "You're having your meeting in a place that has excluded black members for years. Just thought you might like to know."

I hosted *Saturday Night Live* for the second time in 1984. (I like to do it every nine years. For some reason Lorne didn't call in '93 or 2002. I'll give him one more chance in 2011.) This time, unlike the first, I was determined to do sketches, because my acting ambitions had been relit. I felt confident and different enough about who I was by then. I did three sketches, and I have to say I was really good. They were with Martin Short, Billy Crystal and Chris Guest. I did a policeman sketch with Billy Crystal as the father. And Martin Short played this crazy rock guy.

At the cast party, Martin came over and he said, "You know you were terrific in that policeman thing, because you played the middle man." (Which is an old vaudeville term for the man in the middle. And apparently it was a position of responsibility.) I had this wonderful running line where Billy would ask me a question and I would say, "Not to my knowledge. Not that I'm aware of."

I was really pleased Martin had taken that trouble. So now I'm over with Billy. I had done some things in the sketch, small though they were, that came so naturally to me I knew I now had the chops to be an actor. And would get it done when the time for the film acting came. So I said to Billy: "So long, man. The sketch went nice, didn't it?" And since I knew he was going to leave *Saturday Night Live* and go to movies the next year and I was beginning to seriously explore them again myself, I added: "Maybe we'll get to do a movie together someday."

And he gave me this look as if I was some kind of a bug. Like, "Oh yeah? That certainly doesn't work into my plans."

So it was satisfying that I got a pretty fat role in a movie before he did—*Outrageous Fortune* with Bette Midler and Shelley Long—which turned out to be a hit. And I think I got my star on Hollywood Boulevard before he did. Of course, he starred in *When Harry Met Sally* . . . a couple of years later and took off. Still, for that one moment, fuck him.

I had a ball making *Outrageous Fortune*; it was the kind of belonging I'd always longed for. Part of a group I wanted to be part of. It's a cliché that's been used to death, but there is a family feeling when you work with people on an artistic project for four, six, eight weeks; my work wasn't even that long and I still felt it. Like being at camp with good friends and there's this little ashtray you're all making together . . .

I played—of course—a burned-out hippie who's an alcoholic and lives on an Indian reservation and hustles tourists. The part's not huge but the impact is great because in a way he's the hero—he saves the whole situation they get into. I played a fairly broad character and I had just a terrific experience, doing my homework, coming in prepared, working with the other actors, going for those little shadings. It was everything I'd hoped it would be, and it led to *Bill & Ted's Excellent Adventure* a couple of years later, and then a good role in *The Prince of Tides* and more recently *Dogma* and *Jersey Girl* with Kevin Smith. I've always had that same feeling of belonging, working with friends, and enjoying the counterpunching with them. A dream that in a nice little way actually came true. Even if I never did become Jack Lemmon the Second.

My new direction was slowly making itself known to me—by the reading I was choosing and the things I was tearing out and circling in periodicals. I was beginning to keep what amounted to a journal in another form: a record of my reactions to issues.

Every day I take a lot of notes. And the notes go into files in various categories. They can be a sentence, a word, an idea, two things that connect or contrast, an afterthought, a neat phrase. Something I can add to something in a given file; maybe these go together, maybe it could start like this . . . or something that starts an entirely new file. It's an incessant process.

What often happens with these notes is that there's a period of months when they tend in a certain direction or they're about certain topics. I don't review them that often but I add to them all the time, so when I finally take time to look them over, I get a kind of objective view of what my mind really wants to produce.

In the mideighties the notes began to be almost exclusively about issues: capital punishment, rich and poor, abortion, government corruption, official euphemisms, the crimes of those business suits I sat next to on planes. The number of notes about department stores or dogs and cats or driving habits or airlines began to diminish. (Those files were fairly fat anyway.) My mind and heart said, "This is what we're doing now." And it would be new, a new direction, a new sound.

There was a familiarity to these feelings of anticipation. It was how I'd felt in the formative stages of *Class Clown* and *Occupation: Foole*. I knew—just as I had then—that this new material would flow easily and naturally. It had been stored up and was already halfway formed or ready to start forming. It had a life of its own. My process always works like that. I review a file and say, "There's a lot of good stuff in here, but I don't feel this bursting out of my chest yet." I look at another and I get excited: "This shit's going to be GOOD! Can't wait till they hear THIS!"

But something else was happening that had never happened before. Previously my notes and ideas came together the way galaxies do: they just naturally clumped. They clumped simply because they were related—an extended family of ideas around a general topic. Now they were parts that fit and functioned together, which I then gradually formed into a whole. My writing was getting more disciplined, more consciously crafting language and structure. I had that constant laboratory of performance to test things, to strip away what wasn't needed or didn't work. I was taking the first tentative steps toward comedy as art.

The 1986 HBO show, *Playin' with Your Head*, has a piece called "Hello-Goodbye," which is about the ways we say hello and goodbye to one another. The mature voice hadn't evolved fully, but it had pace and urgency and verbal fireworks.

The end of it is "Love and Regards," which in a way is an outgrowth of *Stuff*, narrowly focusing on one word or phrase—treating the trivial as a matter of great significance. The piece is about the implications of trivial phrases like "Give my love to so-and-so," all in the form of almost legalistic questions:

> *Think of the awesome responsibility of carrying one person's love to another person. If you don't encounter that person, can you unburden yourself of the love by giving it to someone else? Even to someone who doesn't know the original person? Does the law allow them to accept it? Does the law allow you to transport the love? Especially across state lines? What form should the actual delivery of the love take, whether or not the person is the intended recipient? Can you tongue-kiss them? What if they're gay?*

It was more an exercise in form than a piece with a particular point, but my mind was beginning to work differently. With my first transformation it was exciting just to speak to my audience one-on-one instead of performing impersonally in front of them—to confide in them who the internal me really was, share insights with them, be their friend.

Now I was driven by a different need: to convey things about the external world—or my version of it. Lead them logically or apparently logically to conclude that my version was correct. Take them step-by-step to the place I wanted them to be.

There was a long piece called "Sports." Once again it had no social or political aim—that would come—but it had a new tone and approach: definitive, forceful and also reflecting a related theme that was showing up more and more in my notes: violence.

It began with suggestions on how to improve major sports by guaranteeing serious injury: in football, you'd have the entire forty-five-man squad play all the time and leave the injured on the field. In baseball, if the pitcher hit the batter with the ball he'd be out, and the outfield would contain randomly placed landmines. In basketball, there'd be a two-second shot clock and you'd score twenty-five points for any shot that went in the basket off another guy's head.

I set out to prove that most other sports weren't sports—another exercise in logically proving the opposite of conventional wisdom.

For instance: *Swimming is simply a way to keep from drowning, so it can't be considered a sport. Having to rent the shoes prevents bowling from being one. As for tennis, what is it really but Ping-Pong played while standing on the table? And then there was golf. Here the point was less that golf wasn't a sport than how inane it is to hit a ball with a stick, then walk after it, then hit it again. Watching flies fuck is a lot more stimulating.*

The noisier the culture becomes, the stronger your voice has to be to be heard above the din. This was a conscious thought—that I'd better raise the level of my voice and therefore the intensity of my metaphors and images and words and topics to get and keep people's attention.

There was another reason to turn up the volume. There was a comedy boom in full swing during the eighties. I was always being told about the hot new guy or the hot new woman. I'd sometimes tense up internally, because you never know. It's like gunfighting, the Old West. New guy in town. Might be faster than you. I'm the big guy on the block, or at least one of them. So they're coming after me. I've always been very competitive about that. But they also come and go. So I was always slow to rush out and catch them; I didn't obsess about the competition as some guys do. But when a stand-up starts breaking from the pack, you have to check them out.

Then one of three things happens. Either: NO THREAT! NO FUCKING THREAT AT ALL! Or: this guy is really good. But he's not on my block. So NO THREAT either.

Or: WHOOOA!

Sam Kinison was a Whoooa!

When he started catching fire in the second half of the eighties I remember saying to myself: I'm going to have to raise my voice. This motherfucker's GOOD! He's got ideas. He's loud. And he's on my block. Definitely on my block.

I loved Sam's mind and the way he went after people and ideas: his piece about world hunger and the Ethiopians—"GO LIVE WHERE THE FOOD IS!"—that was something I'd like to have written. Without wanting to wipe him out, I had to raise my level to where I wasn't lost in his dust.

Be smarter. Be louder. Be on my fucking toes. And though the general proliferation of comedians presented no threat either, the sheer numbers that were happening, the sheer fact that there was a comedy boom, was a spur. You have to run a little faster, show 'em why you're out in front. It's not the accumulated credits, George, not the years you've put in. It's what did you do last week.

My overall reaction to the Reagan years was one of storing up ammunition. Arming myself and storing the armaments away for use later on. I knew this was happening, because I could see the files taking shape, acquiring real structure, meaning and weight. And they were getting fatter and fatter. Before long I was going to be able to back up the things I really wanted to say, the positions I wanted to take. I knew now what I was for and against and I knew why.

The 1988 HBO show, *What Am I Doing in New Jersey?*, was the first use of the stored armaments, the first time that this newfound attention to structure met up with a heightened political sense:

> *I haven't seen this many people gathered in one place since they took the group photo of all the criminals and lawbreakers in the Reagan administration. 225 of them so far. 225 different people in Ronald Reagan's administration have either been fired, arrested, indicted or convicted . . . of either breaking the law or violating the ethics code. Edwin Meese alone has been investigated by three separate special prosecutors and there's a fourth one waiting for him in Washington right now. Three separate special prosecutors have had to look into the activities of the attorney general! And the attorney general is the nation's leading LAW-ENFORCEMENT OFFICER! This is what you gotta remember. This is the Ronald Reagan administration—these are the LAW AND ORDER people. These are the people who are against street crime. They want to put street criminals in jail to make life safer for business criminals. They're against street crime so long as it isn't WALL Street.*

> *The Supreme Court decided about a year ago that it's okay to put people in jail if we just THINK they're going to commit a crime. It's called preventive detention. All you gotta do is just THINK they're gonna commit a crime. Well, if we'd known this seven or eight years ago we coulda put a bunch of these Republican motherfuckers directly into PRISON! Put 'em in the joint where they belong and we could've saved the cost of putting these country-club, pinheaded assholes ON TRIAL! Another thing you gotta remember is these were the people who were elected with the help of the Moral Majority. And the Teamsters Union. That's a good combination: organized religion and organized crime working together to build a better America!*

238

. . . I'm the first to say it's a great country, but it's a STRANGE CULTURE. This has got to be the only country in the world that could come up with a disease like BULIMIA. Where some people have no food at all and some people eat a nourishing meal and then PUKE IT UP INTENTIONALLY! Where tobacco kills 400,000 people a year but they ban artificial sweeteners! BECAUSE A RAT DIED! And now they're thinking of banning toy guns—but they're KEEPING THE FUCKING REAL ONES!

It's the old American double standard. And of course we're founded on the double standard. That's our history. This country was founded by slave owners WHO WANTED TO BE FREE! So they killed a lot of English white people in order to continue owning their black African people so they could kill the red Indian people and move west to steal the rest of the land from the brown Mexican people, giving them a place for their planes to take off and drop nuclear weapons on the yellow Japanese people. You know what the motto of this country oughtta be? You give us a color—WE'LL WIPE IT OUT!

You've got to be evenhanded though. Nothing like road rage for injecting a little populist class warfare:

. . . And then of course, the three most puke-inducing words that man has yet come up with: BABY ON BOARD! I don't know what yuppie cocksucker thought of that! BABY ON BOARD— who gives A FUCK? I certainly don't! You know what these morons are actually saying to you, don't you? We know you're a shitty driver, but our baby is nearby and we expect you to straighten up for a little while! You know what I do? I run 'em into a goddam utility pole! Run 'em into a fucking tree! Bounce that kid around a little bit!! Let him grow up with a sense of reality, for Chrissakes!

I'm supposed to alter my driving habits because some woman forgot to put her diaphragm in? Isn't that nice? Baby on Board!

Child in Car! Don't tell me your troubles, lady! Why don't you put up an honest sign: ASSHOLE AT THE WHEEL! They don't sell many of those, do they? Nah—they give them away free with VOLVOS and AUDIS! And SAAAAABS! Some of these mo-rons have SAAAAAAABS! "We bought a SAAAAAAAAB!" Well, what did you buy a Swedish piece of shit like that for? "It's a safe car." Some of these people think that by buying a safe car it excuses them from the responsibility of actually having to learn to DRIVE THE FUCKING THING! First you learn to DRIVE! THEN you buy your safe car!

WELL, I GET PISSED, GOD-DAM-IT!!!!

16
WORKING RAGEAHOLIC

Brenda, Britt Allcroft and George on the set of *Shining Time Station*

(Copyright 1992 Shonna Valeska. Courtesy of Britt Allcroft.)

The reason I prefer the sledgehammer to the rapier and the reason I believe in blunt, violent, confrontational forms for the presentation of my ideas is because I see that what's happening to the lives of people is not rapierlike, it is not gentle, it is not subtle. It is direct, hard and violent. The slow violence of poverty, the slow violence of untreated disease. Of unemployment, hunger, discrimination. This isn't the violence of some guy opening fire with an Uzi in a McDonald's and forty people are dead. The real violence that goes on every day, unheard, unreported, over and over, multiplied a millionfold.

And it is not sufficient to have a "clever riposte"! A witty song by the Capitol Steps, "Fa la la, oh dear, the killing, hey dilly dilly dilly!" doesn't do it for me.

"FUCK YOU, COCKSUCKERS!" is my approach. To the world, to the leadership. When are we going to start assassinating the right people in this country? (Why is it, by the way, that the right-wing guys assassins have tried to shoot survived? Like Wallace and Reagan? Don't we have any marksmen on our side?)

The 1990 and 1992 HBO shows were when things really gelled. 1990 was the first time that the improvement in my new strengths in writing met up solidly with my heightened political sense. It wasn't a *Jammin' in New York*, but it was a good step beyond what happened in '88, as '88 had been beyond '86.

One reason may have been—don't laugh—that 1990 and '88 were both shot in New Jersey. Yeah, kiss-her-where-it-smells New

Jersey. We'd finally discovered not to do HBO shows on the West Coast. Californian audiences just sit there trying to decide whether they're going to go to the beach tomorrow or Magic Mountain. Not a lot of concentrated energy in a Los Angeles audience.

What Am I Doing in New Jersey? in '88 was taped in the Park Theater in Union City, *Doin' It Again* in '90 in the State Theatre in New Brunswick. The difference in response over the West Coast was explosive. Plus, '90 solidified the new voice with strong, disturbing pieces. One of them was "Rape Can Be Funny," which was less about rape than about being told what you could and couldn't say. The early nineties were the heyday of identity politics, and—especially on campus—language codes were cropping up everywhere, trying to define and prohibit offensive speech. I opened the show by saying I wasn't sure what I could say anymore. Comedians especially were always being told there were off-limit subjects. Subjects that weren't funny. I disagreed.

Take rape. Is rape funny? Yes. Consider Porky Pig raping Elmer Fudd. And Porky's raping Elmer because Elmer had been coming on to him. He was asking for it.

Core point: Men justify rape by claiming that if a woman's provocatively dressed, she's asking for it.

Example: Those news stories where a burglar robs a house, then rapes an eighty-one-year-old granny! Why? Her bathrobe was too tight. She was asking for it!

Keeping the focus on what pricks men are proved my point: that you can joke about anything—even rape. And let me tie the piece up neatly:

Now I've got the feminists pissed off at me, because I'm joking about rape. Feminists wanna control your language. And they're not alone. They got a lotta company in this country. I'm not picking on the feminists. In fact I got nothing against the feminists.

I happen to agree with most of the feminist philosophy I have read. I agree for instance that for the most part men are vain, ignorant, greedy, brutal assholes who've just about ruined this

244

planet. I agree with the abstract that men have pushed the technology that just about has this planet in a stranglehold.

Mother Earth—RAPED AGAIN! Guess who?

" 'EY, SHE WAS ASKING FOR IT!"

1990 was a sign, looking back from the perspective of years, that *Jammin'* was on its way. And when it came—on April 25, 1992, in what used to be called the Felt Forum at Madison Square Garden, in front of 6,500 people—it leaped past all the others. The train had arrived.

Jammin' in New York has always been my favorite HBO show, but it was more than just a favorite. It lifted me up to a new plateau, a good plateau. It became my personal best, the one I had to beat, the template for future HBOs in terms of craft, artistry and risk taking.

We dedicated it to Sam Kinison, who'd been killed by a drunk driver just two weeks earlier.

April 1992 was just over a year after the end of the Gulf War and patriotism was still riding high. A lot of people had seen it and still did as a good war, even though the Pentagon lies in the run-up to it were beginning to come out. Supposed Iraqi atrocities in Kuwait City fabricated by some woman from the Kuwaiti royal family. DOD satellite photos of Iraqi troops "massing at the Saudi border," which actually showed empty desert. There was some risk in doing "Rockets and Penises in the Persian Gulf" on national television, but it was calculated.

I went right into it—at the height of their commitment to me—and it had such pace, such fire, that they couldn't ignore the ideas in it. There was less an unpatriotic ring to it than a loud dissenting one.

America loved war, I said. In our history we've had a major war every ten years. We suck at everything else but we could bomb the shit out of any country full of brown people. Only brown people. The last white people we bombed were the Germans. Because they were trying to dominate the world, and that's our job!

I shifted to my theory that war is just men waving their pricks at one another. We bomb anyone we think has a bigger dick than us. That's why rockets, planes, shells and bullets are all shaped like dicks. America has an overpowering need to thrust the national dick deep into other nations . . .

The ideas came from all directions, piling on joke after joke and idea after idea, the next idea validating the previous one. There was always more shit coming. Including the familiar point that our language always betrays us.

America's manhood problem was typified by the teenage sexual slang we use about war. In Vietnam we didn't "go all the way." We "pulled out." Very unmanly. When you fuck an entire people you have to keep fucking and fucking them—women and children too—till they're all dead.

By the end they were cheering every line. At the beginning I think they were surprised by the sheer performance of it—it wasn't quite like anything I'd ever done. But the combination of laughs and ideas and imaginative flurries of language overwhelmed any resistance they might've had along the lines of "Wait just a goddam minute, I know someone with a boy over there."

I was beginning to realize something: I had a powerful new tool for my tool kit, though I've only made sparing use of it since. Getting laughs all the time *wasn't my only responsibility.* My responsibility was to engage the audience's mind for ninety minutes. Get laughs, of course, dazzle them from time to time with form, craft, verbal fireworks, but above all engage their minds. "The Planet Is Fine," which ended *Jammin',* was the perfect example. Essentially it's an essay on what I see as the futility and narrow-mindedness of environmentalism, symbolized by attempts to save endangered species.

It's probably the most "macro" piece I've ever done. It goes much further than the issues people think of as macro, like saving endangered species or reversing global warming, to the heart of the matter: the arrogance of our species.

The problem was caused long ago by us arrogantly trying to control nature, believing we were superior to our environment. Just as arrogant to think we're needed to save it—especially when we haven't even learned how to take care of one another. Earth doesn't need us to save it. It's survived four and a half billion years through far worse disasters than a species a mere hundred thousand years old that has only been really fucking the place up since the Industrial Revolution.

We imagine we threaten this vastly powerful self-correcting system? The planet will shuck us off like a case of the crabs. Forget about saving endangered species—WE are the endangered species.

The planet is fine. WE are fucked. We're going away. We'll leave some plastic bags behind but, other than that, after the Earth has absorbed them, not a single trace . . .

From the point of view of the performer—the ever-present possibility of going in the sewer—a basically serious piece like this was a lot riskier than "Rockets and Penises in the Persian Gulf," and in my concerts, throughout the months before the Garden show, it would get long, quizzical silences. But it was clear from the response at the end that they were appreciating it. There were considerable stretches when I wasn't getting laughs, but I didn't expect them. (They were where there weren't any jokes.) The laugh-free stretches were acceptable to me and to the audience because they were engaged, or more accurately: we were engaged.

The success of "Planet" gave me new power: the permission to take artistic risks. As long as I kept them interested and engaged and entertained—not bringing them to laughter all the time, but sometimes to wonder: when I could see from their faces they were thinking, "Whoa—what a nice thing he did there!" So long as I did that, the contract between us was fulfilled.

Laughter is not the only proof of success. Boy, what a liberating recognition that was! It grew and grew during those months of testing and practice on the road. And when I got to the Felt Forum, the sheer number of people ensured that even during those quiet moments, there was audible appreciation going on. Not laughs, but some ripple of agreement, a collective "Oh yeah!" Pleasure in sheer ideas! With smaller audiences I hadn't heard reactions like that, because they were less inclined to expose themselves. But here, lost in a sea of people, they let themselves go.

Besides now being freed to write more idea-driven and provocative material, I was learning things about my relationship with the audience too. I don't know if they were evolving along with me or if their willingness to be engaged in this way had always been there and I'd underestimated it. It may have been there all along.

But up till then I had never bothered to think much about my audience's commitment to me. Not even on the basic level, that when people bought tickets to see me in concert, paying twenty, thirty, forty dollars, a week or more in advance, that was a special kind of commitment. It wasn't casual. It's wasn't a brick-wall comedy club, or a Vegas casino. It said a lot about what they were willing to hear, listen to, abide, put up with.

Characterizing audiences is always an imponderable. I do know that if I'm in Chattanooga I don't get the average Chattanoogan. I get the weirdest, flakiest, hard-core-strangest Chattanoogan. The fringe Chattanoogan. Anywhere I go I'm going to get the freer, less risk-averse audience, the ones more willing to go out on a limb. It's too easy to say "left-wing," but one aspect of their collective personality is to be more appreciative of material that attacks authority, takes chances, is experimental or daring. They may not agree with everything I say but I rarely get vocal dissent from the audience.

The "Abortion" piece in the next HBO show in 1996, *Back in Town*—at least during that period of testing and building—was one of the few. There were often walkouts. Never heckling. People quietly got up, turned around and walked out. Jerry would stand in the lobby just to see them. And to hear them if they did say something. We'd laugh about it afterward: "You should have seen the first guy that came out. He was fucking stricken! Almost walked straight through the glass."

I began with a line I'd been using since *A Place for My Stuff* fourteen years earlier: that it was ironic that pro-lifers were the kind of people you'd never want to fuck anyway.

The satirical method was to focus on the meaning of the term "pro-life." What's pro-life about being obsessed with the unborn and then, once it's a child, refusing it health education and welfare? What's pro-life about sending the child off in a uniform at age eighteen to die? Or killing doctors who perform legal abortions? If all life is sacred, why is it an abortion for us but if it's a chicken it's an omelet?

Consistency matters. If life begins at conception, why isn't there a funeral for a miscarriage? If life begins at fertilization and most of a woman's fertilized eggs are flushed out of her body once a month, doesn't that make her a mass murderer? Could it be that "pro-life" is actually code for hating women—the source of life?

This piece had been a while coming, like many of my long-form essay-type pieces. But there was one moment in the original version that I really liked but eventually didn't make it to the HBO show. It says a lot about that relationship with the audience.

My method of argument is not to fuck around responding to one side or the other of a current debate but to go all the way back to the fundamental core of an issue. So in the original version, after "Life started about a billion years ago and it's a continuous process," I said: "And that's a heartbeat in there. So . . . it's MURDER.

"But . . . it's *justifiable homicide*."

I loved that moment. Really risky, really disturbing. And showing why this has always been and will always be such a violent debate. You can't have a totally closed mind or dogmatic opinion about it. And I thought they'd agree, enjoy the thought, the moment. But I was wrong. Audiences wouldn't follow me there. It was one step too far. They didn't enjoy the risk.

I'm a realist. After a while, I dropped the line. And maybe they were right: maybe it was too complex an idea or the phrasing was too harsh. But it shows how the audience shapes the material. They are part of the process. I write, they edit.

I think of thought-provoking pieces—what I call "values pieces"— as taking the audience on a journey with me through my mind. Along the way there are plenty of signposts and reminders of their own perceptions and things that they've assumed, heard, believed and questioned, reinforcing those things for them and reassuring them that I'm not leading them into a cul-de-sac, that the journey is to somewhere new. And if I'm engaging them in forward movement, from a familiar place to an unfamiliar place, I have to do it with marvelous language or some other attention-getting element that transfixes them and moves them along to their destination—and then we can get back to the laughing all night.

That gets away from the most formal definition of the word "teaching," but in a way that's what it is, laying it out for them in an amusing and entertaining way, taking them on an instructional tour. Because there's something you want them to know that they didn't know, or didn't know they knew when they sat down in their seats.

I'd never use the word "teaching" (rhymes with "preaching"), if for no other reason than when new ideas are conveyed via instruction (or speechifying or debate), people seem to have an instinctive defense against them.

But when you're in front of an audience and you make them laugh at a new idea, you're guiding their whole being for the moment. No one is ever more herself or himself than when they really laugh. Their defenses are down. It's very Zen-like, that moment. They are completely open, completely themselves when that message hits the brain and the laugh begins. That's when new ideas can be implanted. If a new idea slips in at that moment, it has a chance to grow. So for that moment, that tiny moment, I own them. That's one of the things—maybe the most important—I seek by following this path: to have that power. To be able to say: stop in your tracks and consider this!

At the same time, I've had to surrender myself to that moment, and it's a communion. A genuine, momentary communion. Which they wouldn't have experienced without me. And I wouldn't have experienced without them.

You have attitudes when you're young, but you don't have the ammunition to go with them. Especially if you're self-educated and you're just trying to find out what you need to know to get through. You haven't had this overlay of other information. I was fifty-five when I did *Jammin'*, already well past fifty—a big turning point for a lot of guys. And I was chasing sixty when I did *Back in Town*. But I've found the perspective of time lends texture to your ideas. The longer you live, the richer your matrix gets and the observations you make have more interesting information against which to be compared.

The difference between what you see and what you know is richer and more full of possibilities. It's an accumulation of attitude and information that people respond to.

And of course, after a certain age you get points just for not being dead.

If you've been paying attention you'll notice there was a four-year gap between *Jammin'* and *Back in Town*. Because as always there was my two-tiered personality to be reckoned with. Just when my craft and artistry and self-discovery were maturing, I started to feel the old longing to belong, to find a group I wanted to be part of. The result was two major diversions in the midnineties, one good, one not so good.

On my Web site it says:

January 1994: *The George Carlin Show* premieres on Fox Television. Lasts 27 episodes. Lesson learned: always check mental health of creative partner beforehand. Loved the actors, loved the crew. Had a great time. Couldn't wait to get the fuck out of there. Canceled December 1995.

For about twenty years before *The George Carlin Show* I'd regularly turn down some offer to have conversations about a sitcom. I was always opposed to it for the usual kind of showbiz-cultural reasons. I'm a stand-up comedian, not a sitcom guy. Movie parts are fine, but it's a commercial wasteland, and so on.

I'd developed a real sense of myself vis-à-vis television, of where I stood in relation to it. If I'd learned anything in the sixties from *Perry Como* and the Two Buddies and wearing the bunny suit in the closing number, the torture I went through, it was: situation comedy was just another form of the same thing. There was a reluctance, on many levels, to get involved in the worst aspects of commercialism.

Fox had been coming after me for about four years and I'd been turning them down. They gradually made the offer so good I had to listen. They gave me 20 percent of the back end and an executive producer credit. Most important, they wanted to put me with Sam Simon, whose pedigree was terrific: *Taxi, Cheers, The Simpsons, Tracey Ullman*. A brilliant writer and shaper of comedy.

What really changed my mind was that the 1992 HBO show was a watershed. It brought me to a new artistic level—that good plateau—as far as the writing and performing. I could afford a pause, a victory lap. I was in my midfifties, I had a great offer, there was a great writer to work with; I thought, maybe I owed it to Brenda—and myself—to see if there was a place I could fit and do something with this form that didn't embarrass me. I didn't want to be in my seventies snarling, "I should have taken that Fox offer, if only I had . . . Christ, look at these fucking kids today!"

I took the chance. And I had a great time. I never laughed so much, so often, so hard as I did with cast members Alex Rocco, Chris Rich, Tony Starke. There was a very strange, very good sense of humor on that stage. The feeling on the set was relaxed, democratic. And the crew was great. No Hollywood ego bullshit from anyone. I loved the acting, the process, learning the lines, shaping them.

But I didn't enjoy the corporate crap. You're dealing with people who are in the business of guessing. Guessing backed up by testing. They test their guesses and if their guesses are correct, they start second-guessing. One another. The studio. The network. Everyone's at odds.

The biggest problem though was that Sam Simon was a fucking horrible person to be around. Very, very funny, extremely bright and brilliant, but an unhappy person who treated other people poorly.

There's a producer-writer in-group culture in television that isn't friendly to outsiders—especially a star who, though he's supposed to be the raison d'être of the project, comes from another area of show business. They keep you at arm's length, keep you in the dark about certain areas. It made no difference that Jerry and I were executive producers—Sam was the show runner, the most important person in getting the show on.

Once a week I'd go to long-rewrite night, after rehearsals and before shooting began. I had to be onstage all the time during the week, so I wasn't part of everything else that happened up in the Executive Office Building. But on long-rewrite night I was. I liked it because I enjoyed having writers around and punching up and shaping stuff.

But the length of time that goes into ordering the fucking food! Ten different menus: the Chinese, the Italian, the deli, the Mexican, they're all over the Valley and, "Okay, who's gonna pick the menu tonight? Joey! Let Joey! No, Joey picked it last week, I'll pick it! Don't order from there, they don't deliver!" Then the food arrives and there's the sorting out whose food is whose and the eating of the food.

I'm old-fashioned. I like to get on with the work. I say: "Hey, Joey, on page thirty—that's where we left off—can we put in so-and-so?" And Joey says, "Mblmblmggmlmmmm. Ya gonna finish that?"

There was ritual, and I don't like rituals. There were unwritten rules, and I don't like them either. For instance, you never criticize or knock down someone's idea, you just let it die in the air. Nobody says it sucks. They don't say anything—just move on to the next suggestion. And even if you fight for a change and win, the rule is, you then have to lose a few. Let others win a few, even if you object to their changes. You end up only half represented.

The producer-writer culture also had a private vocabulary: "Let's not hang a lantern on that," or "Drumroll, drumroll!" leaving me more in the dark than ever. Which is the whole point of private vocabularies.

All trivial considerations perhaps, but important signs of the groupthink that prevents full expression. I hesitate to say "free expression" because it sounds too political, but full expression on a television show you can never have.

Fox wasn't heavily committed to *The George Carlin Show*. I was told the head of promotion didn't like it. We weren't getting much cooperation from on-air promotions and Fox's promotional team. Mainly the network wanted us to retain a share of the audience *Married . . . With Children* left us with.

More unwritten rules. *Married . . . With Children* was considered a Dumb White Show and we were a Smart White Show. A Smart White Show couldn't follow a Dumb White Show. Fox saw itself as a black network, and while blacks liked to watch Dumb Whites, they didn't like watching Smart Whites. (Dumb White Network Executives at work: it turned out we had the highest share of retained audience from *Married . . . With Children* of anything Fox ever followed it with.)

There were pluses. My hellos in the airport, my level of recognition—from black people in particular but also the general public—shot up. But Fox was not the place for me. I was incredibly happy when the show was canceled. I was frustrated that it had taken me away from my true work. I would have done my ninth HBO show in 1994 and I didn't. I had just learned—finally—how to do my work. This wonderful second burst of creative energy was interrupted and hurt in a way. Now I cherished it all the more for that. So Fox was part of a paring down process, getting rid of extraneous dreams and ambitions, once and for all.

Forget weekly television. I'd rather be sitting in a crappy motel in Wisconsin or Oregon going through my files, making notes on the next HBO show, rolling over during the night to write down a note: "Hm-hm-hmmm, that goes with the Kleenex bit for 2002 . . ."

They could get me away from stand-up for a while perhaps, if they said: "There's this wonderful movie role, you costar, big money, great script. You play a priest and you get to strangle six children. Not all in one burst either: in six separate scenes with six different techniques of strangulation." I'd give up a month or two for that.

Which brings us to *Shining Time Station*.

Shining Time Station was presented to me as an acting opportunity. At that point Jerry and I were characterizing the kind of role I wanted as something where my eyes bulged out. I walked away from a lot of stuff because I was looking for somewhere to really stretch my eyeballs.

But when the *Shining Time* lady, Britt Allcroft, a wonderful, creative, concerned woman, came to me about her project, I thought: "Hey, here's a chance to show something quite different: a side that's gentle, childlike." Britt was careful about what her team did, and this was PBS. Jerry and I had always tried to associate ourselves with strong brands: HBO, Atlantic, Warner Bros. Records—PBS was one of them. Plus I took the place of Ringo Starr (who did the first season). So that made me the anti-Pete Best.

The nicest thing about it was I didn't have to deal with actors—adults or children—because it was all green-screen. I was the only actor there, which made the acting a little harder, but it was more pleasant not having to deal with everybody's little story-of-the-day.

It won me a whole new generation of admirers who knew nothing about George Carlin except that he was a little man in a little blue suit. When I ran into one of these kids at the airport and the parents would say, "That's him, that's him! Go over and say hello," the child was always completely fucking traumatized. I was out of uniform and way too big. I had to say gently, "I'm not on the Island of Sodor, I'm not working today. But I am Mr. Conductor." Then that wonderful look would come on the child's face: "What the FUCK is going on?"

I must say, like most adults, I find kids fascinating one-on-one. Just watching them drool or look at you funny. Or even saying something bright. But as a class—far too much attention.

Now, ten to twelve years later, some of Mr. Conductor's little fans are beginning to show up at my concerts and HBO shows. To complete their education.

After Fox died, we did some one-hour specials for PBS with guest stars like Jack Klugman, and a series of half-hours, a few of them where Mr. Conductor was the central person and told several Thomas the Tank Engine stories. There was talk about a feature film, which never came to anything, but I do remember a fascinating series of discussions out at the studio—casual but with a purpose—talking with Britt about what the movie ought to be and how to keep the core of *Shining Time Station* intact.

She pointed out how the stage in *Shining Time Station* began over on the right with a lot of mischief: Schemer and his arcade, the moneymaking schemes, always creating hassles and anarchy and chaos. Then, as you moved leftward on the set—she didn't plan that you move leftward but some right-wing asshole could see a subliminal message there, I guess—you came to the center, the information booth, with Stacy Jones, the female stationmaster. She was the embodiment of order and reassurance: "It's all right, it's okay, this is going to work. The train comes in at eight and it leaves at nine." Then, moving farther left, you got to Billy Twofeathers, the engineer, an American Indian, who represented a spiritual and nurturing side.

There was a combination in *Shining Time Station* of nurturing, freedom, lesson learning, chaos. I pointed out that Mr. Conductor didn't quite fit into any of those roles but could be part of any of them—even chaos, in his evil twin. None of them explained why he was so fascinating to children. And Britt asked, "Why is he the most fascinating?"

The director had been Jesuit-trained as a kid and I'd been attacking them and religion in children's lives and we'd been enjoying that. There seemed to me a connection. I'm aware this is a well-known theme, but bear with me.

And PAY ATTENTION!

When we're in the womb, we're in the oceanic state, we are completely part of nature. We are attached to nature, literally, physically. Everything comes through tubes, you don't have to do a goddam thing, everything's cool. You are at one. You are in union with nature.

Then you get torn out of this fucking place and there's pain and screaming and the violence starts. The slapping on the ass, the acid wash, the circumcision. You are out of there, not attached, not cool, not at one with anything. And INDIVIDUATION starts! You are JOHNNY PHILLIPS and you are going to be a LAWYER. And you're going to be just like your FATHER and you've got RED HAIR and you're gonna have a TEMPER and a whole bunch of other shit will be true of you. You better SHAPE UP and have a goal and work for it and achieve things. UNION is OVER.

The rest of your life is spent yearning for reunion. To join the One again. That's where religion perverts a very natural longing in people. More primitive people have found a way of having for themselves a communion with nature, balance and harmony with it.

Not: "I am DISTANT from nature and SEPARATE from nature

and I will change the course of that river and I will tear up the land and make freaks out of animals and take milk out of them." Instead, it's: "We won't control nature, we can't. So let's live at one with it."

But we *civilized* people have this loss, this loss of union, this loss of oneness. And we look for it and dream of finding it, but in all the wrong places. In religion, in sex, in success . . .

Back to Mr. Conductor. I said, "He's got two things combined. He's small like a child. He's childlike, like a child. But he's fully developed like an adult. And he's wise like an adult. These things are joined, so there's a unity in him that is complete." That's one of the reasons I did him so unself-consciously—even in those silly outfits and with the propeller on my head. I didn't feel the need to use one of my voices. He was natural to me.

I said to Britt: "I think he's fascinating to children because he's got the things children need from adults, experience and information (and gold dust). At the same time, he's totally unthreatening. He's even smaller and more powerless than they are. He's a baby adult."

I loved doing *Shining Time Station*. But part of it was—I also like presenting a moving target. I liked the idea of people saying, "Well, that's nice. Now he's on *Shining Time Station* educating two-year-olds. Hey, but . . . doesn't he say 'cocksucker' and . . . 'the Virgin's bleeding from her cunt?' " Yeah. Keeping them a bit off guard.

And being on the series gave me a great line for the '99 HBO show *You Are All Diseased*. It was a reprise of riffs I'd been doing for some time about child worship in America.

Kids were getting FAR TOO MUCH ATTENTION! And whatever people thought about kids they had to listen to an expert . . . This was *MR. CONDUCTOR* talking!

17

DOORS CLOSE, DOORS OPEN

George and Kevin Smith on the set of *Dogma*
(Courtesy of Scott Mosier)

One last story about material. About just how long it can take for stuff, even stuff I love, to see the light of day, or in this case HBO. And why I hate topical humor.

Sometime in the late eighties I began to see things in my files like, "Hey, let's just kill everybody." That was only one brief thought, but I remember thinking, "Here's an opportunity to create some art." Obviously I don't think it would be a good idea to kill everybody, but at the same time it was a good idea to *let loose in the world*. If I could come up with enough semi-, quasi-, pseudo-reasons and methods for getting rid of everybody in the world (except for a nice workable two hundred thousand, including me), I've got a great piece.

The boilerplate definition of satire is taking on the mentality of your enemy—at this point it was still Reagan and his gang—and taking it to extremes in an ingenious way. I guess that's what this was— instinctively anyway. Reagan's basic worldview was that to save the American way of life everybody had to be ready to die in a nuclear holocaust. (Except of course a nice workable two hundred thousand Republicans, including him). So being 1000 percent *for* that kind of ultraviolence, really enthusing about it, relishing it, was fun. It appealed to the extreme in me. Some part of comedy is always about excess.

Over time the idea grew in my files. Other similar ideas attached themselves to the core one. I began testing them out in shows on the road. One variant was that because the world is so fucked we should just kill everybody and start over. Another was essentially the introduction to "The Planet Is Fine." Television news about disasters, the worse the better, was my favorite entertainment. I couldn't give a shit about the budget or where the Pope was. Give me screaming people on fire being crushed by falling masonry. Now that's fun!

Some offshoots became pieces in their own right. One of them—the same basic idea—is "Capital Punishment" from *Back in Town*. The idea was that we shouldn't abolish capital punishment. We should expand it, kill far more people, in far more entertaining and time-tested ways like crucifixion, beheadings, boiling them in oil—in all cases the slower the better . . .

As I played out the piece onstage a character began to emerge who wasn't just an advocate of death on a massive scale but a real lover of it. Finding this out was wonderful. I used a very calm voice and manner, a really friendly, really open and honest clinical sociopath:

> *I have a confession to make. If I confess my secret to you, I would hope that you would not judge me—not think of me as a bad person. Maybe many of you, if the truth were known, would have to make the same confession. Here it is: I kinda like it when a lot of people die. I really do. I can't help it. It makes me feel really good.*

> *. . . Every time there's a big disaster, I always wish it were bigger. I always wish it happened in rush hour. And—forgive me for this, but . . . near a school? Or a hospital? Or a nursing home? I apologize if that bothers you . . . I know some of you will say, "Well, you'd feel different if someone close to you were killed in some big disaster." I say: "No, I wouldn't."*

What was great was that now I could *be* the clinical sociopath, play his glee at all the carnage, enjoy it, not just suggest it. And, by getting them to go along with my glee and laugh at it, driving home that this was something deep down in our psyche. That was confirmed by hearing this certain laughter of complicity from the audience, a knowing, accepting laughter.

Things have a way of telling me when they want to be done and this piece wasn't bursting out of me yet. It would need a lot of writing and polishing, stage time to get all the parts working together. Plus a major memorizing job, which doesn't get any easier when you'll never see sixty again.

I already had enough stuff for the HBO show in '99, including a great closer: "There Is No God." But there was no question that this new piece would be ready to go for the next HBO show, two years later.

I honed it all that time and it evolved into a complex catastrophe leaving millions dead in every possible kind of disaster, unfolding across the continent, disrupting the laws of nature, full of a kind of grisly poetry, a real tour de force, along the lines of "The Planet Is Fine," but darker and madder.

I had big hopes for the next HBO special. It would be my twelfth and twelve is a magical kind of number. And it had the makings of an explosive show, with a big fat target in the White House: Governor Bush and his Christian fucks. I had a sledgehammer values piece: "Why We Don't Need Ten Commandments." And I had this major new tour de force.

Taping was set for the Beacon Theatre on November 17. I named the entire show for the new piece. I had a hunch it was going to be the first HBO in a decade to equal, maybe even surpass, *Jammin'*.

I held on to that hunch right up to 8:46 a.m., September 11, 2001, when the first plane hit. Because the show was called:

I Kinda Like It When a Lot of People Die.

Who says there was nothing funny about 9/11? There were a couple dozen eggs on my face that day. Osama bin fucking Laden hadn't just blown up the World Trade Center. He'd blown up the best piece I'd written in ten years.

I'm a realist. We changed the name of the show to *Complaints and Grievances*. (If there were such a thing as generic George Carlin, that title would be stenciled on the box.)

Hard-core fans were probably hoping I'd do something about 9/11. I did mention it—the elephant in the living room no one was talking about—which got a kind of hopeful laugh. But I left it at that and kept the focus on strong observational stuff with the basic theme, Assholes of Our Time: "People Who Wear Visors," "Parents of Honor Students," "Guys Named Todd." And "Ten Command-ments" killed.

But there was a hole in the show the size of Ground Zero.

When I'm on the road doing promotional interviews for concerts I love it when someone from the *Great Falls Gazette* or the *Pitts-burgh Post and Nasal Drip* says: "You must have a lot of stuff about Cheney and *American Idol* and Hillary's pantsuits." And I pull the rug right out from under them: "I never talk about events or people in the news."

I hate topical material because I hate to throw anything away. I don't want to develop a nice little thing about Bush and Scooter Libby and it kills, then I do it for a month or so and really tighten it, add three more jokes, get the whole fucking thing down cold, but it's not getting laughs anymore because it's old news. I'd have to abandon it! I fucking hate that. I like to polish, polish, polish, get it perfect, put it on tape and keep it forever.

The fate of "I Really Like It When a Lot of People Die" is a re-verse example of why I hate topical humor. A piece based on stuff we see on the news was killed by stuff we saw on the news.

At least I didn't have to abandon it. It made it into the next HBO show in 2005, *Life Is Worth Losing*. That would be about seventeen years after it had first come down the birth canal. But I wasn't tak-ing any chances. I called it "Coast-to-Coast Emergency." It was the finale and the best thing in the show. So—now I have it, polished, perfect and put on tape. And I'll keep it forever.

The piece had evolved into a narrative of a nationwide cataclysm with small beginnings in L.A. A downtown water main breaks and floods an electrical substation. At the same time, a monthlong global-warming heat wave hits. Because everything in L.A. runs on electrical power, including air-conditioning and hospitals, social chaos soon spreads through the city, bringing with it cholera and smallpox and fires that firefighters can't fight with no water, until the entire city is ablaze . . .

Everybody panics and tries to leave the city at the same time and they trample one another to death in the streets by the thousands and wild dogs eat their corpses and the wild dogs chase the rest of the people down the highway and one by one the dogs pick off the old fucks and the slow people because they're IN THE FAST LANE WHERE THEY DON'T BELONG . . . And big sparks from the city have lit the suburbs on fire and the suburbs burn uncontrollably and thousands of identical homes have identical fires with identical smoke, killing all the identical soccer moms and their identical kids named JASON and JENIFERRRR . . .

Now the fires spread out beyond the suburbs to the farmlands . . .

. . . and thousands of barns and farmhouses begin to explode from all the hidden METHAMPHETAMINE labs! The meth chemicals run downhill to the rivers where wild animals drink the water and get completely GEEKED on speed. Bears and wolves amped up on crank start roaming the countryside looking for people to eat—even though they're not REALLY HUNGRY . . . And now the forests burn furiously and hundreds of elves and fairies and trolls come running out of the woods screaming, "Bambi is dead, Bambi is dead!!" and he is! He is! Finally that FUCKING LITTLE CUNT BAMBI IS DEAD!!

All the regional fires come together into one huge interstate inferno which engulfs the West and Midwest and races through the South, then turns northeast and heads for Washington, D.C. . . .

. . . where George Bush can't decide if it's an EMERGENCY OR NOT . . . And the fire moves to Philadelphia but it's a weekend and Philadelphia's CLOSED on weekends! So the fire moves to New York City and the people of New York tell the fire TO GO FUCK ITSELF! And while all this is going on Canada burns to the ground but NOBODY NOTICES! . . .

With the entire North American continent on fire the thermal updraft causes an incendiary cyclonic macrosystem that forms a hemispheric megastorm . . .

. . . breaking down the molecular structure of the atmosphere and actually changing the laws of nature. Fire and water combine, burning clouds of flaming rain fall upward, gamma rays and solar winds ignite the ionosphere . . . and bolts of lightning 20 million miles long begin shooting out of the North Pole. And the sky fills up with GREEN SHIT!

Then suddenly the entire fabric of space-time SPLITS IN TWO! A huge crack in the universe opens and all the dead people from the past begin falling through: Babe Ruth, Groucho Marx, Davy Crockett, Tiny Tim, Porky Pig, Hitler, Janis Joplin, Allen Ludden, my uncle Dave, your uncle Dave, everybody's uncle Dave, an endless stream of dead Uncle Daves . . .

And all the Uncle Daves gather around a heavenly kitchen table and they light up cigarettes and they begin to talk about how they never got a break, their parents didn't love them and their children were ungrateful and how the Jews own everything and the blacks get special treatment. And their hatred and bitterness forms a big pool of liquid hate and the pool of liquid hate begins to spin, around and around, faster and faster. The faster it spins, the bigger it gets until the whirling pool of hate is bigger than the universe and suddenly it explodes into trillions of tiny stars and every star has a trillion planets and every planet has a trillion Uncle Daves.

And all the Uncle Daves have good jobs, perfect eyesight and shoes that fit. They have great sex lives and free health care. They understand the Internet, their kids think they're cool . . . And every week without fail Uncle Dave wins the lottery. Forever and ever until the end of time every single Uncle Dave has a winning ticket and UNCLE DAVE IS FINALLY HAPPY . . .

Awards and honors started coming in the nineties. Awards and honors are nice. They feed a part of me I don't consider that important, the superficial showbiz ego. If there's any reason I do what I do, it's not to win awards.

Isn't there SOMETHING I can say that WON'T make them want to give me an award?

Most awards are just an excuse for a television show. Showbiz congratulating you but also congratulating itself for being so relevant and important and having the good judgment to pick the best. There's more than a whiff of that empty showbiz bullshit I used to hate in my sixties nice period, the celebrity club pretending to know and admire and care for one another in their acceptance speeches. And where there are acceptance speeches, you can be certain that pretty soon *children* will enter the picture.

The Aspen Comedy Arts Festival in '97, where I was honored for forty years in comedy, had a little of that. Not totally: I was proud of the HBO compilation of my work to date—*40 Years of Comedy*, my '97 HBO special—and it was my first taste of Jon Stewart. He was just a kid at the time and he did a great interview. Maybe a little too respectful, but he soon got over that. Boy, did he go on to do brilliant things.

There were a bunch of us: Dennis Miller, me, Laraine Newman and Janeane Garofalo thrown in for gender equality, and an *SNL* contingent: Chevy, Lorne, Martin Short, Steve Martin. I have a lot of respect for Steve Martin. I think he's got a great mind. He's made some good choices. And I like Martin Short's talent. But it's a club.

I had something in my head for each of them: you fantasize these encounters beforehand and prepare. A little personal thing I wanted to say to each one, Chevy, Lorne, Martin and Steve. Just to make human contact, because I'm out of this club. Steve Martin came by. I hadn't seen him since 1967 on the *Smothers Brothers* show, where he gave me an eight-by-ten signed: "Not just another pretty face." I pulled him aside and said, "Steve, you know I haven't seen you in a long time. And I want you to know how happy I am for your career and the things that you've done."

He was touched, I could see, a little taken aback, but kind of touched. I'd made human contact. I told him about the photo—that I still had it and occasionally have it out to show people.

Now I see Lorne, for whom I have no respect, because he's a fucking hands-and-knees cocksucker, but I wanted to make contact so I put on a nice face and I said, "Lorne, all these years I've wanted to apologize to you for making that first week so difficult because of the cocaine." He nods and thanks me. Like he's accepting my apology and that's that. No clear human contact like I got from Steve.

By now we're in a big briefing room that looks like the Council on Economic Affairs; everybody has a pad and a glass of water and a pencil. The room is largely empty and is where they're supposed to brief us before we go to the dais for the press conference.

So it's Lorne, Martin, Chevy, Steve and me. That's it. And HBO's camera. I do a little thing with Lorne that's funny, we laugh, there's a couple of good cocaine jokes. But then it becomes Lorne telling the others Famous Cocaine Stories From *SNL*: "Gary Busey in the countdown to air . . . he snorts . . . 5, 4 . . . he snorts . . . 3, 2 . . . he snorts . . ." Okay, fine. But I never got another glance, never another word.

Martin Short came over. When I'd done *SNL* the second time, Martin had been nice and I'd never told him I was grateful. So I said, "I always wanted to tell you—I saw you in Toscana a few weeks ago and I didn't get a chance—how nice that was of you on *SNL* and how touched I was by your words." And he said, "Oh, I didn't know that." Some empty words. Just—WHOOSSSSSHHH: no contact. And Martin is a person who, when I see his work, I feel has something really human in him. I forget what I said to Chevy.

Then it's just movie talk, yuppie talk. Nothing stuff and still not a glance or a word. And I'm realizing that this group of people, who were once considered radical and revolutionary, has become just another fucking Hollywood celebrity club. The Lorne Club. That their chitchat is a modern version of the fraudulent showbiz crap I was expected to do forty years ago in Mike Douglas's gazebo.

We move on to the press conference and first of all there are a lot of *Saturday Night Live* questions. Chris Albrecht from HBO, who's moderating, tries to direct a question or two toward me so I'm included, but I dismiss them with short answers. The press is not interested in me at all. Now people start asking these pretentious questions about the effect of television on CHILDREN. Dennis Miller's next to me, who I think is an arrogant person but I kinda like his mind. Dennis occasionally says something and I occasionally say something. But they're all talking about CHILDREN.

Steve and Chevy were very funny. They're very funny people, though Chevy might not want to be doing so many pratfalls now that he's a little larger than back when he was doing Ford. But they're quick and bing! they land on each other and the banter was wonderful.

I'm letting it go whenever it's CHILDREN this and CHILDREN that. Now it's the Internet and THE CHILDREN and we can't protect THE CHILDREN and porn and THE CHILDREN. This goes on and on and even Chevy, when he's not doing structural damage to the building, is being self-important and pretentious about THE CHILDREN.

They finally call on me and I say: "There's TOO MUCH AT-TENTION TO CHILDREN in this country! Leave them ALONE! They're gonna BE ALL RIGHT! They're SMARTER THAN YOU ARE!"

There was a big laugh on it. HBO used it as the punch line in their on-air version of the event. Fuck the Lorne Club.

On April 5, 1997, Brenda was diagnosed with cancer of the liver. They said the cancer had metastasized from her breast cancer and attacked her liver, always vulnerable because of the hepatitis C. A liver transplant was not an option because of her previous cancer.

Some part of me probably knew it was the end. The part of me that always looks for the brighter side got the better of it. The doctors fed that a little, sugarcoated it, I think—that she might have three to four months. I wanted to believe them. Maybe even that she was going to live. They'd given her only a few weeks to live when she got sober in '75, and ten years later worried that she'd have a recurrence of her breast cancer. Yet here she was: she'd survived so often. With all the progress in chemo and radiation, new drugs, protocols, treatments, why not again?

I decided to keep working.

I'd always been disturbed that my actions in the 1970s concerning my money and other behaviors had put me in the position where I had to be away from Brenda so much. I have a thoughtful nature—as a child I did—and I'd always tried do extra things for her that would be described as thoughtful acts, unprompted, unbidden. First, to make her more comfortable in every way in her physical feelings and her emotional world; and second, to let her know I was trying to compensate, consciously trying to atone—my mother's word, very Catholic of course—for these absences.

And '97 was an unusually busy season, with the normal work schedule plus Aspen in February and the book tour for my first book, *Brain Droppings*, which was to begin in May. I'd said to her: "I'm working on our retirement. We're close to being even. I'm trying to get ahead of the game. Set some things in place that will make us less likely to be eaten by dogs later in life." I saw that as part of the atonement.

But the initial diagnosis had been incorrect. The cancer hadn't metastasized from her previous one. It was new, separate and aggressive. In fact the oncologist told us—afterward, of course, when it was too late to act upon—that under the microscope it was the most aggressive cancer he'd ever seen. Brenda deteriorated rapidly, and on the morning of May 11—Mother's Day—she crashed. She was already unconscious when Kelly got her to Saint John's. At midday all her systems shut down and her heart stopped.

I was in New York. I grabbed the first plane I could find. The doctors restarted Brenda's heart and Kelly had them put her on life support till I could get back.

I hadn't seen her for a week or more. Jaundice had made her skin yellow. All her hair was gone from the chemo. She was unconscious and unresponsive but . . . her eyes were open. I have no idea if she was aware of anyone, but I saw her eyes were tearing up a little.

I took a tissue and gently wiped away her tears.

My own health troubles seemed to be on hold. I'd had a third, pretty serious heart attack in '91 while driving to Vegas and a follow-up one—less serious—in '94. I believe that the '94 one was related to the '91 heart attack. They tried to do an angioplasty after that one and it failed, an artery went into spasm and I had a lot of angina. I went to San Francisco to my guys there and they said they didn't want to touch the lesion. It was a little immature, not well formed. They said: "We don't want to work on this artery, so we're going to send you back to your cardiologist in L.A. and treat you with medicine." For three years that was fine, and then I began to get a tiny bit of angina—my usual kind in the throat—but only at the highest point of exercise. It would go away when I stopped exercising.

But I don't fool around. I checked into the hospital and they took a look and did an angioplasty with a stent. A stent is a mesh cylinder, like a Chinese finger puzzle, made out of very fine wire. They insert the balloon with the stent, the balloon is expanded, the stent expands and then they deflate the balloon and take it out. The stent remains in the artery to keep it open. This prevents restenosis, which is the biggest problem with angioplasty—the dilations they make can reclose, either immediately or within six months. Stents had a much higher rate of keeping them open. I'm quite sure that the lesion he fixed was the one from '91.

One strange thing about my heart problems is that I've always gotten in on, if not the leading edge of technology, things that were still in the experimental stage. When I got my stent, the procedure hadn't yet been approved by the FDA. It was only in use in six hospitals. I was lucky again—as with the streptokinase—that they were experimenting with it in that particular hospital. At the time, the only other person I knew about who'd had a stent was Mother Teresa. Mother Teresa had a stent—I had stent. My mother would have been so proud.

It always seems to me when I have these heart attacks or angioplasties that it's just mechanical work. It may have an organic origin—the plaque builds up because of a chemical reaction—but essentially it's Roto-Rooter time. Let's get in and clean out that clogged pipe. Everything I've ever had healthwise involved something that could be moved around. That's lucky. Even the ablation I had in 2003, which is a procedure to correct arrhythmia, where they intentionally scar your heart to control the signals from your brain, is really just a kind of tune-up. Your heart's not firing properly and needs adjustment. I've always felt optimistic and comfortable about my heart. Even with an attack, once it's over you don't feel any pain. With angioplasty, the only result is the incision they made and you just want to get home.

I sort things out well. I place things in my world where they ought to be mentally as well as physically. In fact I move my physical world around in order for my mental world to be a little easier to look at and work with. People ask me in interviews sometimes: "Didn't the heart attacks change your life? Didn't they change you?" And I say no, not really. Obviously I had to start exercising because I'd been sedentary my whole life. I had to start eating correctly because I'd been an American slob eater my whole life. Those were the only two changes. I've never lived with a sword of Damocles. I guess I knew another can strike at any moment so I don't know how much of it is this wonderful thing we've discovered, denial. I don't think so: denial has a different flavor. This is just being sensible about yourself and not being a fucking martyr and a victim.

One reason that I don't worry too much about these things is that I'm happy in love.

I met Sally Wade about six months after Brenda's death. She was a comedy writer based in Hollywood who'd always wanted to meet me, but was a bit shy about it. So her dog Spot made the first move for her. We fell for each other—I've always been lonely for people like me and she was a kindred spirit. Still, with Brenda's death so recent, I wasn't ready yet. Sally waited for me, and when we got together, I knew she would be the love of my life. And she is.

A big part of my job is exploding clichés. But it seems impossible to talk about what Sally and I have without them. I've already used a couple. So here's a couple more: it was love at first sight, we're crazy about each other, we have a great love together. And there's more where those came from. The weird thing is, they're all true.

At my age, I'm allowed a little inconsistency.

Throughout the nineties and whatever we call this decade—"the zeros" works for the Bush years—I've had a constant sense of growth and growing strength. I've always had the path ahead of me as my artistic life unfolded, sometimes with side roads and cul-de-sacs, true, but in spite of them a sense of growing internally, intellectually, emotionally, of constantly finding a better way to craft my work. And thanks to Jerry, I've always had plenty of shit to do out there, always had 125, 150 dates a year. There's always an audience waiting for me in Topeka or Eugene or Orlando or Stevens Point, Wisconsin. There'll always be a roomful of people somewhere, willing to sit quietly in the dark. Not too quietly, obviously, but at least sit in an orderly fashion and appreciate me and listen to my stuff and pay. That has a life-giving aspect. That is what I live for.

People always ask questions like: "How can you go on? Aren't you anxious to retire? Aren't you tired of the road?" But I realized something very simple a long time ago. I can't do what I love to do without these people. I have to go where they live. They're not going to come to my house. Even if I pay them.

Sure, there's always bad stuff. The fucking Bide-A-Wee Motel or the rinky-dink airport where a wing's fallen off the plane, all the bad shit about traveling we all know. And I've never liked being backstage. That's the worst fucking place in the world. It's like being in a boxing ring and the match hasn't started yet. That's where I used to get a lot of my drinking done. But I will say this: once I get onstage—not every night and not every minute of every night, but damned close—once I'm onstage, it's a transformation. All the bad stuff just drips away when you step onstage.

You may have thirty, forty years under your belt. You may feel really good about your shit. You may know exactly what you're going to do and that they're predisposed to like you . . . But the instant I get out there it all starts over again. Right from the beginning. Win them over, and get 'em where I want 'em! That's living! That's the thing that feeds me, that's my nourishment.

I don't know if there'll be any more movies. I did two with Kevin

Smith, *Dogma* in '99 and *Jersey Girl* in '04, where he wrote me a great part as Ben Affleck's dad. I like working with Kevin; there's a lot of great counterpunching and the Catholic thing is a strong bond. Acting is fun to do, a worthy fraternity and a great tradition to have had a tiny speck of a part of. But stand-up and acting are like running versus strength training. You work aerobically running, that's what you need to feel good. Sometimes you do strength training—a completely different set of muscles—and you feel good for completely different reasons. I'm a runner who makes occasional visits to the free weights.

I prefer rewards over awards. There's something I like about having done so many HBO shows. Thirteen so far. It's throwing down the gauntlet to the rest of comedy. Comedians who come later: this is the new standard! Thirteen one-hour shows on HBO and you're in the club! And it's rewarding to be able to say: "All right, now, I have proved to myself and to whoever's watching what I wanted to prove in this form."

Which is stand-up comedy in live performance. Long ago I described my job as being "a foole"; that's still what I do. Once, this kind of comedy was called the people's art, a vulgar art. Maybe all comedy is. I prefer live stand-up comedy to any other form. Since my changes in the early seventies I've only used television as an advertisement for myself. I've been blessed—and cursed—by events and circumstances that have made me, I think, one of the principal stand-ups of this era. The stand-up who has stayed longest with the stand-up form as his prime thing and made it what he does. Therefore I've had a chance to take some forward steps with it, at least for myself.

A lot of people who use stand-up to get them to movies let their stand-up work wither or forget about it altogether. Or they go out for a few dates to put together a special, then forget it for two years. The only other guys who did stand-up all their lives were from what I call the Jackie-Joey era—the forties and fifties, when they got their act to a certain level and just stayed at that level for the rest of their lives. I think I can say I'm one of the few people who, in the absence of a movie career and/or a television career, have taken this form to higher levels. That feels good, that feels special. If I were a Jackie-Joey still doing an act exactly as I did it twenty years ago, I'd be ready for a large blunt weapon. Instead I have a feeling of progress and of achievement. I've contributed a little to the vulgar art.

18

BEING, DOING, GETTING

George and Kelly Carlin
(Courtesy of Kelly Carlin-McCall)

On 123rd Street, when I was young, we had a gang called the Gripers. (That struck terror into the neighborhood. Watch the fuck out or we'll come gripe at you.) But even though I was in the Gripers, I wasn't a Griper. Belonging to any group for me was always an ad hoc thing that filled some immediate need—in this case smoking pot—but not what you'd call a deep existential hunger. As soon as I started going steady with my first girlfriend, Mary Cathryn, I left the group. I was still a card-carrying Griper, but it was always: "Georgie's up in the hall with Mary Cathryn." The only gang I wanted to be part of was the Loners, membership restricted to one: me.

In the air force, where they enforced group thought, I got around it by hanging with the black airmen, completely cutting me out from being any part of the white guys. I was out of that group—and happy to be. Then I became a disc jockey, downtown, off base: I'm already edging away from air force group thought. I'm apart, different. Alone in front of a mike. Almost back to my gang of one.

It always seemed to me that the reasons groups came together were superficial. The group didn't feed me, and I had nothing to contribute to it. I had a deeper goal, this giant puzzle to work on, which was only going to happen if they left me alone. "No one but me can figure me out. No one can help me with it." All the group stuff: rules, uniforms, rituals, *bonding*, was a distraction. It denied me the chance to solve the giant puzzle: "Who the fuck am I, how did I come together? What are the parts and how do they fit?"

The aloneness of the stage makes groups irrelevant. Few things dramatize the face-off between loner and group more starkly than the artist before the audience. And there's an irony here. If this loner can't get the audience to act as a group—laugh together—he's fucked.

When things go well onstage I don't just think: "They like me. They accept me. They think I'm clever." All those things happen, but I'm also looking inside to see what else is going on. And when I do, there is a sense in those moments, I am more than alone—I am the only thing in the universe. I am the only thing that's happening in it. No way to escape the progression of moments as they come up onstage—the next line and the next line, the next laugh and the next laugh. Which include my hands and the tilt of my jaw, how wide I open my eyes, whether I put more energy into it or slow it a little with my voice. There is nothing happening in the universe outside of that reality and that experience. When besides that I'm being rewarded with all this approval, attention, approbation, for something that is solely mine and only I can do . . . There can't be anything better than that. To be intensely alone, intensely myself, in control of everything, the center of a self-created universe.

The creation of material is the ultimate freedom because that's creating the world I want. I'm saying to people: the world you imagine isn't really true: THIS is what's happening: "Booogadee! Booogadee! Booogadee!" Even if I'm just babbling I'm saying: THAT is what's true. What *is*. Here and now. Whatever you think to be true, you with the suit and the hat, on the subway or the freeway, is bullshit. THIS is true: "Booogadee! Booogadee! Booogadee!" I am momentarily changing the world to THIS. I am reinventing the world because I can. So long as you're down there and I'm up here, freedom is: WHAT I SAY GOES!

That's the freedom I always have. I'm alone, nobody wrote it but me, there are no amplifiers, no counting off, no staying in the same key. There are words I have to know but I made them all up. My job is making up things that AREN'T and telling people that they ARE. That's what I do. What greater freedom can there be? To say, "The world is upside down. It's not what you think at all. It's my world! I invented it! FUCK YOU!"

I loved it when I was a kid and other kids would say, "Georgie, you're fucking crazy." "You ever see Carlin? He's fucking crazy!" I still love it. When people say, "You're weird, you've got a *strange* mind," it means way more to me than if they say, "You're a very funny man." Of course, when they say, "You're a very funny man and you have a strange way of looking at things," I swell up: it's just the greatest thing I can hear.

So part of me wants to let them see my weird side. And part of me wants them to see the serious craft it takes to dig this stuff out and turn it into art. And there's some need for me to connect with them. This whole thing is probably about connecting. Standing up in front of people is saying: "Hey, folks, look at me, ain't I great? Please induct me into your imaginary club of people you like. I want to be in that." And there's the need to find things out about them. To make kinships: "I feel this way about abortion, Volvos and farts." "Yeah! Me too!" "You too? OKAY!"

Is there any connection between gradually leaving drugs behind and gradually discovering this process, devouring it, living for it? I would absolutely give that credence. During my drug period, the only thing that was important was getting high—and fulfilling dates when I could. I don't recall these feelings of pursuing and appreciating artistry, the increasing ability to create. I'm sure the drugs blocked that sort of thing out, if it was there at all.

At the risk of sounding psychobabbly, maybe it's that once the drugs are gone as artificial stimulation, thrill, high and escape, the real stimulation, thrill, high and escape can make themselves known. Whether or not such things are needed in the first place drives the whole prohibition versus nonprohibition debate. But for me it could be that stimulation, thrill, high and escape are legitimate human needs and have now shown up in a more benign suit of clothes.

Whether performance is or isn't addictive, it's certainly habituating. (Even though a lot of the show doesn't change from night to night. But then, nor did the drugs.) I'll find myself in the middle of something I've done five hundred times and it's intoxicating, totally consuming. There are nuances, little ways to play with each word in a sentence. And simultaneously I'm thinking: boy, wait until they hear "House of Blues" or "Guys Named Todd" or whatever it is, at the same time as I punch home the lines I'm doing.

Sometimes I'll be in the midst of a list—I love to rattle off twelve things in a row—and I'll be around the third or fourth and one part of me will say to me: "You don't know what the last one is." And I'll reply, "I know, but we'll know it when we get there. And we're getting to Number Twelve and I say the word before it with no clue what comes next. I couldn't consciously tell you the next word is "Wilhelmina" but boom! there's "Wilhelmina" right on cue. There's an electric, magical, mysterious thing about that. Nothing to do with the audience, it's not about performing. It's watching one corner of your mind work from another corner of your mind. That happens a lot to me. And—I vaguely recall—happened a lot on drugs too.

Outside of these internal divisions of attention is a paradox. The reality is that the only thing that is happening for the audience also is that same line, that Wilhelmina moment. When they laugh, we're acting as one. In that moment, they're part of me, another aspect of me.

An audience is the only group I can tolerate, because the audience wouldn't be a group if it wasn't for me. Which extends to every other audience that has ever liked me. More and more as I get older, when people come up to me in public places to tell me how much they enjoyed some piece at a concert or club as long as forty years ago, I mentally see an audience of millions stretching away into the darkness. Individuals who in a sense I've met and some spark has passed between us, actual humans in whose presence I've been and who've been in mine, 1,500, 2,000, 3,000 at a time, but also one-on-one. Whenever they laughed, in that moment I was speaking to them directly. Faces with favorites; I overhear them in the lobby sometimes: "Wait till you hear 'There Is No God.'" Or someone who loved Al Sleet when she was little. They're part of the family. We're kindred. Live performance does that for you as nothing else can. And I think very few other comics in my lifetime can say that.

Outside of my audience, groups repel me, because for the sake of group thought, they kill individuality, that wonderful human oneness. I'm wide open to individuals. Fine with individuals. Individuals are just great. Even the most evil man on earth, who's just eaten a whole dog, I find fascinating and interesting. I'd love to spend a minute or two with him. Discuss the preparation. "You put a little salt on that? Used a little cream?" I'd look in his eyes and his eyes would be from someplace God knows where in the universe and yet for that reason fascinating.

Every individual set of eyes you look into gives you something, whether it's a blank wall or an infinite regress of barbershop mirrors. Just as fascinating. There's something in all individuals. I make room for them psychically—even though I might want to get away after a minute and a half. People are wonderful one at a time. Each of them has an entire hologram of the universe somewhere within them.

But as soon as individuals begin to clump, as soon as they begin to clot, they change. Sometimes you have a friend and you say, "Gee, Joe is a great guy. But when he's with Phil he's a real jack-off." Or, "Now that he's with Linda, the fucking guy is different. He's changed, he's not the same old Joe."

Groups of three, five, ten, fifteen—suddenly we have special little hats, we have arm bands, we have a marching song, a secret handshake and a list of people we don't agree with. Next we have target practice and plan the things we have to take care of Friday night.

One of my lists once was: "People I Can Do Without." Near the top: "People who say, 'Long live Such-and-such!' and then kill someone to accomplish it."

The ideal grouping for human beings is one. With the occasional sexual visit to the lady in the next group. Temporary twosomes are fine. Once upon a time people might have been good up to ten or twelve, or one hundred or so, whatever the ideal tribal unit was. When everybody took care of everybody else's children, there were no last names, no patriarchy, no patrimony, when property was unheard of. You might have personal stuff: this is my favorite rock, I got an ax I made. But no one owns the tent, everybody belongs in that tent as long as we have our fire. What buffalo there are belong to everybody if we can kill one. Something about that is awfully compelling. But we lost it long ago.

The larger the group, the more toxic, the more of your beauty as an individual you have to surrender for the sake of group thought. And when you suspend your individual beauty you also give up a lot of your humanity. You will do things in the name of a group that you would never do on your own. Injuring, hurting, killing, drinking are all part of it, because you've lost your identity, because you now owe your allegiance to this thing that's bigger than you are and that controls you.

It happens in police culture. You get talking with individual cops and they're the greatest fucking guys in the world. But you know that when they're making a domestic disturbance call in the black section of town, they're going to hit first and ask questions later. And if you happened to be there and called them on it, you'd be the enemy, right or wrong. That great fucking guy would be gone. It's the same with military men, with corporate assholes, the same anywhere on earth. And by the way, America's groups are no better than anyone else's.

The worst thing about groups are their values. Traditional values, American values, family values, shared values, OUR values. Just code for white, middle-class prejudices and discrimination, justification for greed and hatred.

Do I value a flag? No, of course not. Do I value words on a piece of paper? Depends whose words they are. Do I believe in family values? Depends on whose family—most are pretty toxic and that plural already has me suspicious. So I have a few holdings concerning potential behavior that an outsider could define as values. It's received beliefs, received wisdom, received values I have trouble with.

My affection for people as individuals and the fact that I identify with them doesn't extend to the structures they've built, the terrible job they've done of organizing themselves, the fake values that supposedly hold society together. Bullshit is the glue of our society.

I love anarchy. Anarchy and comedy are a team. But along with anarchy's hostility toward authority, I have a deep suspicion man is not on the right path. Man went wrong a long, long time ago. The private property thing—"This is mine! You don't own that!" Religion backing up property, religion backing up the state: "We say this king will be fine." The king saying: "I am the king and the moon is my uncle and he tells me when to plant the crop." All this mass hypnosis. Which is certainly akin to the hypnosis caused by Mass.

I no longer identify with my species. I haven't for a long time. I identify more with carbon atoms. I don't feel comfortable or safe on this planet. From the standpoint of my work and peace of mind, the safest thing, the thing that gives me most comfort, is to identify with the atoms and the stars and simply contemplate the folly of my fellow species members. I can divorce myself from the pain of it all. Once, if I identified with individuals I felt pain; if I identified with groups I saw people who repelled me. So now I identify with no one. I have no passion anymore for any of them, victims or perpetrators, Right or Left, women or men. I'm still human. I haven't abandoned my humanity, but I have put it in a place that allows my art to function free of entanglements.

My job is to watch the ludicrous dance down here for the humor and entertainment it provides and drop in every now and then to show my former species how fucked up they are.

Years ago I began to recede past Jupiter and its moons, out to the Oort cloud of trillions of comets, beyond the planet formerly known as Pluto, back home with my fellow atoms. All of which originally came from some star or other, and not necessarily the one we're circling.

I believe I am bigger than the universe, smaller than the universe and equal to it. I'm bigger than the universe because I can picture it, define it in my mind and everything that's in it and contain all that in my mind in a single thought. A thought that's not even the only one in there: it's right between "Shit, my ass itches!" and "Why don't we fuck the waitress?"

That thought, with all the others, is inside the twenty-three-inch circumference of my cranium. So I'm bigger than the universe. I'm smaller than it because that's obvious: I'm five foot nine and 150 pounds and the universe is somewhat taller and heavier. I'm equal to it because every atom in me is the same as every atom the universe is made of. I'm part of that protogalaxy five billion light years away and of that cigarette butt in Cleveland. There are no differences, we're equal. Unlike our fake democracy, the democracy of atoms is real.

Depending on my given mood on a given day, I can reflect on one of these three relationships for a moment or two and find comfort in it. And know that I'm really at one with the universe and will return to it on a more fundamental level someday—my reunion with it—and all the rest is a journey, a game, a comedy, a parade . . .

After I die I'd love to be fired into space. That's probably not practical given the crowded nature of the upper atmosphere. So one of the codicils of my will is: "I, George Carlin, being of sound mind, do not wish, upon my demise, to be buried or cremated. I wish to be *BLOWN UP*."

I'm sure there are people who see these attitudes as a form of escapism. My response has always been: "I don't care. Leave me alone. I'm not going to give you any threads to pick up here, folks. This is all temporal bullshit." Of course, once you tell someone, "This is all temporal bullshit," you've retreated to the realm of the angels. (I realize "temporal" and "angels" are Catholic terms, but as I've always said, I did use to be a Catholic. Until I reached the age of reason.)

Kelly has taken exception to some of them. She feels that if you don't vote you shouldn't have a say when it comes to complaining. Then there's golf. Her husband is from a golf family—his dad managed country clubs—and she plays golf. Sometimes on public courses, so a whole different experience than the corporate one I attack. It uses up a lot of land, but there's trees in the middle of the city and it's a nice way to spend the afternoon. Does that make her a golf asshole? Of course not. On occasion she's also questioned that I'm antiauthority and anarchist, with no belief in any system or political wing. That I often showed myself to be a very traditional—even conservative—father. Like when I took a baseball bat to her abusive boyfriend.

I don't think the world is that neat; none of us is that neat; none of us falls into categories. There are differing aspects of ourselves, not all of which point in the same direction. I'm a collection of liberal, conservative and anarchist. Different parts of me emerge when I'm outside my common mode, permissive left-liberal. I guess menacing some punk with a baseball bat for messing with your daughter is what you'd call traditional conservative behavior. So fine, part of me is conservative.

I do hide stuff from myself. I deny a lot, in current terminology. If someone isn't on fire, actually standing in front of me in flames, I'll say, "Everything's fine." I don't want to know stuff that isn't real apparent, right out in the front parlor. Leave it alone unless it explodes. When it's not exploding, it doesn't attract my attention. I don't take a few random clues and construct a complex problem out of them to obsess about.

I am very single-minded and preoccupied about my career, my art, my craft, my writing, my entertainment, whatever this package is. I'm accustomed to going out into the world and talking to thousands of people and being applauded for it, then coming home and debarking emotionally.

Doing that night after night, for decade after decade, may have made those other personal connections unnecessary as psychic food. I get so much satisfaction out of my work, I pour so much of myself into it and get so much approval back, it's a circular process that's going on, a closed system; and maybe some percentage of the normal need to connect with people, even those I'm closest to, has always has been satisfied.

But boy, nature is exacting! It has a balance sheet that just won't quit, and if someone leaves before the end of their balance sheet . . . it may never be balanced up. The longer time goes by, the closer to even numbers it's going to come out in the end. And someone has to pay. There is no way that the stand I took long ago—I will exist alone and write my own things and steer my own ship and tell everybody what I think with just a microphone, no instruments, no band, no director, no writer, no producer, just me—isn't singularly selfish.

No way that the other side of the ledger doesn't fill up with all sorts of debits. I've never had to look at that. I've thought about it intellectually, but I've never really looked at it in human, emotional terms.

When Brenda was alive I used to have a fantasy of Ireland, the southeastern parts so that it would be a little warmer, and the two of us there, close enough to Dublin that you could go buy things you needed and not have to clean yourself with . . . wire or whatever— I don't know much about the countryside, I guess I know they're not poor—and just e-mail my shit to the publisher and go sit in the garden.

I often wonder if things had turned out differently whether I would have acted on that fantasy. I think I might. Give up performance. Make that sacrifice.

The most important lesson I've learned from nature, and I don't necessarily apply it well, is balance. There's a part of me that's unfed and unnourished. It needs the light of day, it needs some encouragement. And that is, not doing what I do now. I'm not even going to call it by its name. The opposite of what I do now.

Time to be and not do. I learned that early on from my shrink, Al Weinstein, whom I loved and trusted but who died suddenly on me. He had a stroke. (It's a really great feeling when your appointment gets canceled because your therapist died.)

But that doesn't alter or affect his code of life, which was: Be. Do. Get.

And I don't be enough, Jack.

I do plenty. I get some. But I don't BE.

19

NEW YORK BOY

George at The Comedy Hall of Fame Awards, 1994
(Courtesy of George Schlatter Productions Comedy Hall of Fame)

Clean and sober seems like the ending of a journey I've been on since I was a kid. Not a happy ending, I've never believed in those, but not an unhappy one either.

On December 27, 2004, during my Christmas break from the road, I made a decision I'd been putting off for a while. I went over to Jerry's house and told him I wanted to go into rehab. For a long time—since giving up pot in the late eighties—I'd been addicted to an opiate called wine-and-Vicodin. I was up to a bottle and a half and five or six Vikes a day. May seem like small potatoes compared to the planeloads of coke and pot and truckloads of beer I'd ingested in the seventies, but it was my personal bottoming out. I couldn't control it and I needed help.

Jerry had booked a lot of dates for the first part of 2005 and it would cost a small fortune to cancel and reschedule them. Not a consideration. I checked into Promises in Malibu the same day—another small fortune—and went into a thirty-day detox program. The details aren't important. What is important is that I developed a new appreciation of the AA techniques that had helped Brenda so much—whatever skepticism I'd had about them or the people who used them. And that they worked. (Although I can do without that Higher Power stuff.) At the age of sixty-seven I put an end to five decades of substance abuse, beginning with my first toke in the hallway of a building on 122nd Street when I was thirteen. That's a fifty-four-year-old high.

I don't miss it. I feel better than those mornings when I dropped a couple of Vikes to feel better. Wine sections and liquor stores hold no temptations for me. That's all in the past. Which is good. I have plans.

I have thousands of notes and ideas in hundreds of files on four Apple computers. And the notes keep coming. Probably there are other HBOs in my future, and there'll always be stuff for them. But my mind and focus have been elsewhere for a while. The reason I want to spend less time on the road is so I can develop the next form for myself.

If I live long enough and still have my wits about me, I believe there's going be a Broadway period for me. What form it takes will evolve, but the basic structure is becoming clearer.

Over the years I've had an increasingly accelerated anticipation of, and speeding toward, the moment when I begin to use my characters. This multiplicity of identities inside me that I've never had the opportunity or moment or chance to unleash. Or rather, I've never had the courage to force the moment and opportunity into being, so that they could be unleashed.

Some of these characters are onstage already, when I use an occasional voice to accentuate something. For instance, when I'm doing a language piece, the misuses of it or clichés or absurd expressions, voices come out with the misuses, clichés or expressions. I don't ask for them, a character just appears and speaks.

When it's ready, I always print material out so it's there in black and white. Once I've memorized it and start running it, I often find that suddenly I don't want to do a certain speech or passage. Something about it says: this is not mine. Maybe it's as basic as: if I do it in my own voice I'm going to sound like a speech giver or teacher; maybe it's just that everything is going to sound too much the same. But almost without my being aware of it happening, a blue-collar voice is growling: "It's the quiet ones you gotta watch." Or a gritty, world-weary one is explaining why all the Uncle Daves in the universe felt life had dealt them such a shitty hand.

The biggest family of voices are West Siders. The voices of my childhood. An older, throaty West Sider has always been my default voice, the voice of the Indian Sergeant and his extended family of NCOs, of numerous low-grade authority figures who show up in many pieces. A variant of him appeared in the Fox series. But there are many others—aggressive, noisy, quiet. Some are street crazies, speedy, high-pitched or deep, slow or menacing, confusing or confused. Some are funny and some aren't, some old, some young. There are priests, cops, shopkeepers, all of them real, not impressions of actors onscreen doing priests, cops and shopkeepers. There are southerners from the air force, westerners from my radio days.

But what all of them do when they start talking is invent this magic fucking material. In the past, when they appeared in the stand-up pieces I was running, I would sometimes do a couple for myself just to see where they went and I'd actually get scared. First of all, that they were going to completely overtake and overwhelm and possess me. And second, that I would be never be able to capture them. That they were all one-time people, that sentences would pour out and I wouldn't be able to get them down, and they'd be gone forever. So I didn't even let them get started.

But they weren't one-time people—they're all still here inside me. And they are bursting at the tethers, trying to get out. I'm a thousand different people that I can climb into in an instant and really inhabit. I don't want them to be inhabited by other people's words. I found that out long ago. Nor, to the extent that I can think for them, would I ever put them in a script to be acted by others.

The constraints of my left-brain-organized, carefully constructed stand-up material won't allow them to be themselves. But they have to be allowed to be who and what they are. I have to let my people go.

What I've realized is that I've been writing a Broadway show all along. I've had this dream for a while now and I'd often worry that being on the road would never leave me time to fulfill it. Among the notes I write and file all the time are many I put away because I can't find a place to use them, but in effect are at a stage well past notes: they're the beginning of a narrative. Theater is a different form and not every word has to be scripted. My characters will write their own words when the time comes. Their words are not the words of my stand-up—commentary, lists, observation—so much as stories. So what started as notes is becoming a narrative, linear flow.

It'll be more a case of finding out where they fit in the larger story and how and why. A Broadway show has been growing organically out of the stand-up process. This is going to be the one place where my stand-up meets my acting. That's good, because it will reassure people: here's something you're not expecting, but not so unexpected that I'll have to prove myself to you all over again.

The organizing principle will be my childhood—in effect the first chapters of this book. So in a way we're back to the autobiographical burst of the seventies—more familiarity—except that instead of the class clown it will be the rest of the rich, wonderful, gritty world of the solitary boy who whiled away his school hours by disrupting class.

The priests and nuns, the beat cops, the Irish gangs, the Moylan regulars, the Columbia interlopers, the shopkeepers and street hustlers and so many more, a whole vanished neighborhood with its sounds, music, accents and smells, its fights and joys and loves and prejudices, all seen through the eyes of that same boy.

His home life and mother—yes, I can do my mother—a set of characters in herself, a lace-curtain Bernhardt who can soak you in guilt but also tell you a story with six characters, do a voice for each one of them and come up with a punch line. And beyond home and neighborhood: the magic island of Manhattan—wartime Manhattan—just an IRT ride downtown.

I'll tell that boy's tale, even though by the time we get this on I could well be an old fuck of seventy or more. But that will be as it should be. I'll be old man and boy. The boy who will one day be the old man, the old man looking back on the long-ago boy he once was . . .

Reunion, in fact. What we seek all our lives: returning to the One, no longer separated. The capstone of my life.

It'll be pretty good, I think.

I'm calling it: *New York Boy.*

ABOUT THE AUTHOR

Born in New York City in 1937, **George Denis Patrick Carlin** was one of the greatest and most influential stand-up comedians of all time. He appeared on *The Tonight Show* more than 130 times, starred in an unprecedented fourteen HBO specials, hosted the first *Saturday Night Live* and penned three *New York Times* best-selling books. Of the twenty-three solo albums recorded by Mr. Carlin, eleven were Grammy-nominated, and he took home the coveted statue five times, including a 2001 Grammy win for Best Spoken Comedy Album for his reading of his best seller *Brain Droppings*. In 2002, Carlin was awarded the Freedom of Speech Award by the First Amendment Center, in cooperation with the U.S. Comedy Arts Festival in Aspen, Colorado, and he was named the eleventh recipient of the Kennedy Center Mark Twain Prize for American Humor in June of 2008. George Carlin passed away at age seventy-one on June 22, 2008, in Santa Monica, California.

Tony Hendra was recently described by the *Independent* of London as "one of the most brilliant comic talents of the post-war period." He began his comedic career with Graham Chapman of Monty Python, appeared six times on *The Ed Sullivan Show*, was one of the original editors of *National Lampoon*, edited the classic parody *Not the New York Times*, starred in *This Is Spinal Tap*, and cocreated and coproduced the long-running British satirical series *Spitting Image*, for which he was nominated for a British Academy Award. He has written or edited dozens of books, most of them satirical, with the exception of two *New York Times* best sellers: *Brotherhood* (2001) and *Father Joe* (2004). He is a senior member of the board of the nationwide storytelling community the Moth.